Euan Uglow

This second edition of the Euan Uglow Book of Paintings follows that published in 1998, which is now out of print.

We have added an interview with the artist by Andrew Lambirth conducted in the Spring of 1989.

As before, the volume is not a *catalogue raisonné*. It is a book of paintings selected by Euan Uglow and ourselves.

William Darby
March 2003

First published in Great Britain in 1998 by
Browse & Darby Ltd
Revised second edition published 2003

Printed by Oldacres & Co Ltd, London

A catalogue record of this book is available from the British Library
ISBN 0 9533862 1 X

Snatches of Conversation

The following interview, reproduced courtesy of The Artist's and Illustrator's Magazine, is based on three conversations which took place in 1989 between the artist and Andrew Lambirth.

Why did you first start to paint?
I've always tried to make things. I find making things a relaxation from painting, but the two are caught up together. As a child I was always making objects even if they were boats with too many nails in that sank. Then at sixteen I went to Junior Art School at Camberwell.

Whilst at Camberwell, I came into contact with many influences like Bill Coldstream and Claude Rogers, Johnny Minton, Keith Vaughan, Pitchforth, Sam Carter, Victor Pasmore and John Dodgson. Also the sculptor Carl Vogel who wanted me to make sculpture; however, I preferred painting. I found myself in a hive of activity that did me nothing but good. It was a very stimulating atmosphere, activated by many ex-servicemen who wanted to make full use of the art school.

Then I went to the Slade and although most students did what was roughly called 'working from nature', I felt it wasn't so much a personal attitude but an accepted tradition. I wanted to be much more extreme, and work in a more intensified situation. The other painting students were people like Mike Andrews, the Cohen brothers, Martin Froy, Craigie Aitchison, Myles Murphy, Norman Norris and Victor Willing.

Did your interests form a focus at the Slade?
Oh yes. I was interested in appearances and in making a proper order with conviction. But I don't think it was wholly to do with the Slade. This idea of drawing that was supposedly handed down via Tonks and Augustus John was a legend that had died out thirty years before.

Was it a very structured or formal art education?
There was some structure, one had to do perspective and art history and anatomy, but it was all pretty loose; in anatomy I did the psychology of seeing. Of course, that was interesting, learning all about *gestalt*, though I don't know if it ever had any influence on me. And the learning of perspective was good, though it has no importance to me now. I tried to do a painting which was constructed from the idea of using perspective to give an imagined idea a greater reality. That's the picture called *Musicians* (1953). On the other hand in *Summer Picture* (1972), I found the perspective was so violent that I had to build a table much wider at the back than at the front so that when I looked at it the angle wasn't so violent. I couldn't just make the adjustments in my mind, I had to have a visual proof.

Did Coldstream have the most influence over you?

He was a friend, and it's difficult to know how friends influence one. We'd go to the boat race together, very rarely did we talk about painting. It was only much later, in the 1970's and 80's, that he used to get me to look at his pictures and we'd talk as equals about painting. At the Slade, he was this strong *eminence grise* we had around.

How do you stand in relation to the Euston Road School?

I really don't think I've got much to do with it now. Obviously I learnt from all those people, but you can't call Claude Rogers' late pictures anything to do with the idea of the Euston Road School. If you think of the burning of stubble pictures, the night pictures he did from Highgate or the pictures he did in hospital, they look nothing whatsoever like Euston Road paintings. Critics' pigeon-holes aren't much use. Obviously there are other people's paintings that I find interesting, but I don't think I'm part of a school in the same way the Impressionists were when they met in Parisian cafés.

I love the painters of the Italian Renaissance. I wouldn't think of going to Florence without calling in to see the *Trinity* by Masaccio at Santa Maria Novella. It would be like going past a friend's house, seeing the light on and not going in. Masaccio's *Trinity* is a perfect example of using geometry, in this case the Golden Section, relating to a spiritual idea. I like the Japanese printmakers a lot. Utamaro is very fine. I think the Lorenzettis are marvellous, they mean a great deal to me. And, of course, Cézanne does, Piero, Poussin, Ingres, Rembrandt, Uccello, Mantegna, Goya and Velazquez.

Do you consciously draw inspiration from those kind of sources?

I don't think it's inspiration, except that the Royal Academy show of early Cézanne paintings was very inspiring, I think it's just pleasure. I think one gets inspiration from looking into oneself and from looking around. I can see a Poussin every time I walk down the street.

Is there a science to the way you look, a science of picture construction?

No, it's new every time. Somebody asked me to teach how to start a painting once. I've no idea. There are no generalisations, every picture is different. Sometimes I start with a lingering idea, an idea that's been forming in my head for some time. There's a painting I'm working on at the moment, of a man chasing a girl up the road. It comes from a kind of flashed image on the retina. Whereas *The Diagonal* (1977) was a very formal picture.

Now I like to have an ordered rectangle, a shape with reason. The whole picture is glued together with the shape of the canvas and the appearance of the subject. The measurements will be to do with the shape of the rectangle. I take measurements so that the subject has a real link with the rectangle; it also gives me freedom to make a whole surface.

Some of the marks are there to be able to go on with the painting. There are probably more marks on the more precarious poses. They are to do with what happened today, yesterday and the month before. They may be in different colours so I can see what happened. It's a chart or diary of what happened, while still trying to keep to the idea of what the painting is. I don't know what the end of the picture is going to be like, but I'm trying to find out why a subject does look so marvellous, and trying to make that sensation manifest on a flat surface.

Why do you make these marks?
It's the most immediate way of getting something down. They're obviously two-dimensional, which again is related to the rectangle. I don't do it for fun; it's absolutely necessary. I'd rather drink good claret for fun.

Why do you leave some of the measuring marks on the final canvas?
How can you lose those marks when the next second you may need them? I don't really finish a painting, it stops. Then, if I were to paint out those marks it would be another picture.

As you have spent up to five years on a painting, have you ever been accused of over-perfectionism?
I don't see how anyone can be over-perfectionist. If you've got an idea, you've got to get it down. Sometimes you think you've got there, but if you're not careful you go too far and start to paint another picture. Stopping has nothing to do with putting highlights in or gloss of hair. In most of the pictures it seems to have been the case that they had to go through a revolution before getting there.

At Camberwell I tried to paint analytical Cubist pictures in a very unintelligent way. A few years ago, the Georges gave me this toothbrush and I thought it was very sexy. I was wondering how I could say what I wanted to say about it, and I was also thinking about analytical cubism. So I fixed up two mirrors to paint her back, her side and her front. As far as I'm concerned *The Three Graces* is a modern equivalent of an analytical Cubist picture.

I'm painting an idea not an ideal. Basically I'm trying to paint a structured painting full of controlled, and therefore potent, emotion. I won't let chance be there unless it's challenged. I don't make a brush mark and think, 'oh, that looks nice', if I don't mean it as a statement. I'm not interested in that. Painting's too serious to take flippantly. I think one should behave morally with paint, though that doesn't stop one taking risks.

Do you avoid the evidence of brush marks?
I try not to think about it, because that's not the important thing. I love painting with a new sable brush, so there's obviously some pleasure in the physical process of painting.

Do you use geometry in your paintings?
All the pictures are different in construction. *Double Square, Double Square* (1980-82) is a double square rectangle, and a double square in space. It's a very beautiful idea and very simple. I only use geometry if I think it's going to be to do with the idea.

How do you respond to colour?
Colour is very important, very limited, and is one of our senses that we should try to use.

Our colours are limited because of the palette; it would be nice to find a new kind of colour just as it would to find a new kind of meat. You can't go much further than the pigments you've got at the moment, though you can make colours behave differently. I get more and more excited about the idea of colour. I want colour to play a very important part in what I'm making.

What about movement?
Quite a lot of my pictures are concerned with movement. I don't think you have to paint swirls to show movement. Perhaps my paintings are more about implied movement. I'm not interested in the kind of movement of the Futurists, for instance, because I think it's too much to do with a concept of movement. Whereas I have more sympathy for Duchamp's *Nude Descending a Staircase* because it's more analytical, it's more to do with trapping movement.

What is your objective?
I'm trying to make something new. I'm trying to make an image, or give an image to an idea. I like to paint in the light of a high grey London sky. In a wider sense, I don't know what's going to happen tomorrow.

Andrew Lambirth
1989

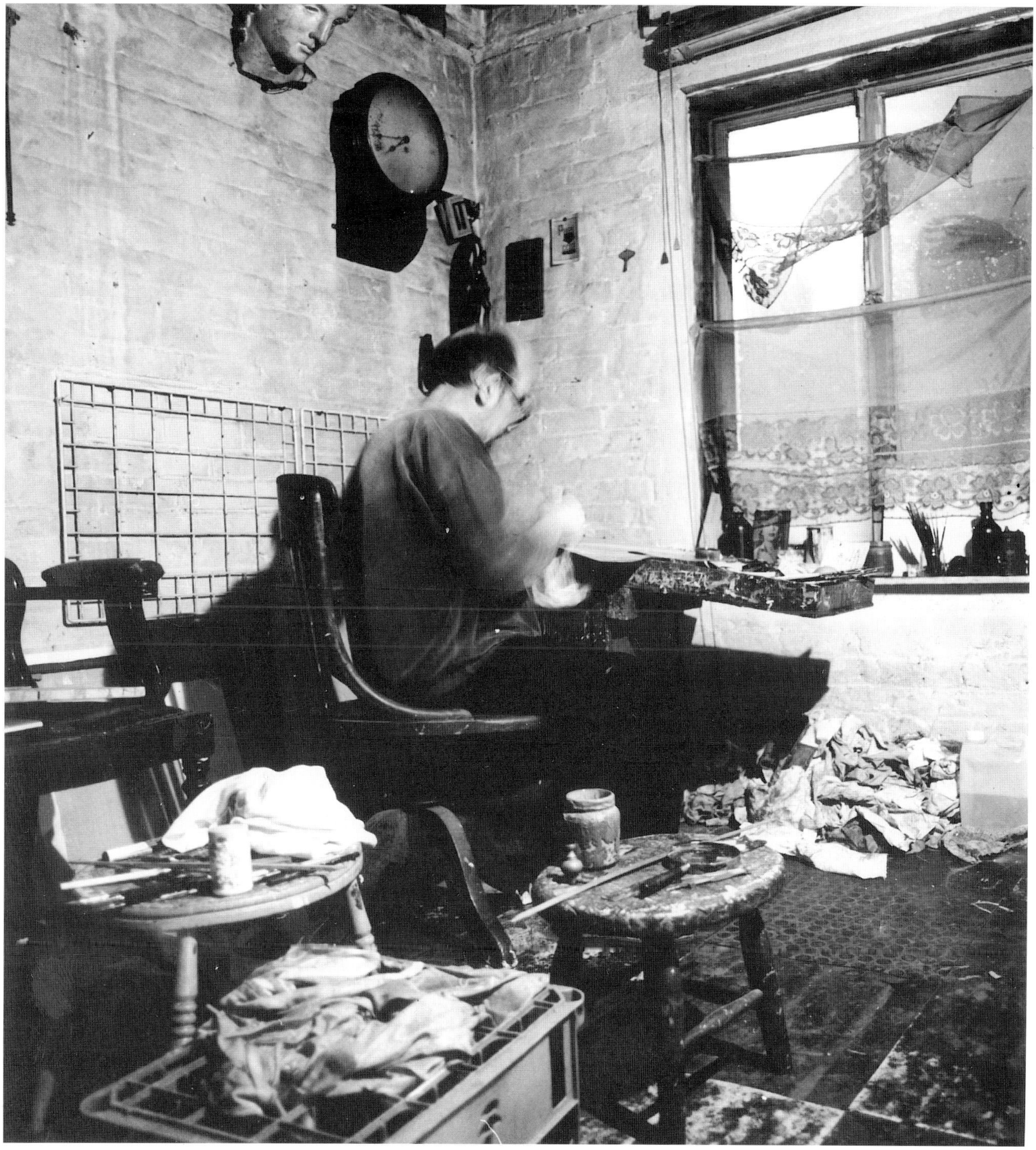

The Studio, Spring 1997 *photograph by Matt Pia*

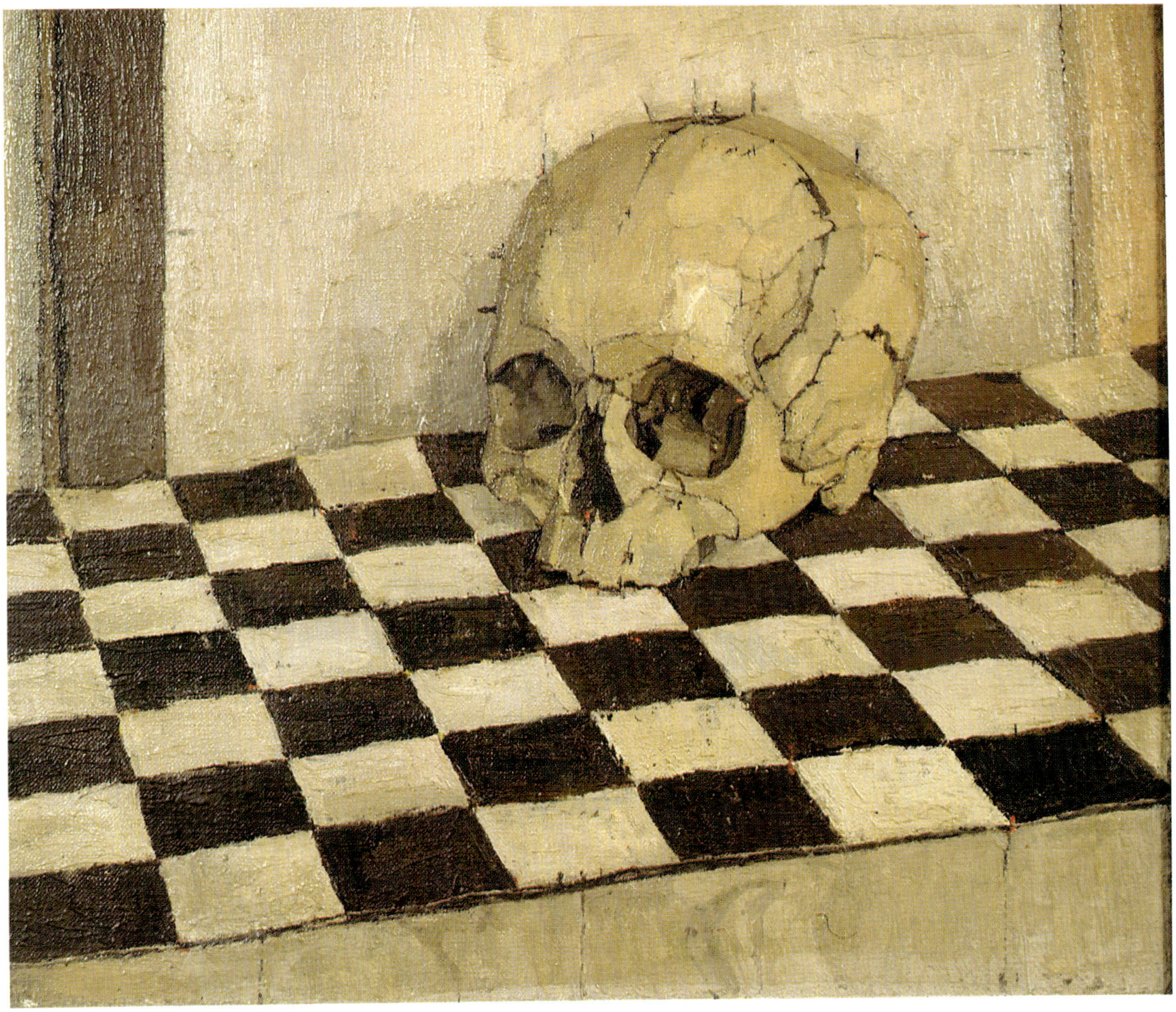

Skull, 1952
oil on canvas 12 x 14 inches

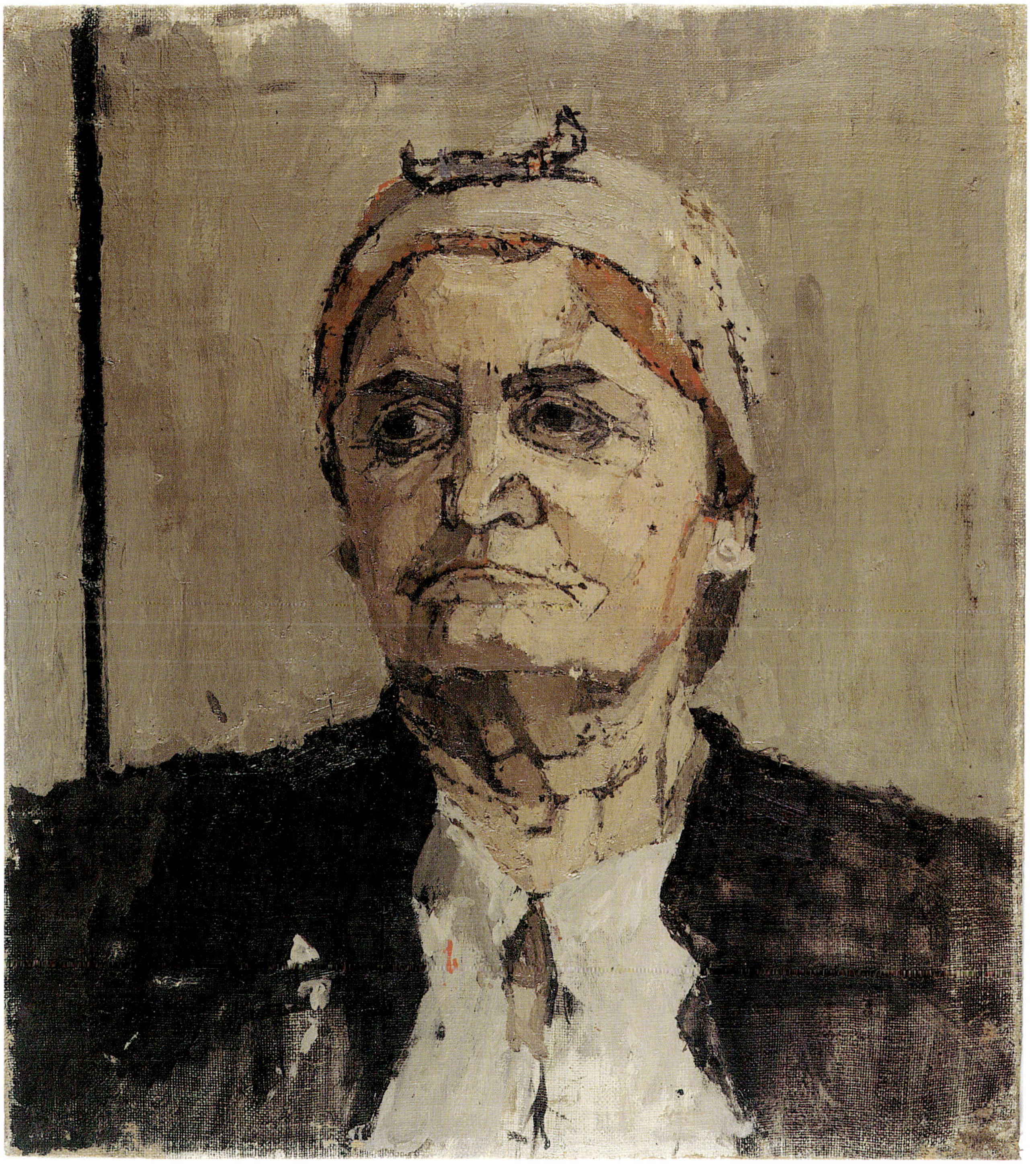

Portrait of an old woman, 1952
oil on canvas, laid on board   14 x 12 inches

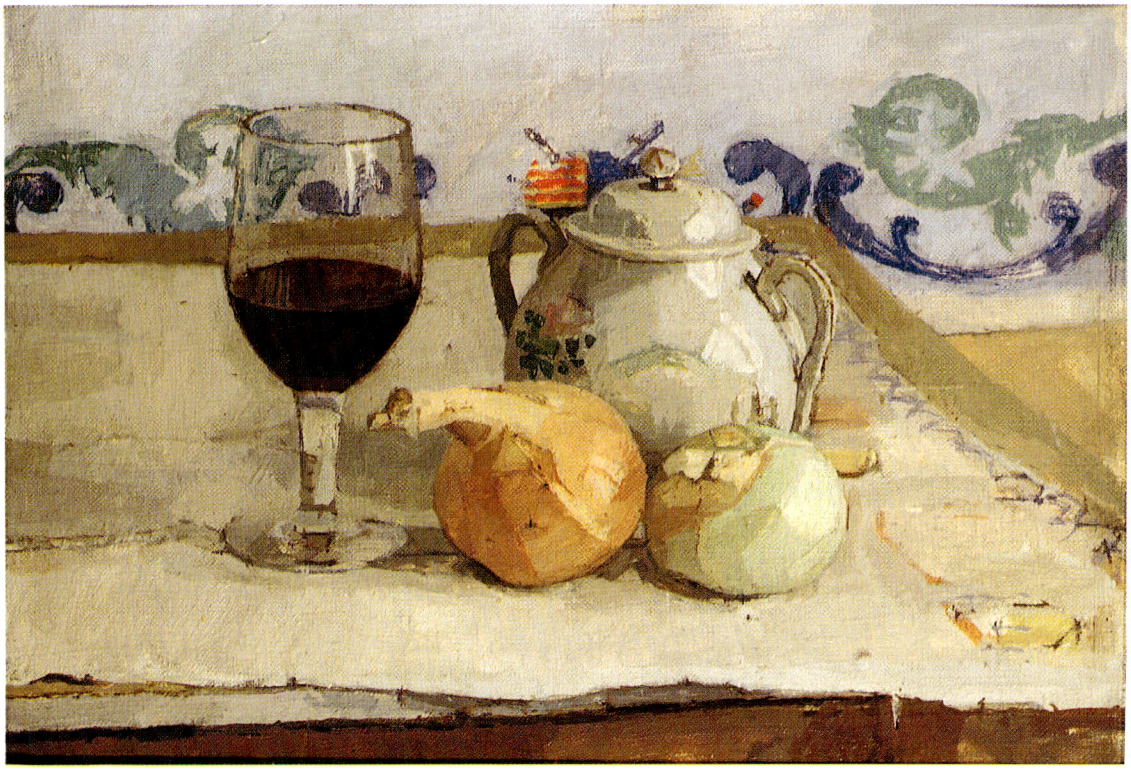

Still life with onions and wine glass, 1962

oil on canvas   8½ x 12 inches

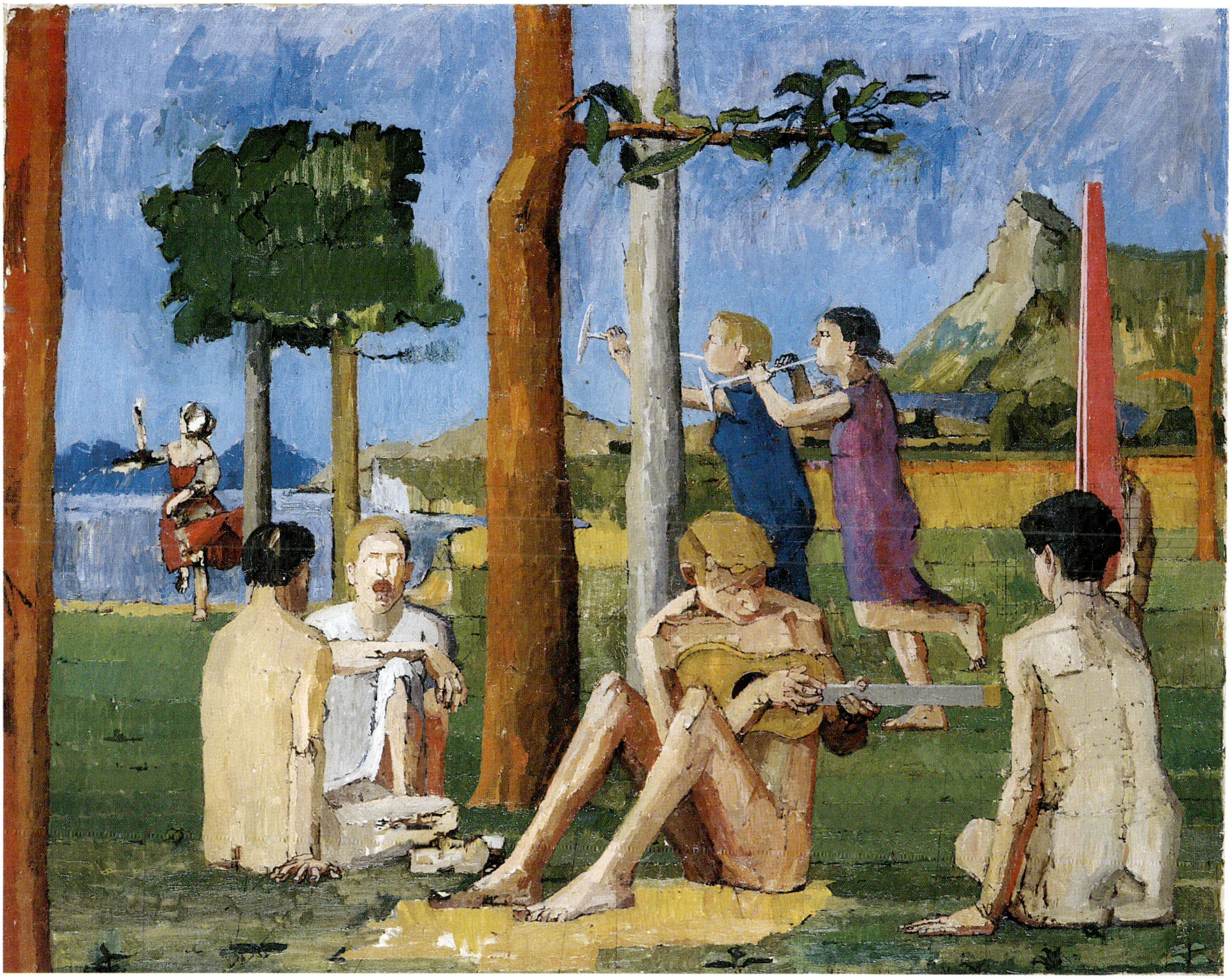

Musicians, 1953
oil on canvas 40 x 50 inches

National Museums & Galleries of Wales

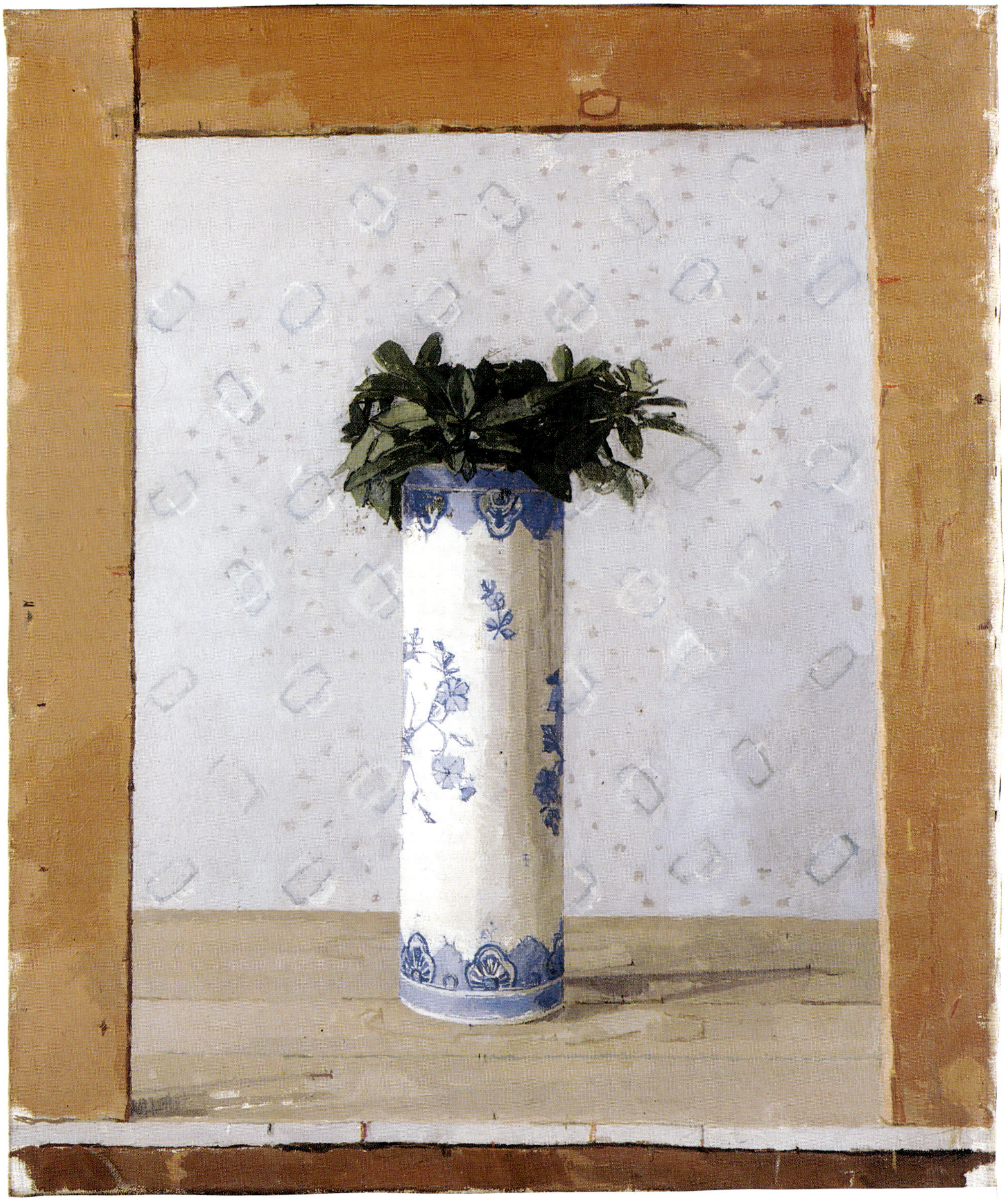

Leaves in a Delft vase, 1960
oil on canvas   22½ x 18½ inches

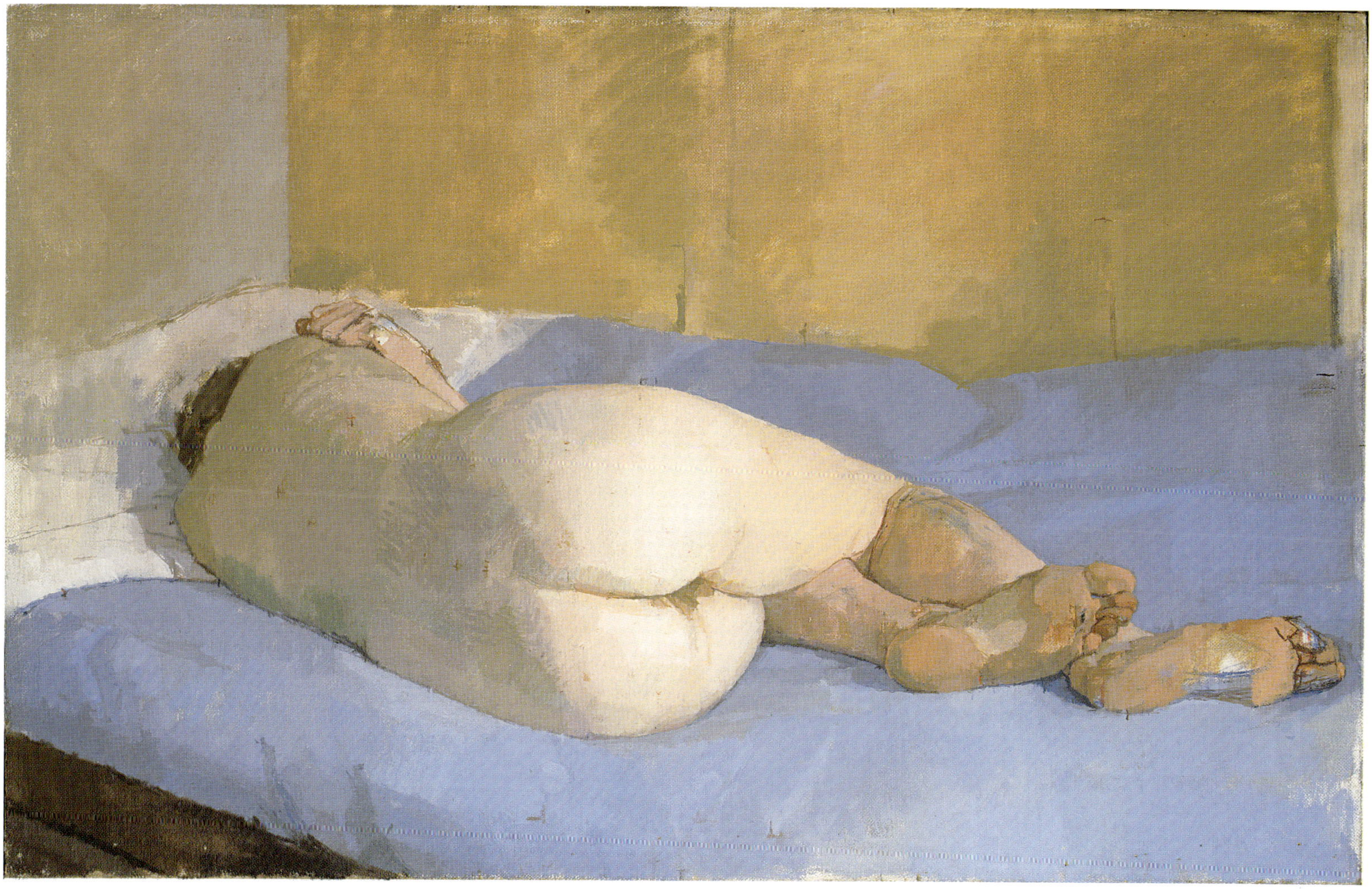

Beautiful girl lying down, 1959
oil on canvas 28 x 40 inches

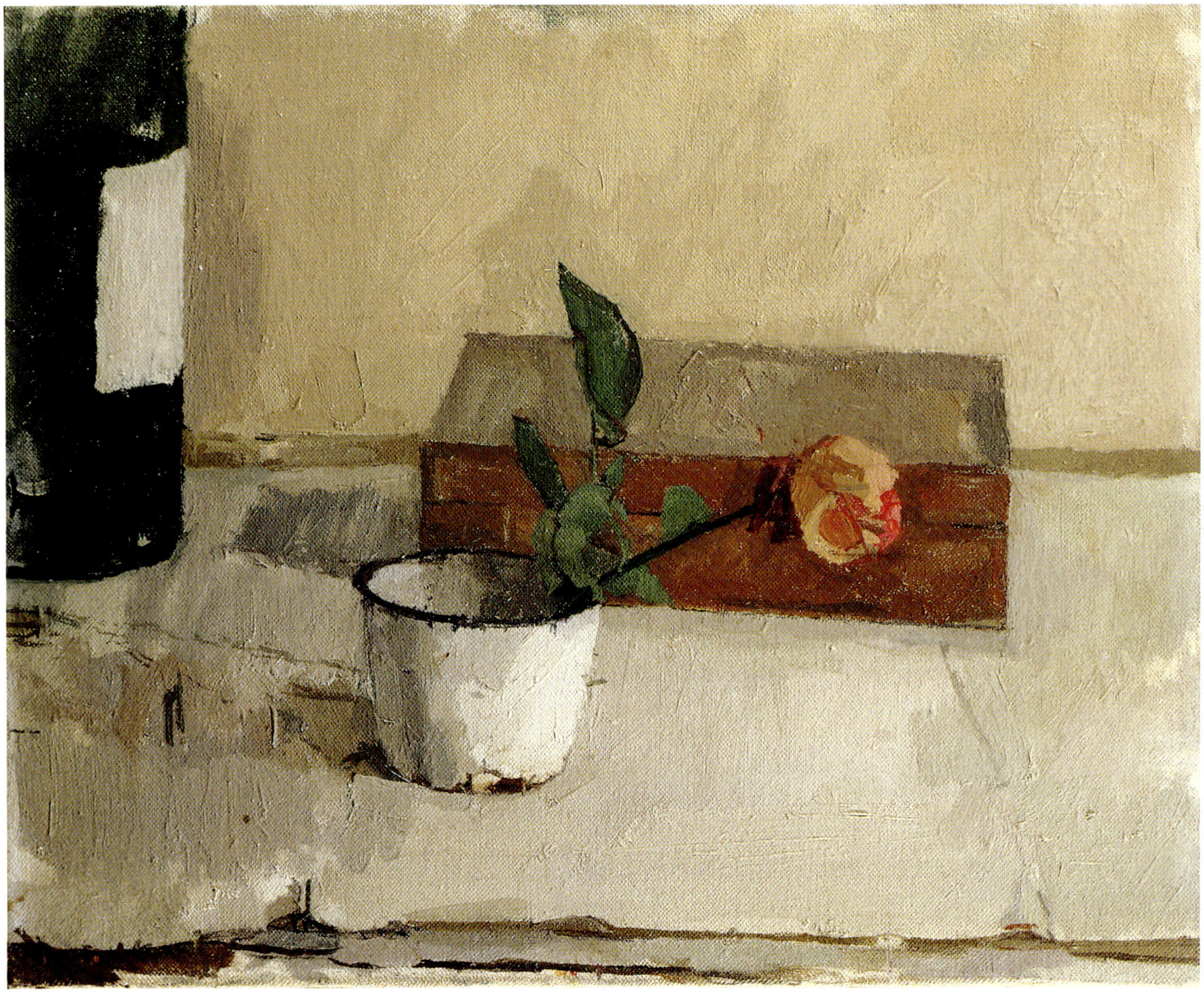

Still life with rose, 1957
oil on canvas 12½ x 15½ inches

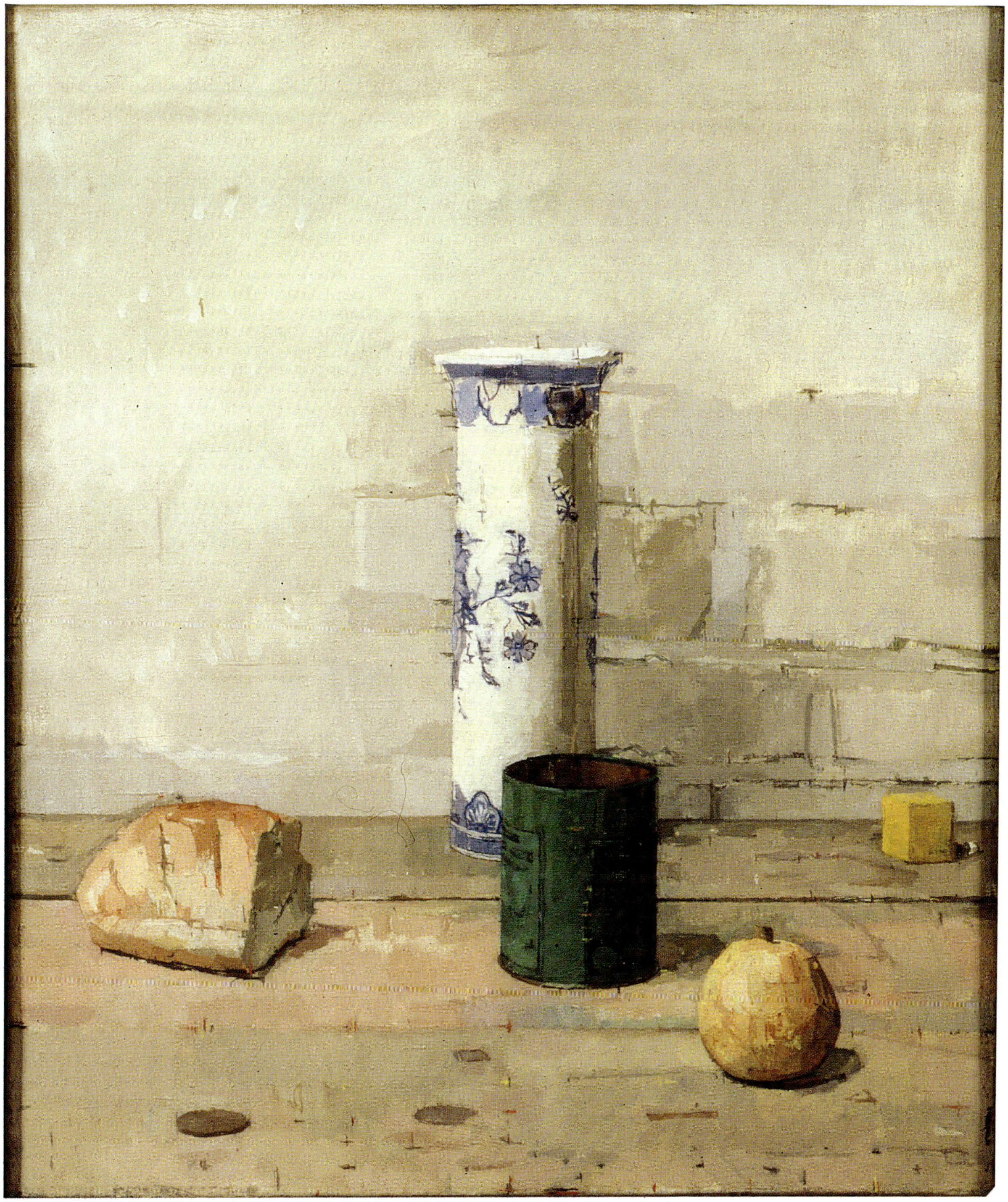

Still life with Delft jar, 1959
oil on canvas   24 x 20 inches

The Arts Council of Great Britain, Hayward Gallery

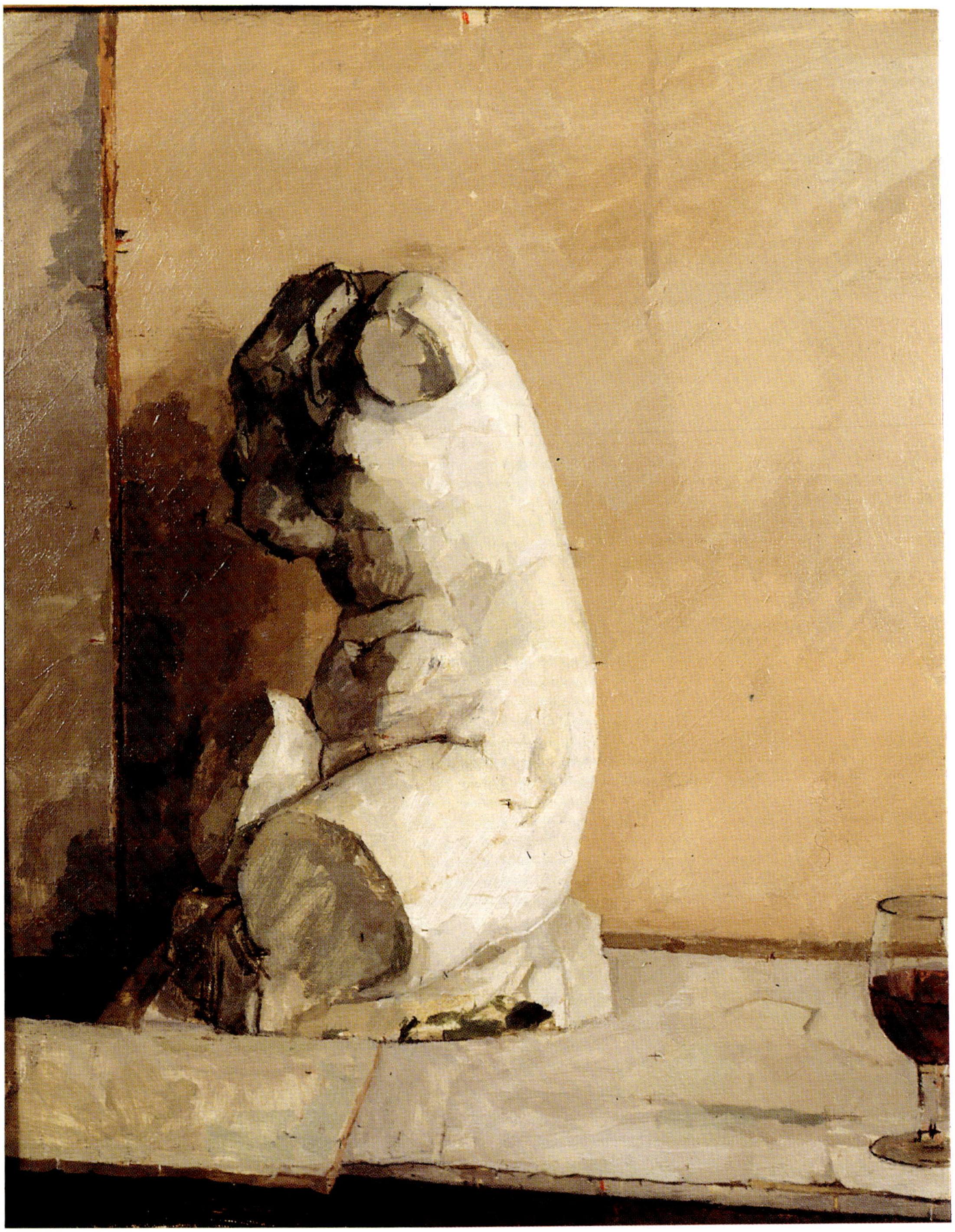

Still life with cast, 1960
oil on canvas   20 x 16 inches

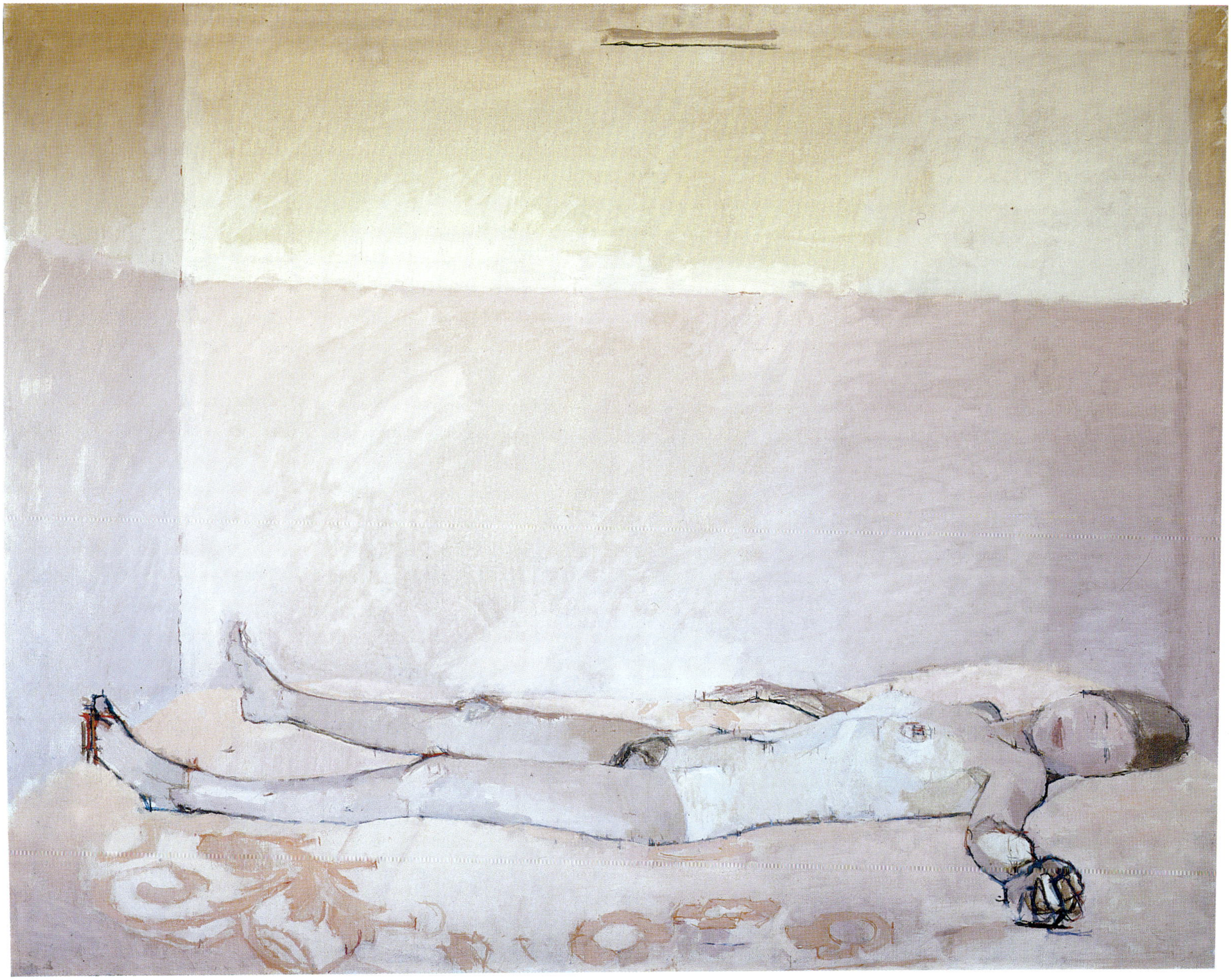

Girl in the South of France, 1961
oil on canvas 40 x 50 inches

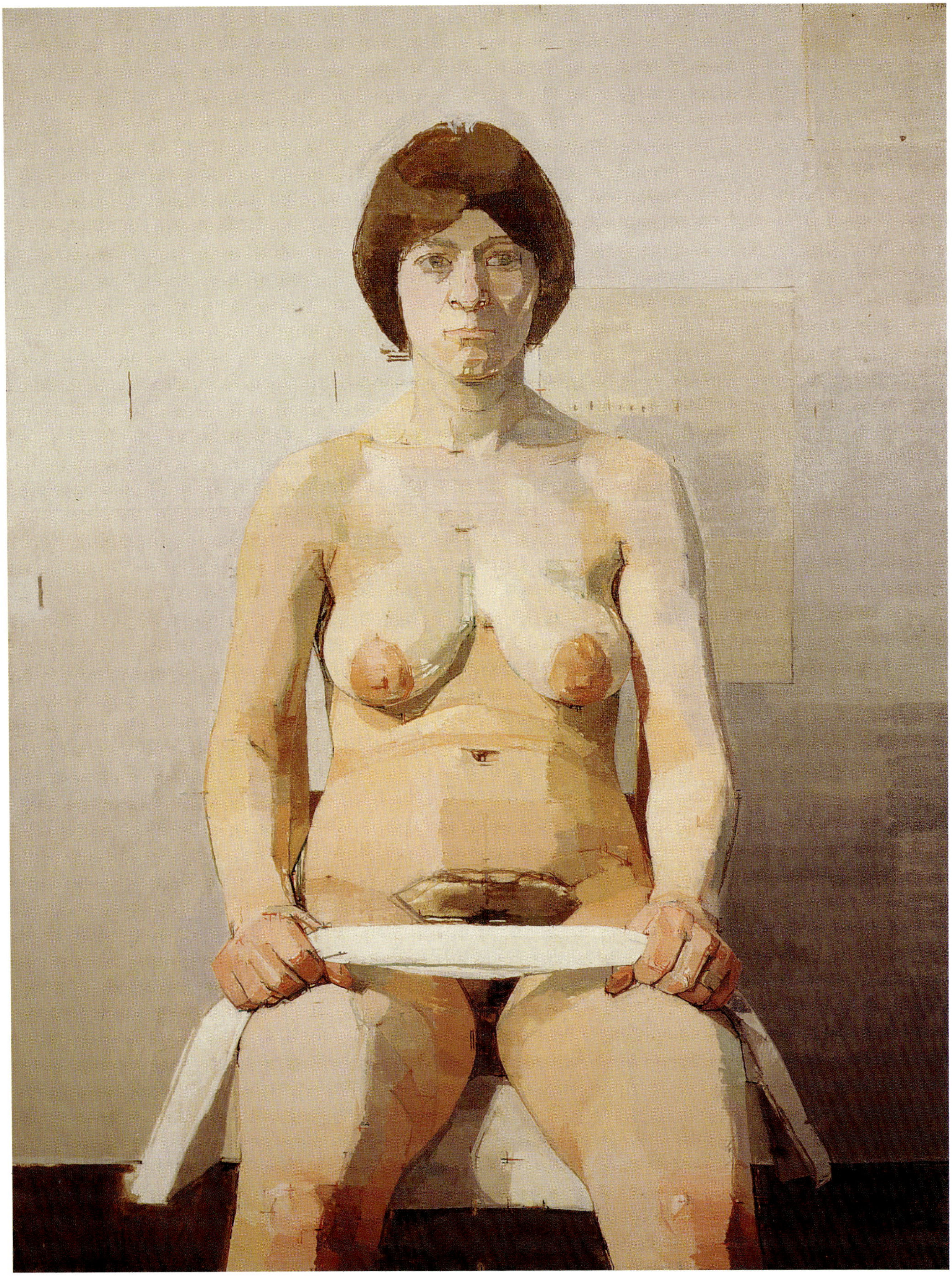

Miss Venne, 1963
oil on canvas   39½ x 29½ inches

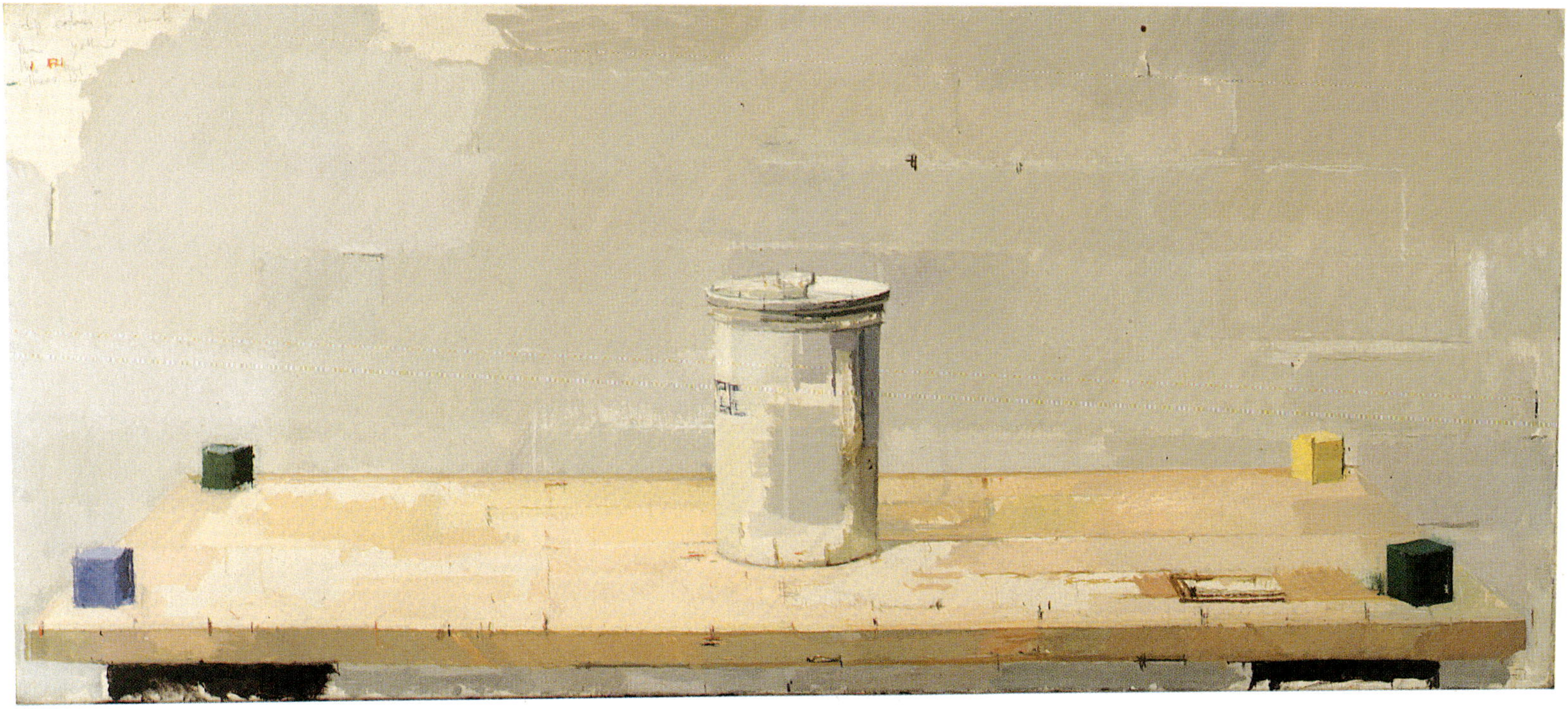

Passionate proportion, 1964
oil on canvas 18 x 39½ inches

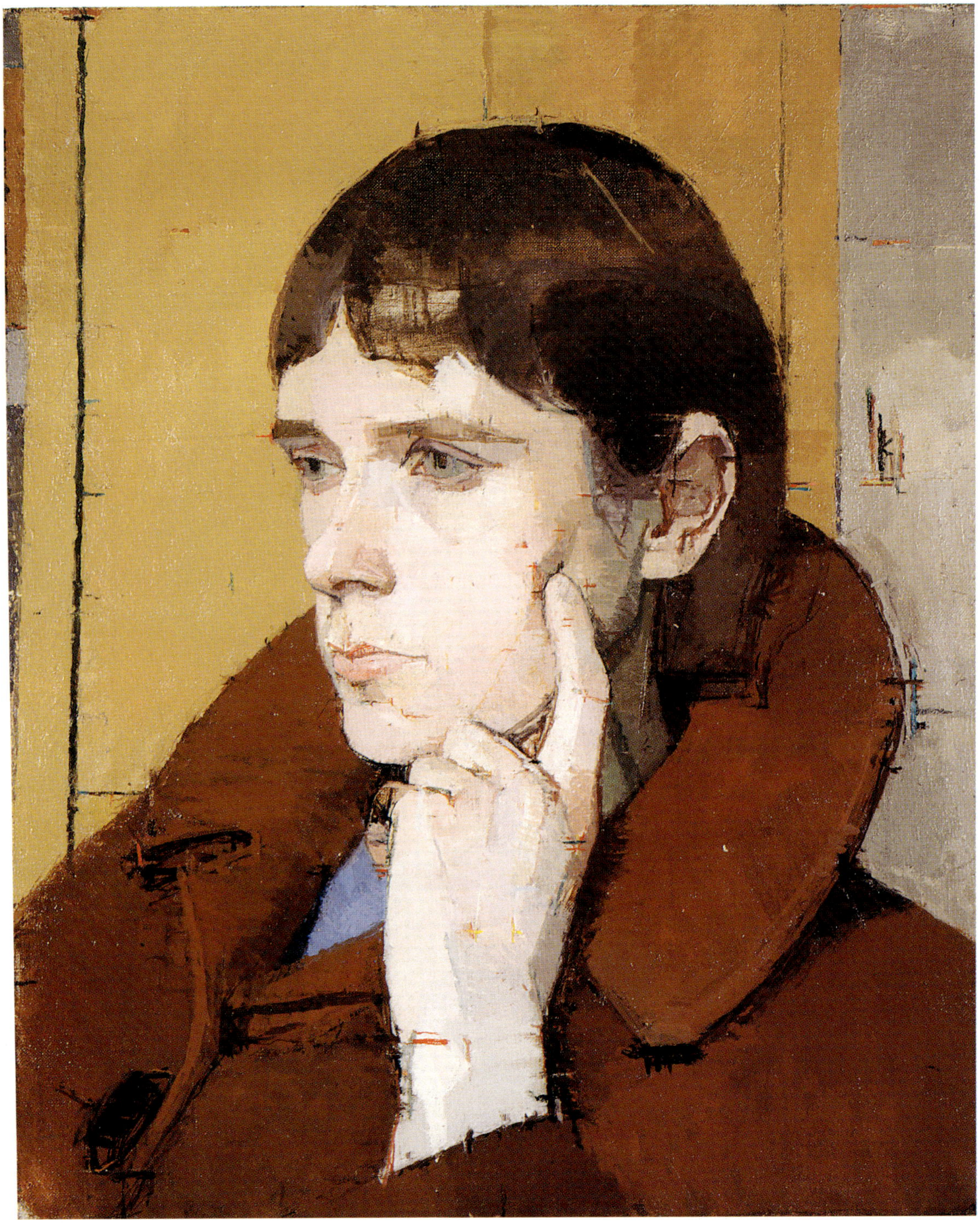

Head of Christine, 1966
oil on canvas   20 x 16 inches

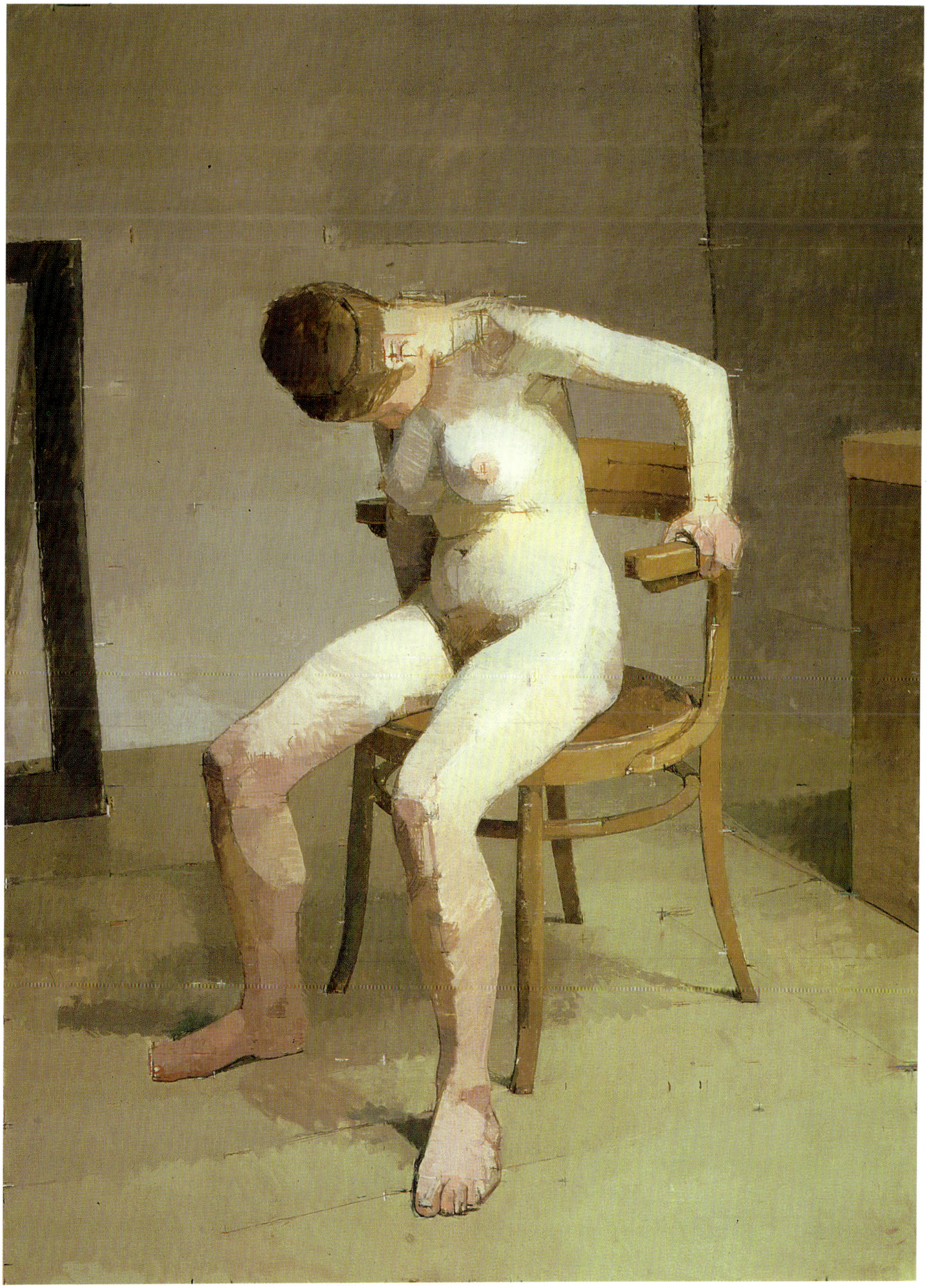

Nude, 1962-63
oil on canvas   64½ x 46 inches

The Trustees of the Tate Gallery, London

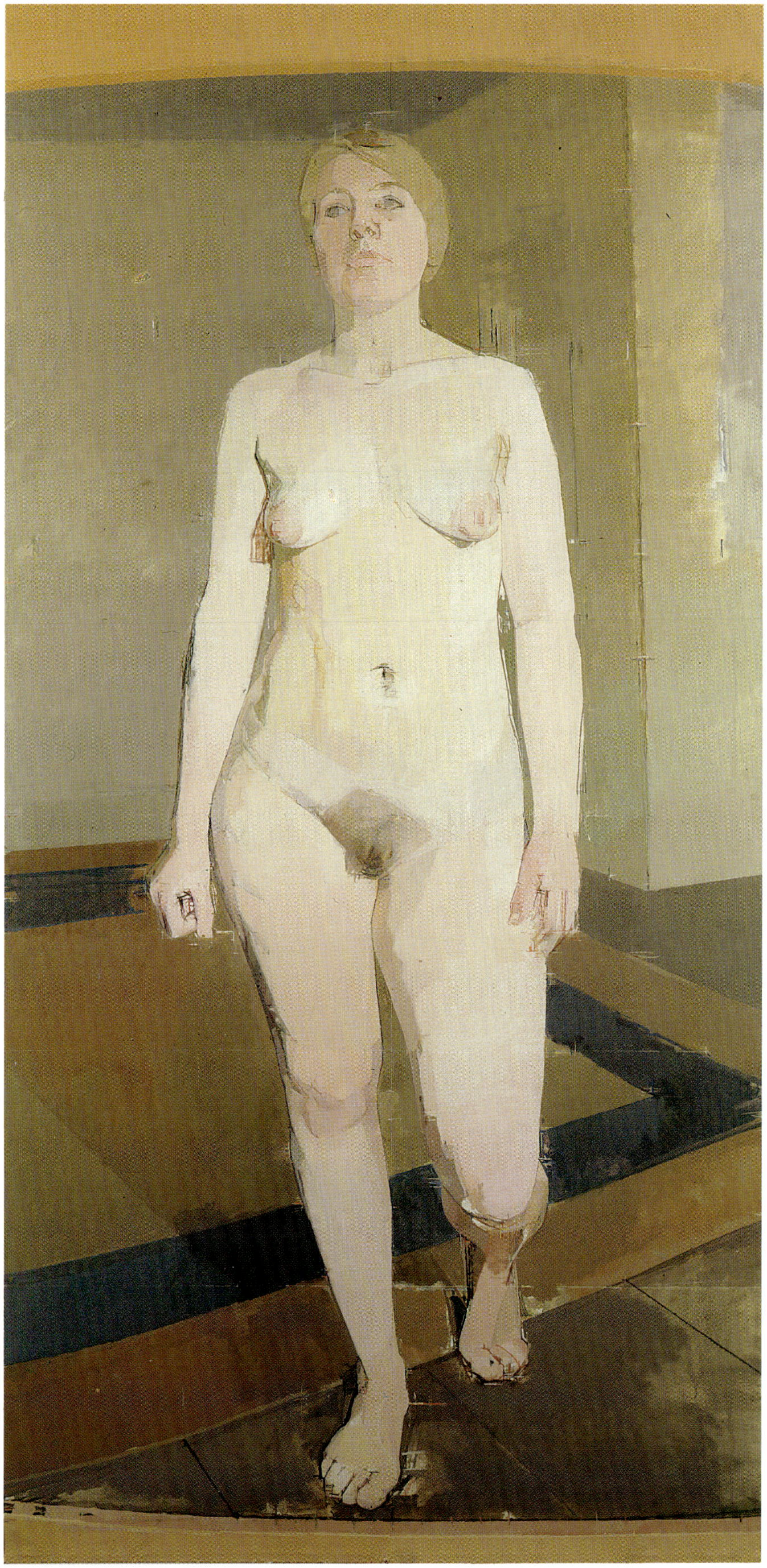

Large nude walking towards you, 1971
oil on canvas   72 x 36 inches

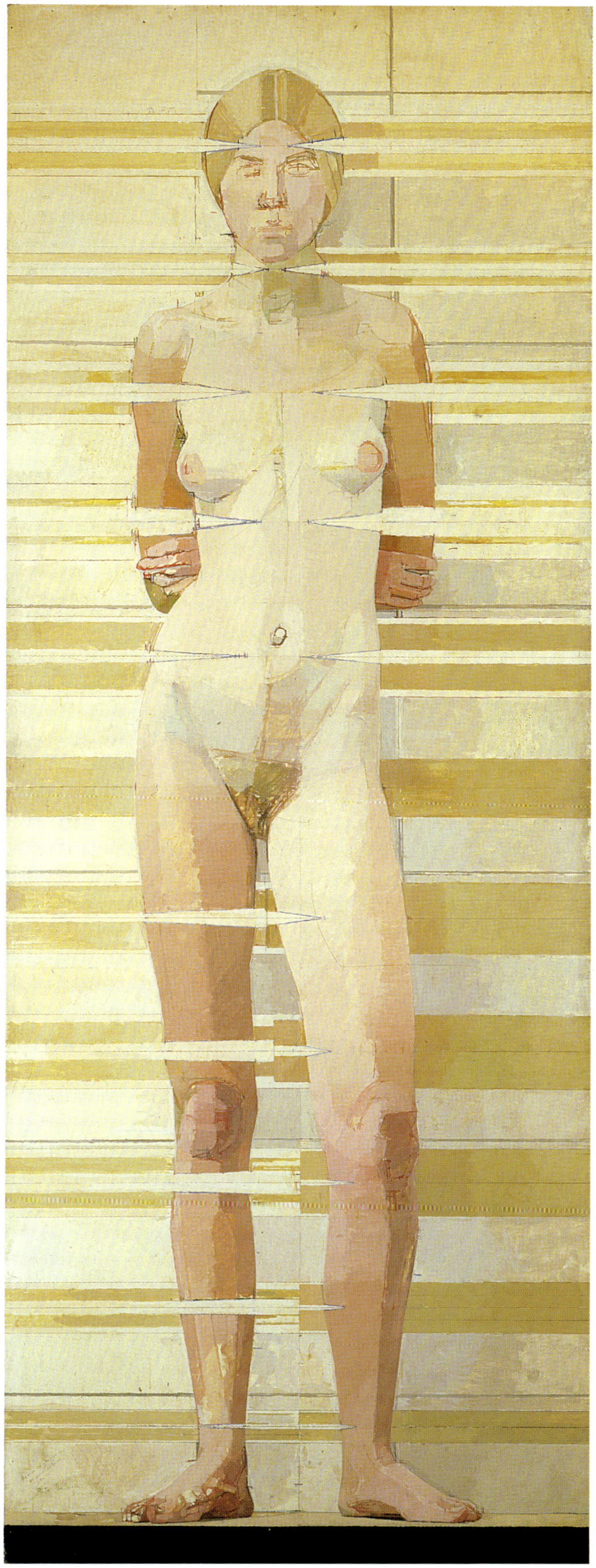

Nude, from twelve regular vertical positions from the eye, 1967
oil on board 96 x 36 inches

University of Liverpool collection

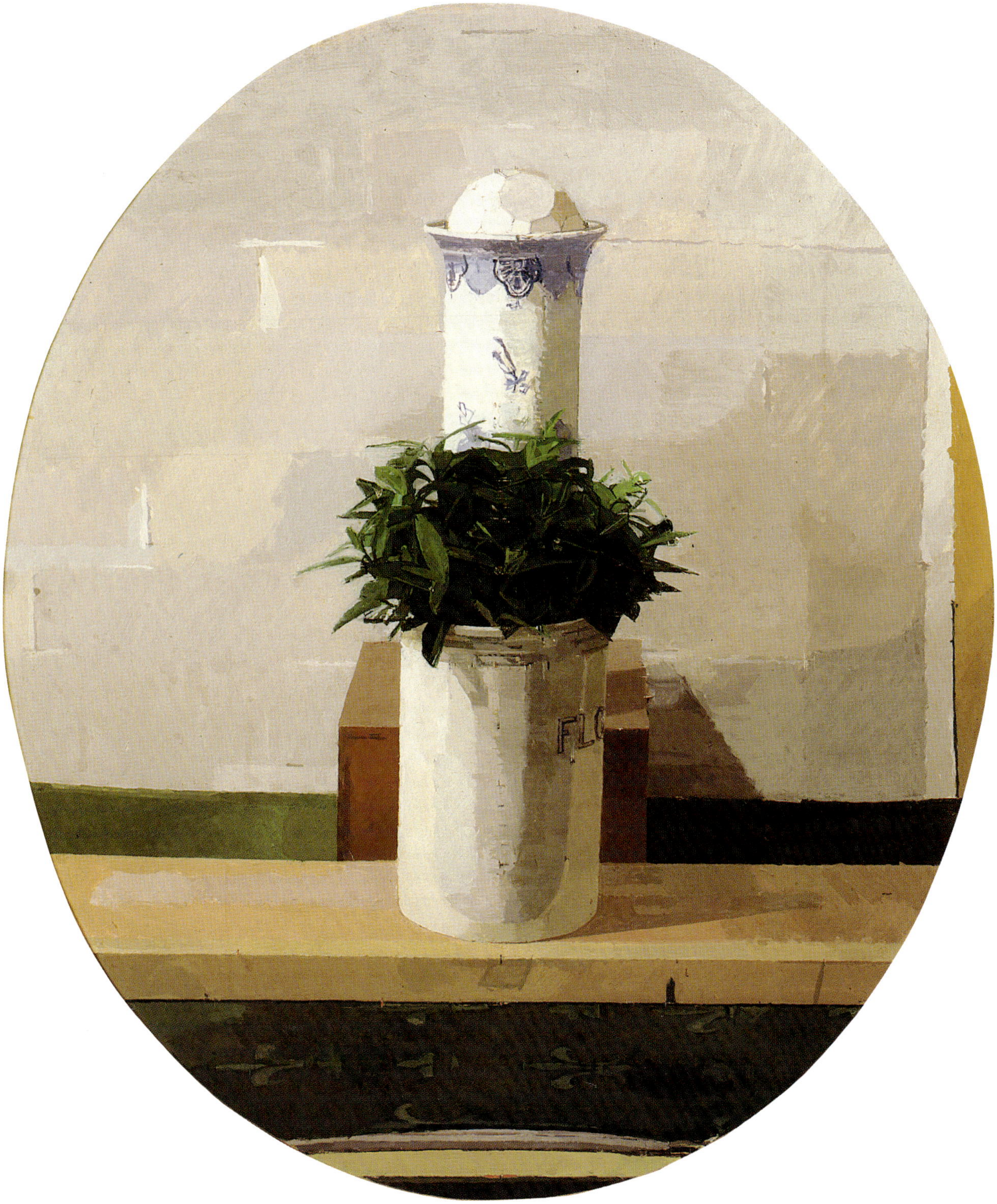

Large oval still life, 1968
oil on canvas 28 x 23 inches

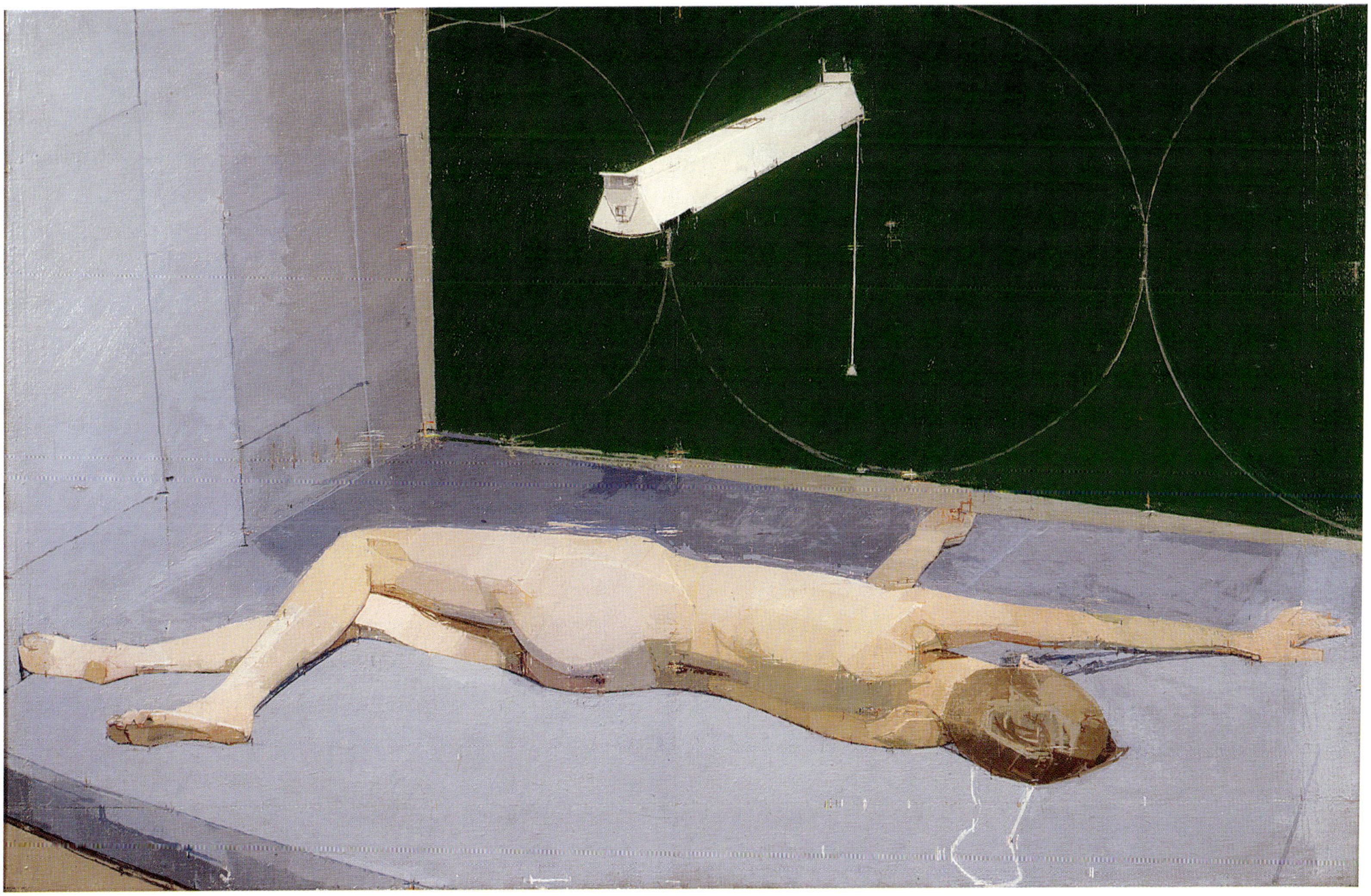

Three in one, 1968
oil on canvas   36 x 56 inches

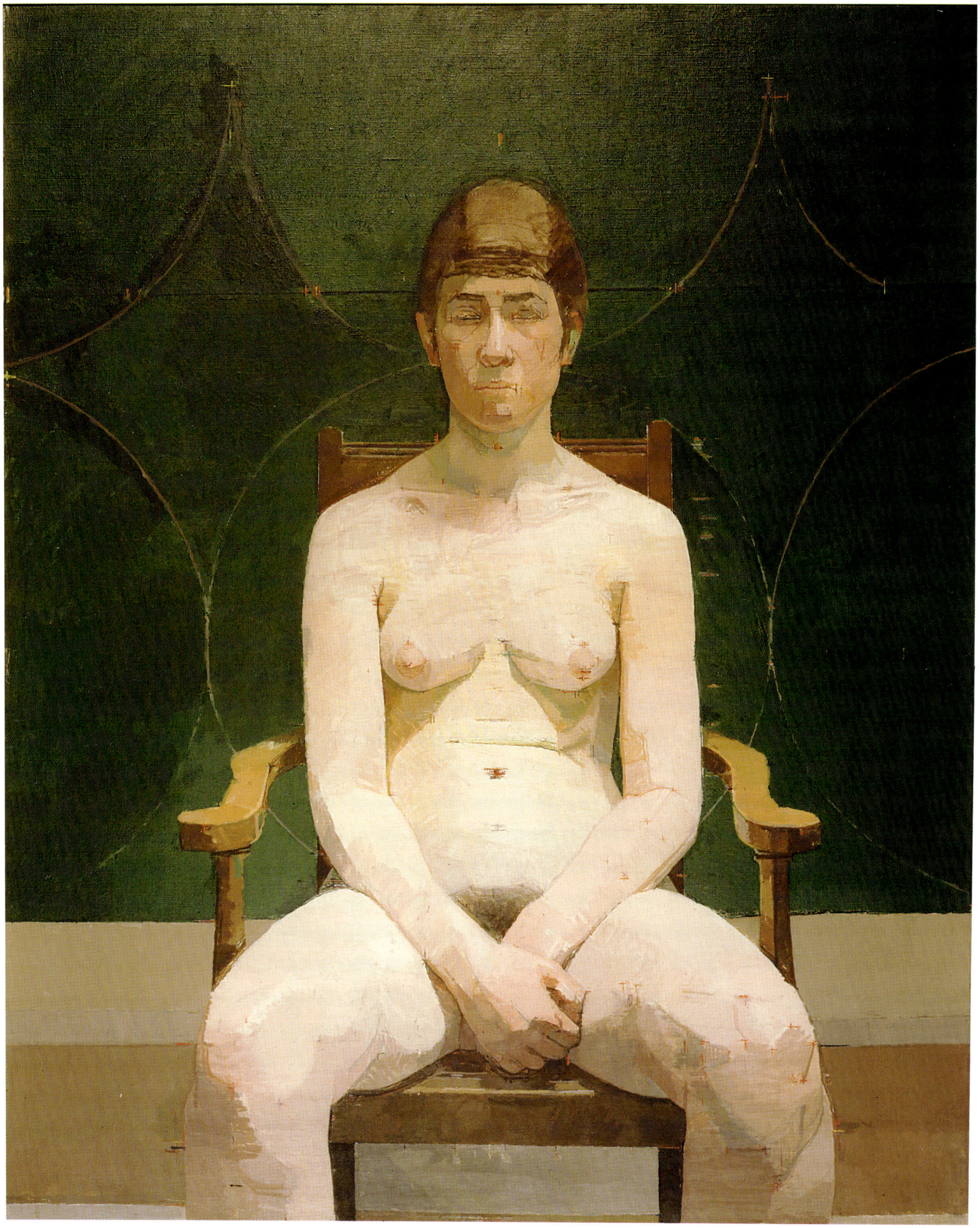

Nude with green background, 1966
oil on canvas 44 x 35 inches

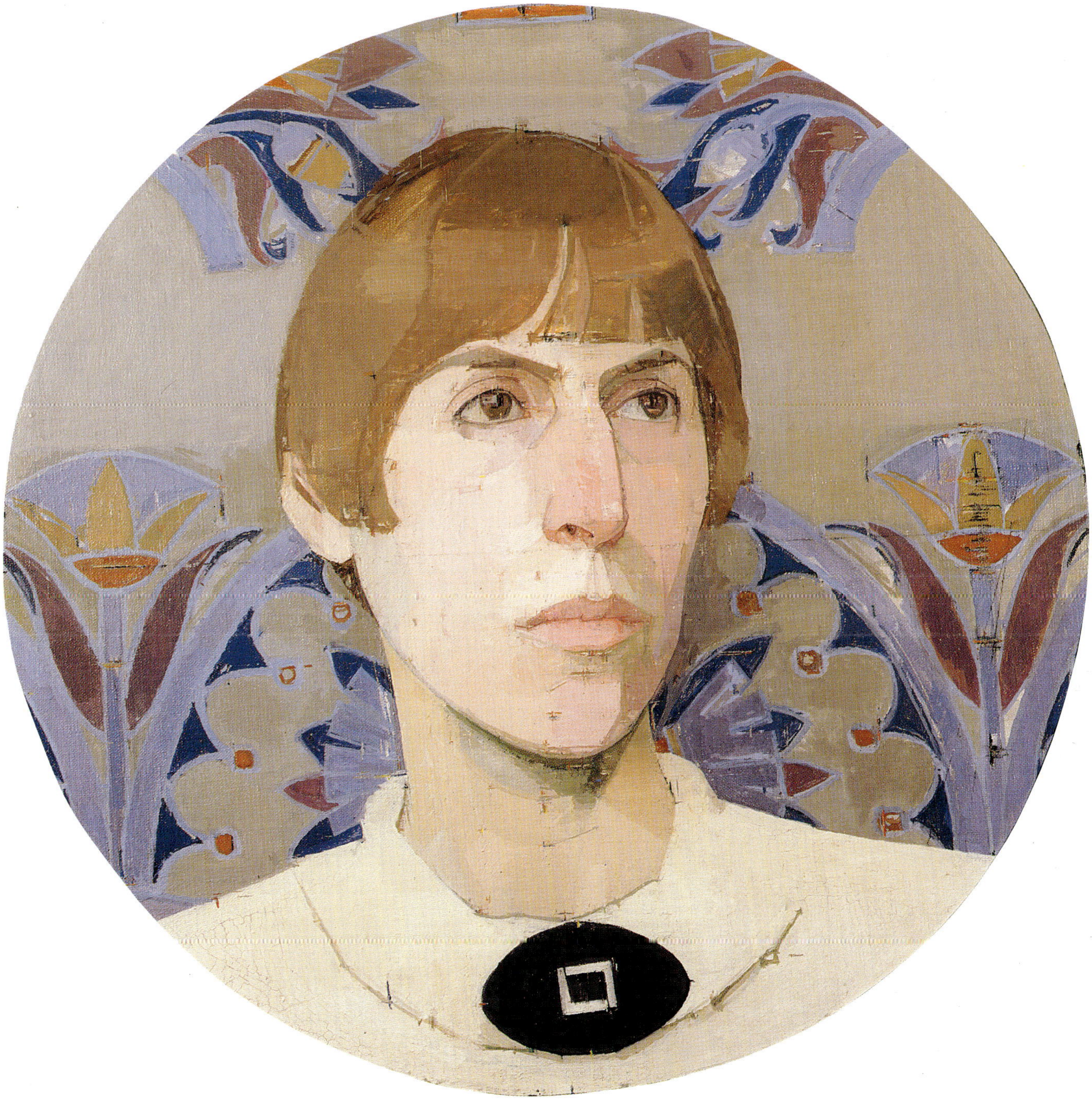

Portrait of Eve, 1969
oil on canvas, laid on panel 18¾ inches diameter

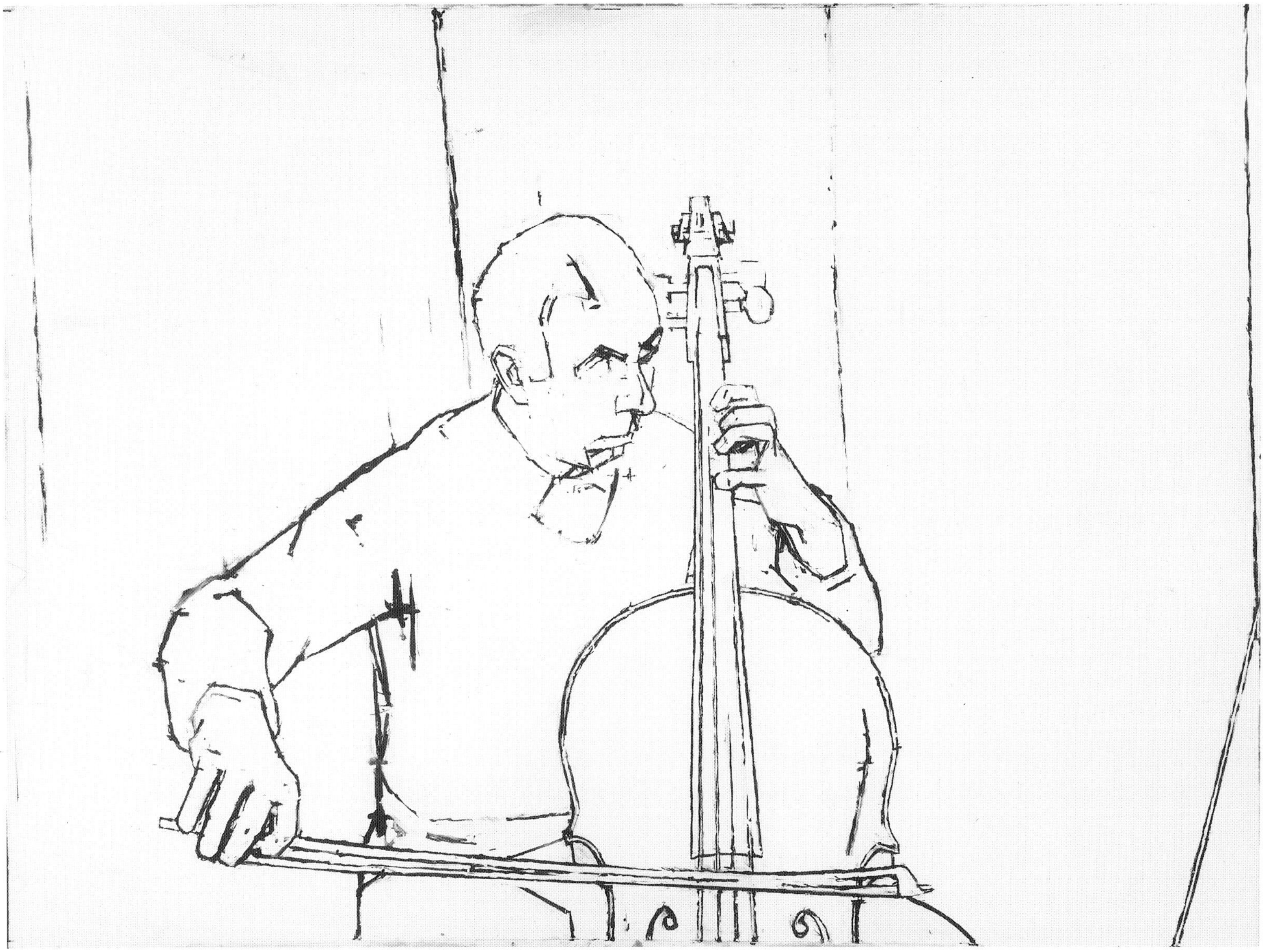

Portrait of Patrick Symons, 1969
oil on canvas 36 x 48 inches

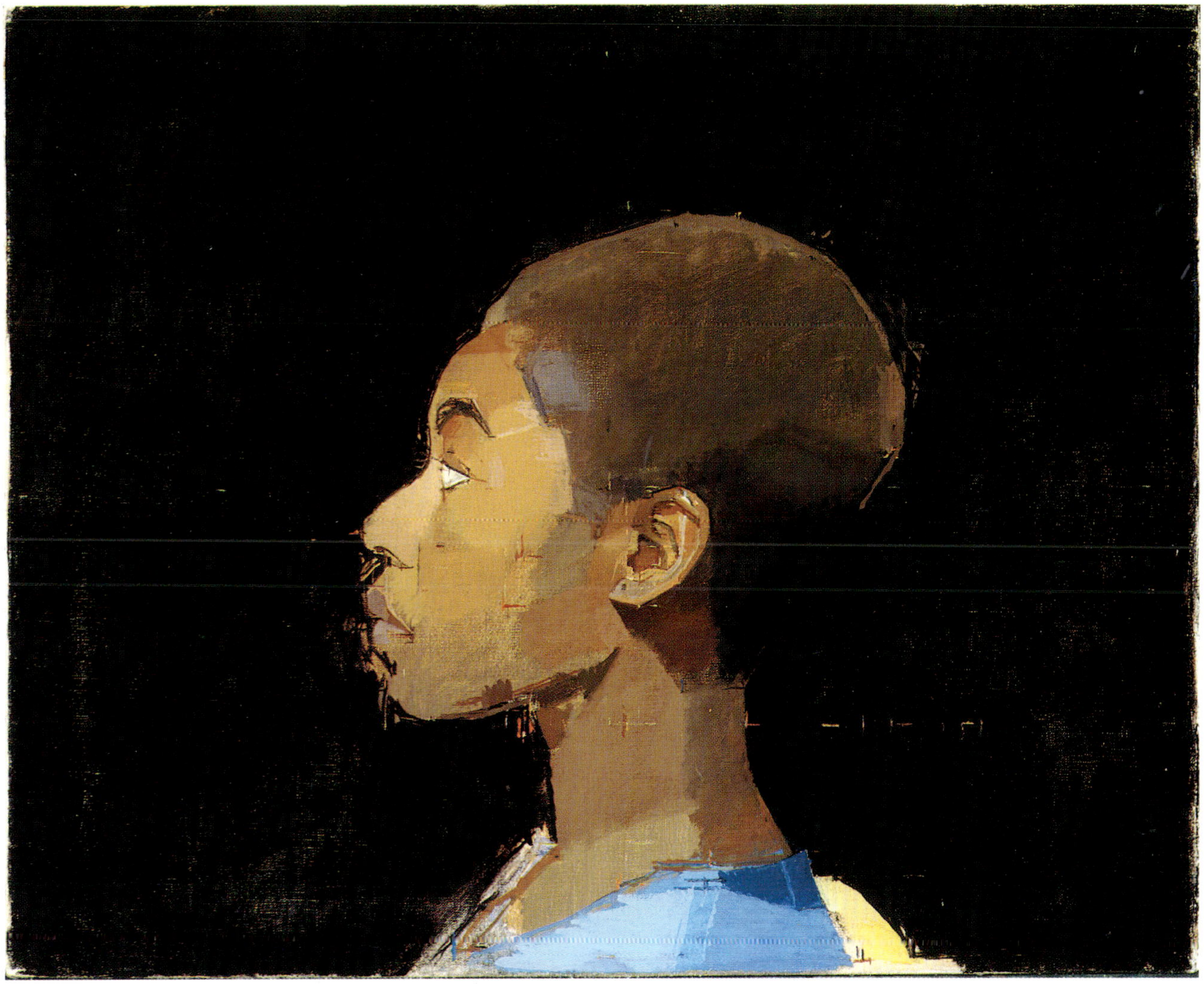

Marigold, 1969
oil on canvas   20 x 24 inches

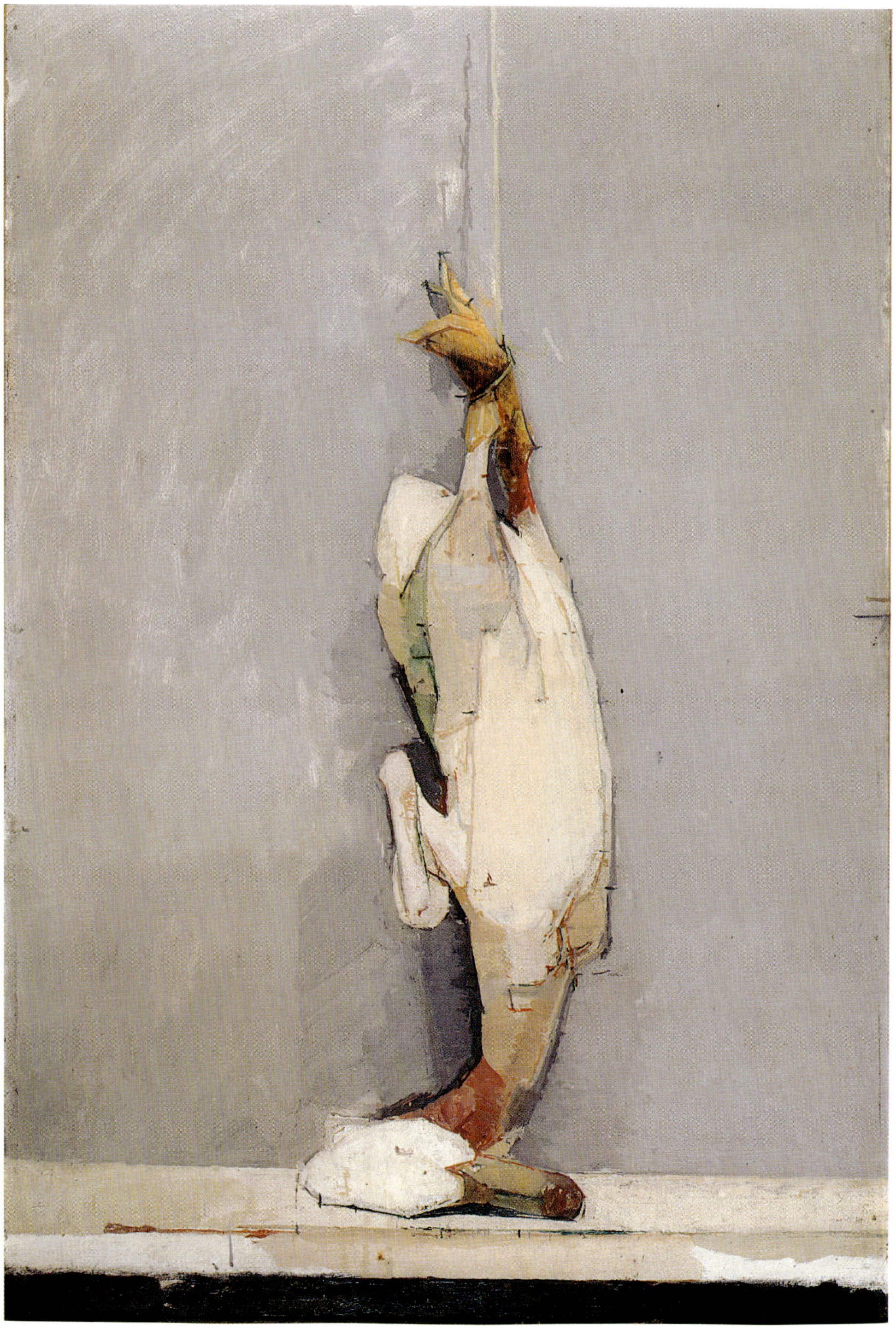

Duck, 1968
oil on board   29½ x 19½ inches

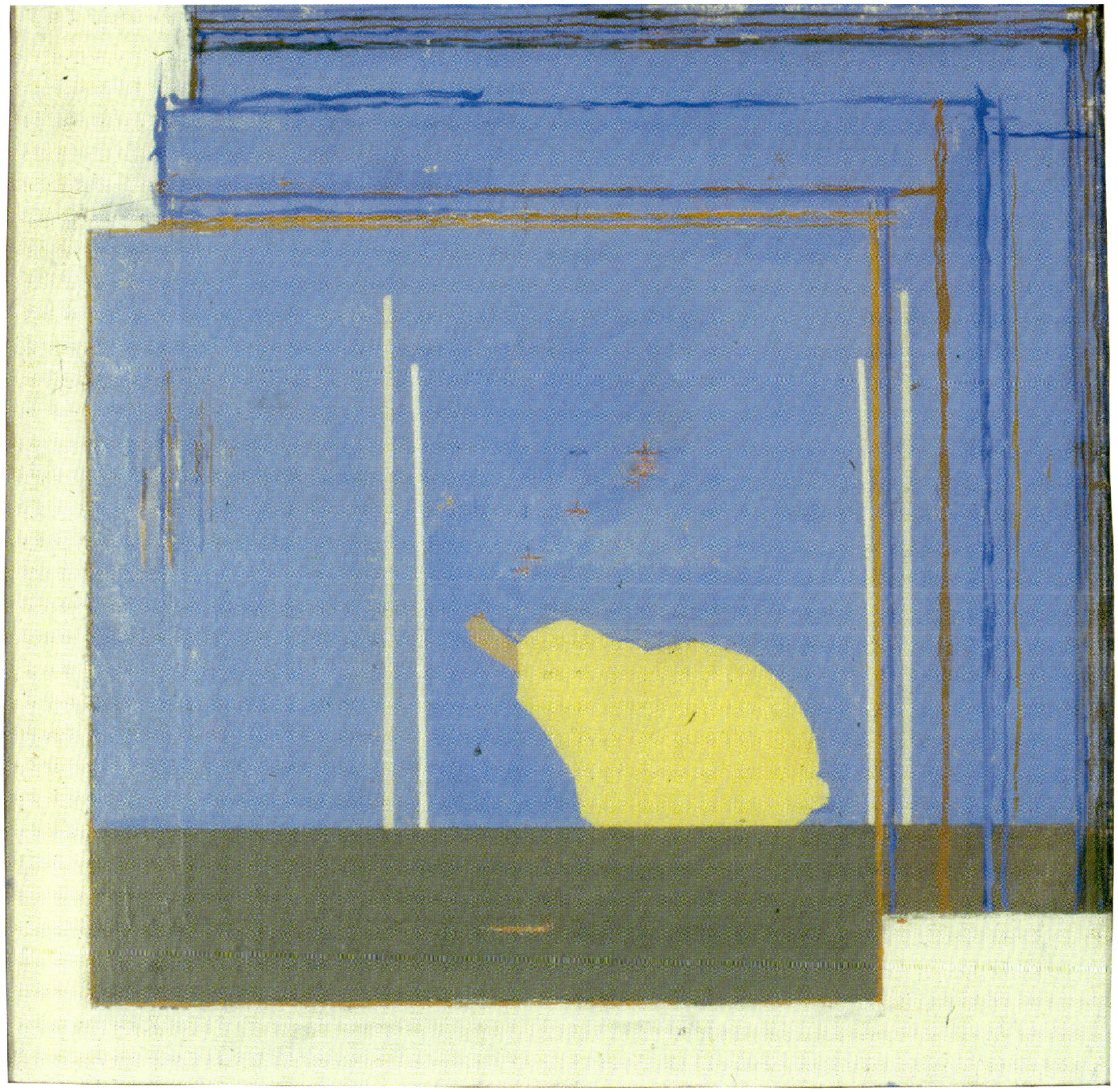

Diary of a pear, 1972
oil on board 16½ x 16½ inches

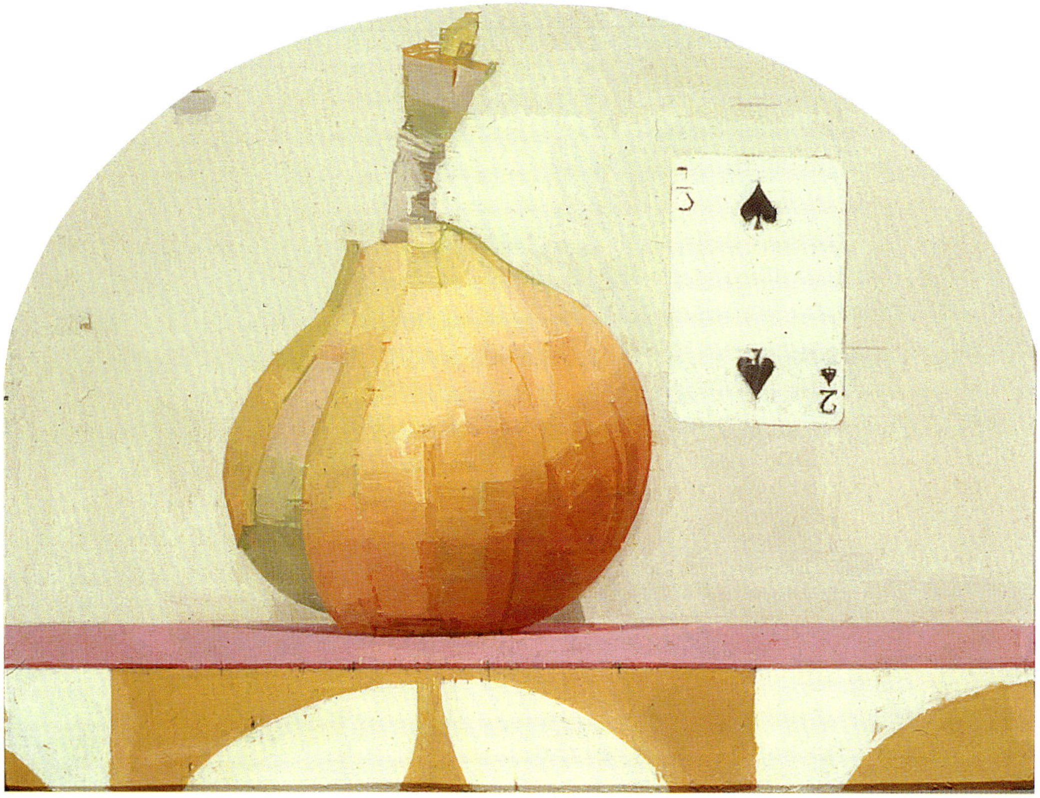

Onion with playing card, 1972
oil on canvas   12 x 15 inches

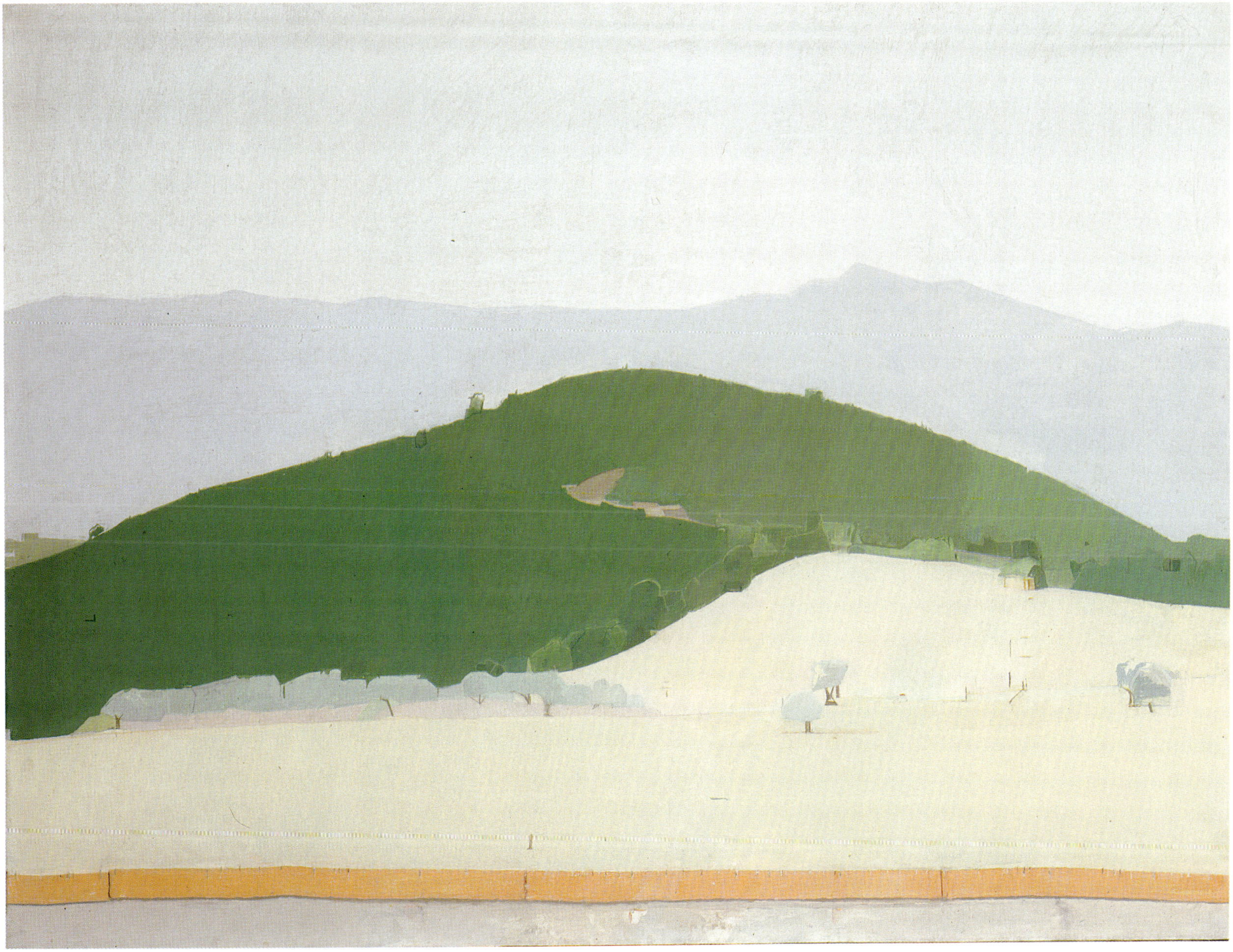

Italian landscape, 1972
oil on canvas 34 x 44 inches

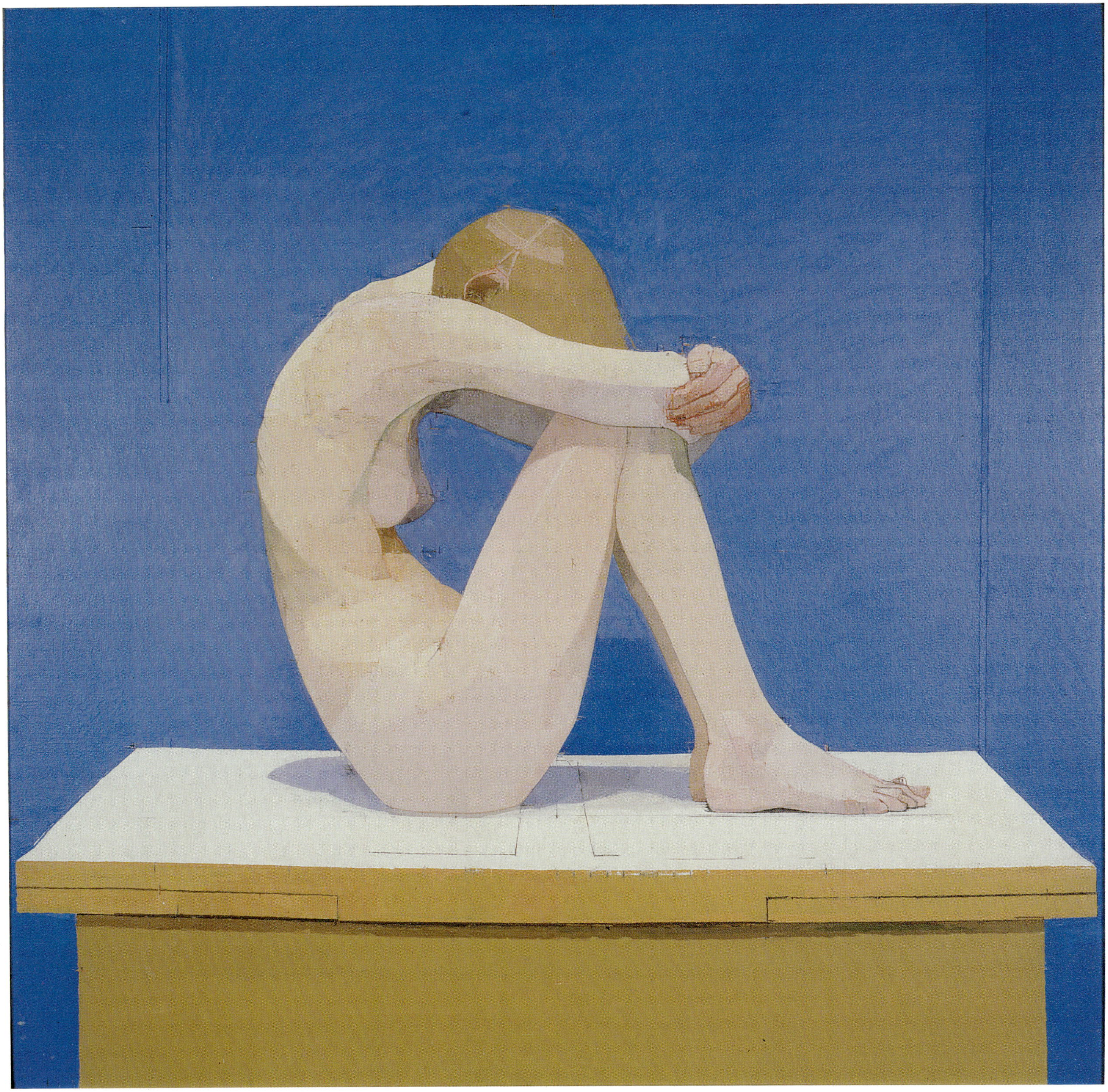

Summer picture, 1972
oil on canvas 43 x 43¼ inches

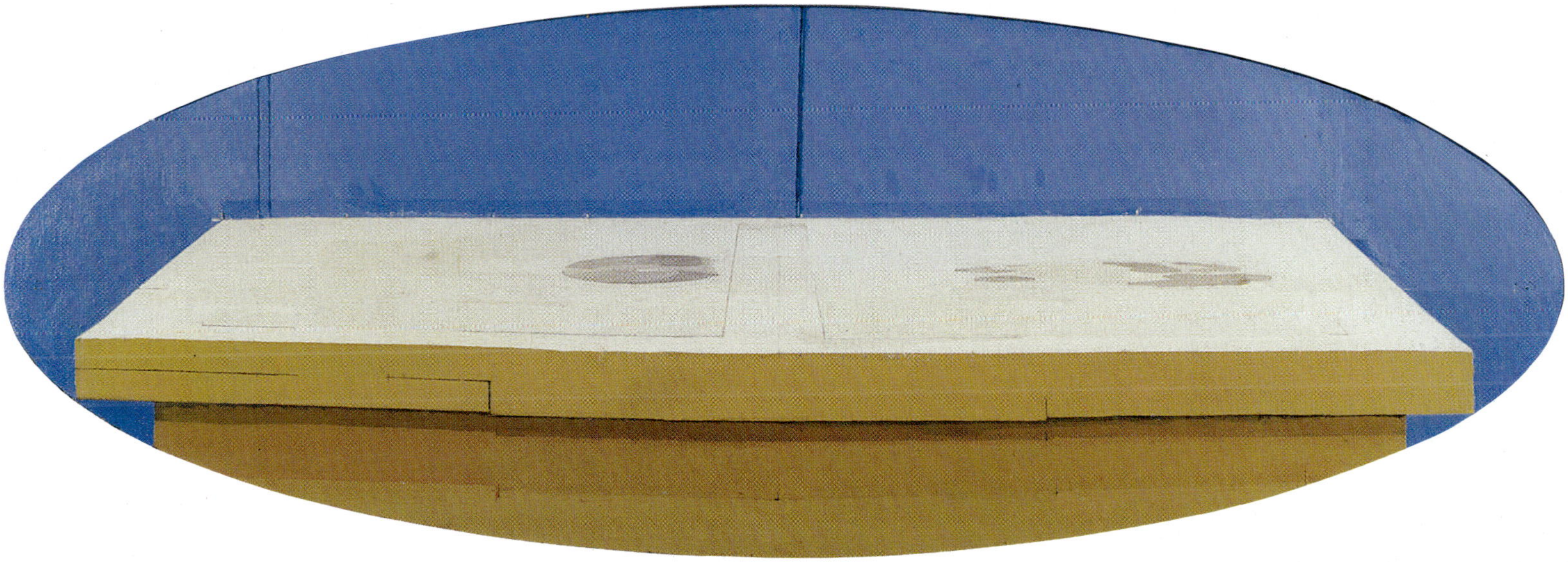

Still life with model marks, 1971-72
oil on canvas, laid on panel 16 x 40 inches

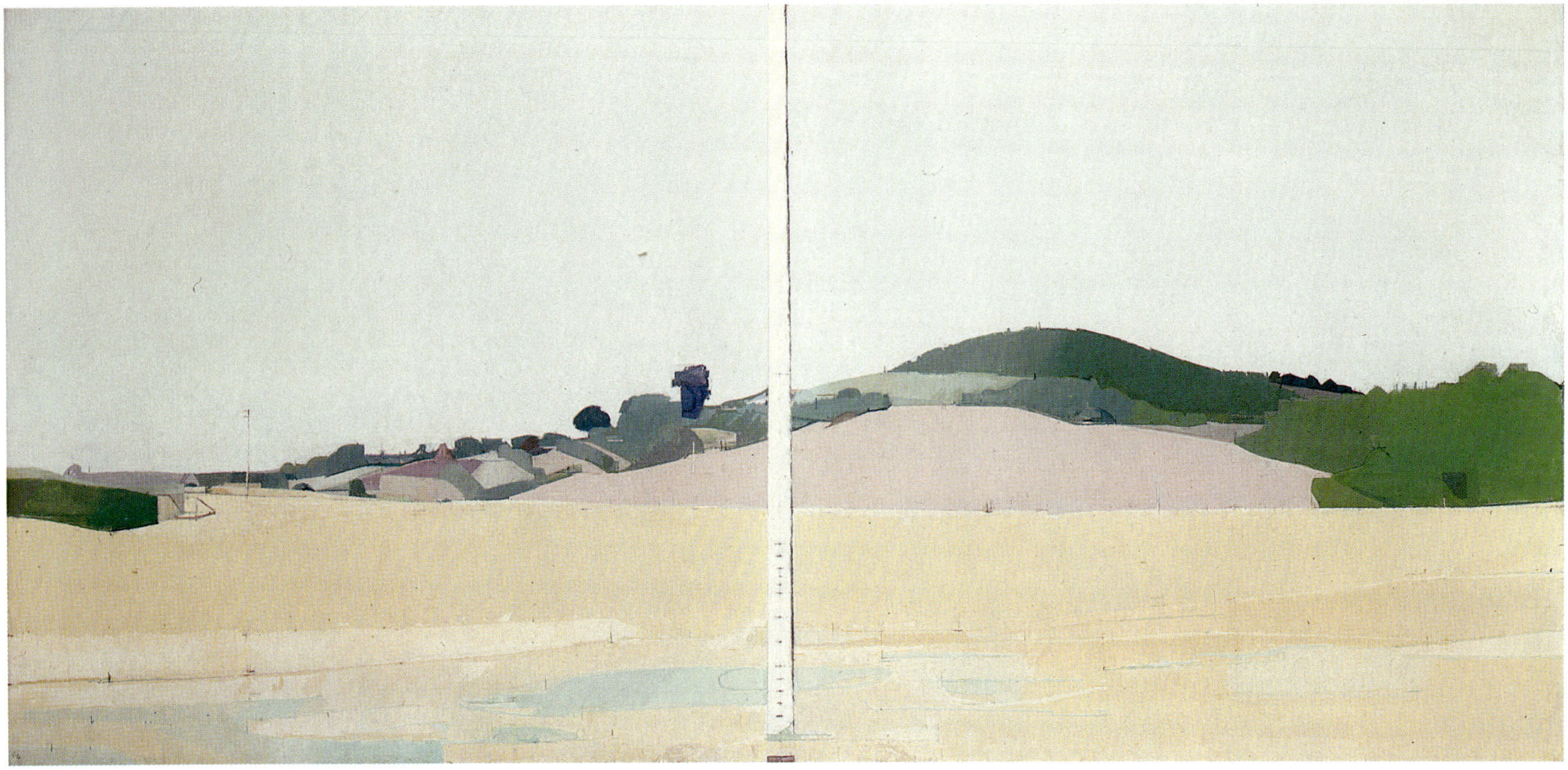

Pignano, 1973
oil on canvas 25 x 50 inches

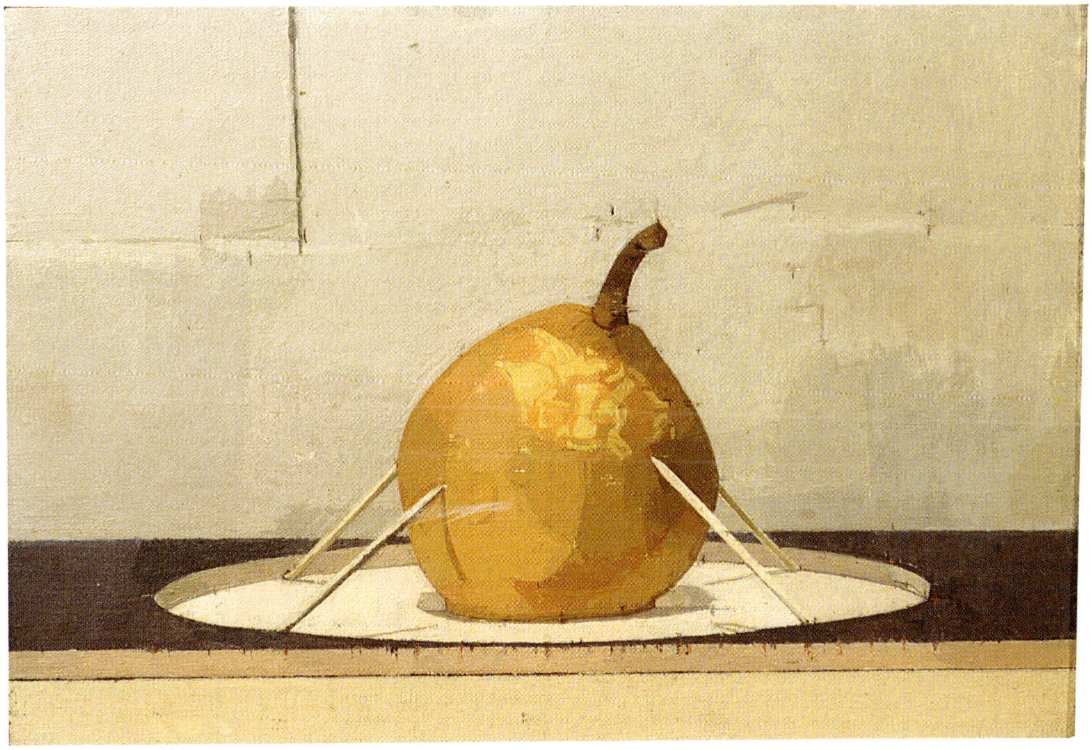

Wax fruit, 1973
oil on canvas 7¾ x 11½ inches

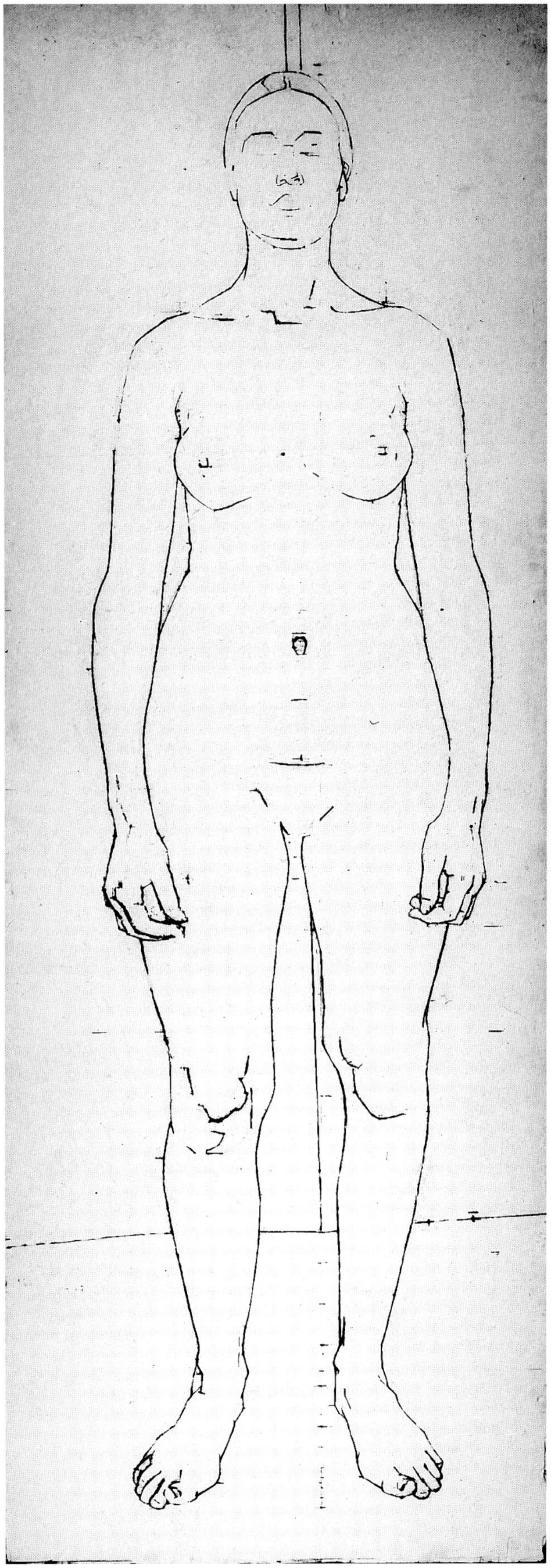

Stevie, PVA drawing, 1972
PVA on panel 74 x 26 inches

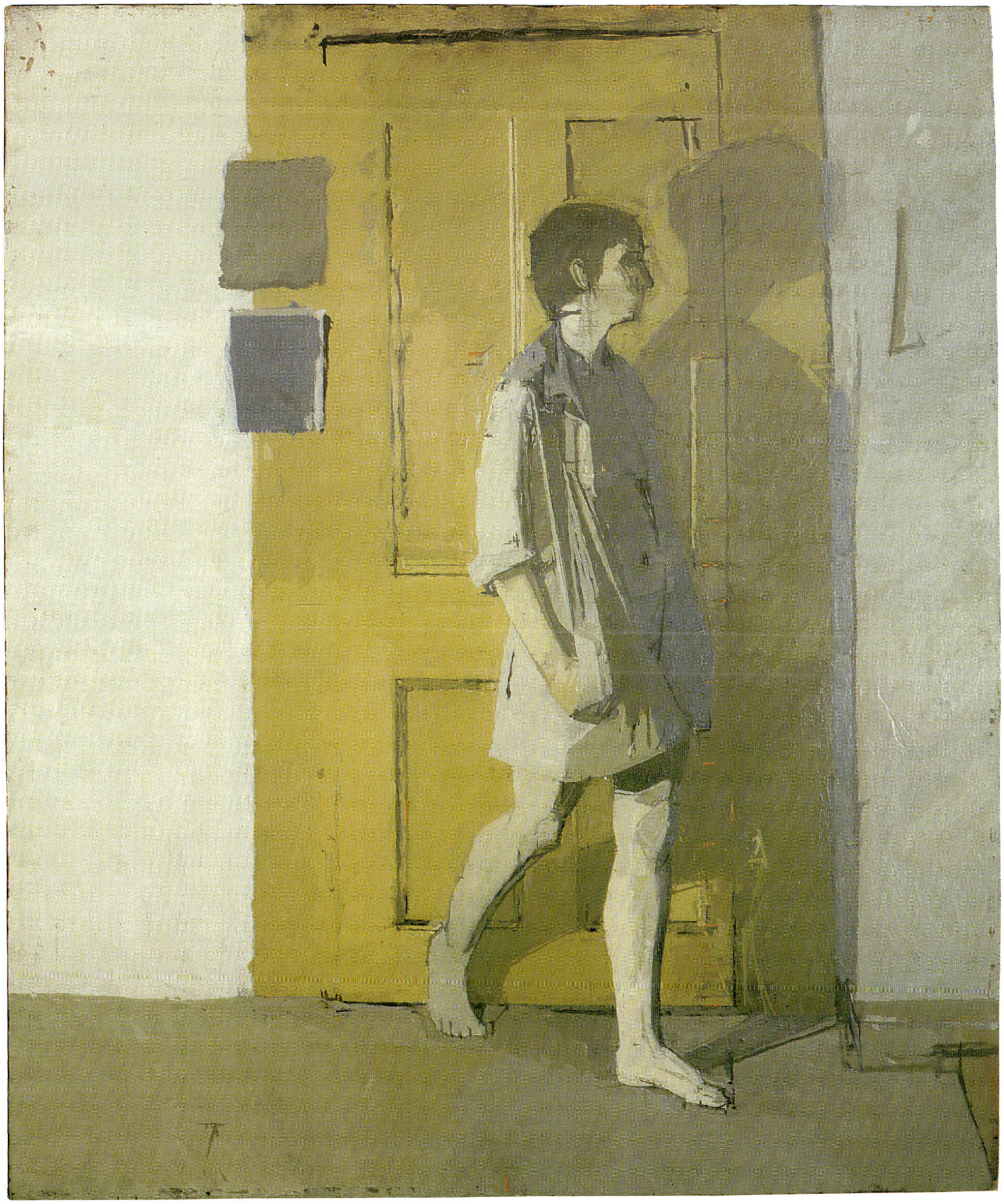

Jenefer by a door, 1971-74
oil on panel   24 x 20 inches

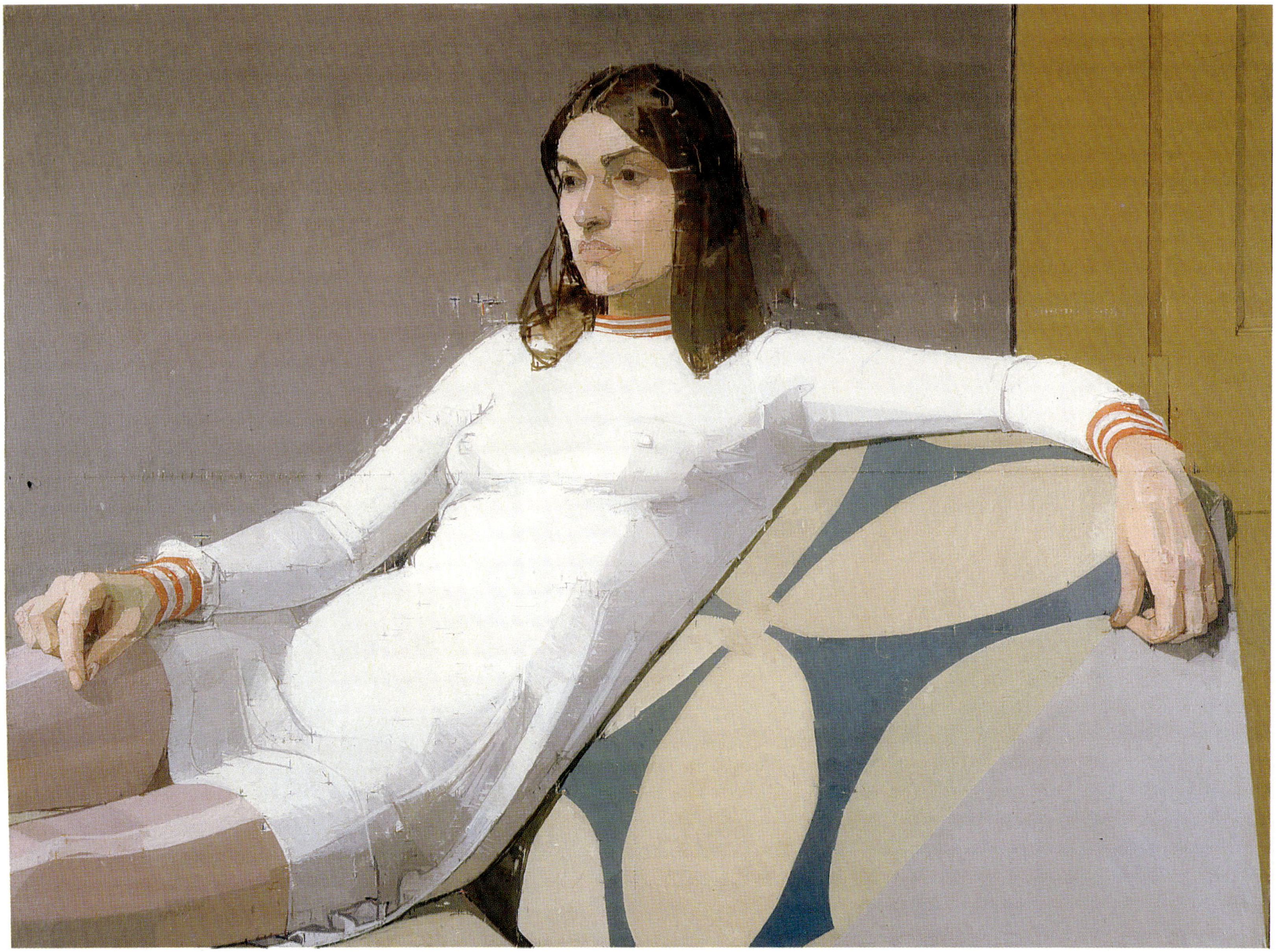

Georgia, 1973
oil on canvas   33 x 44 inches

The British Council collection

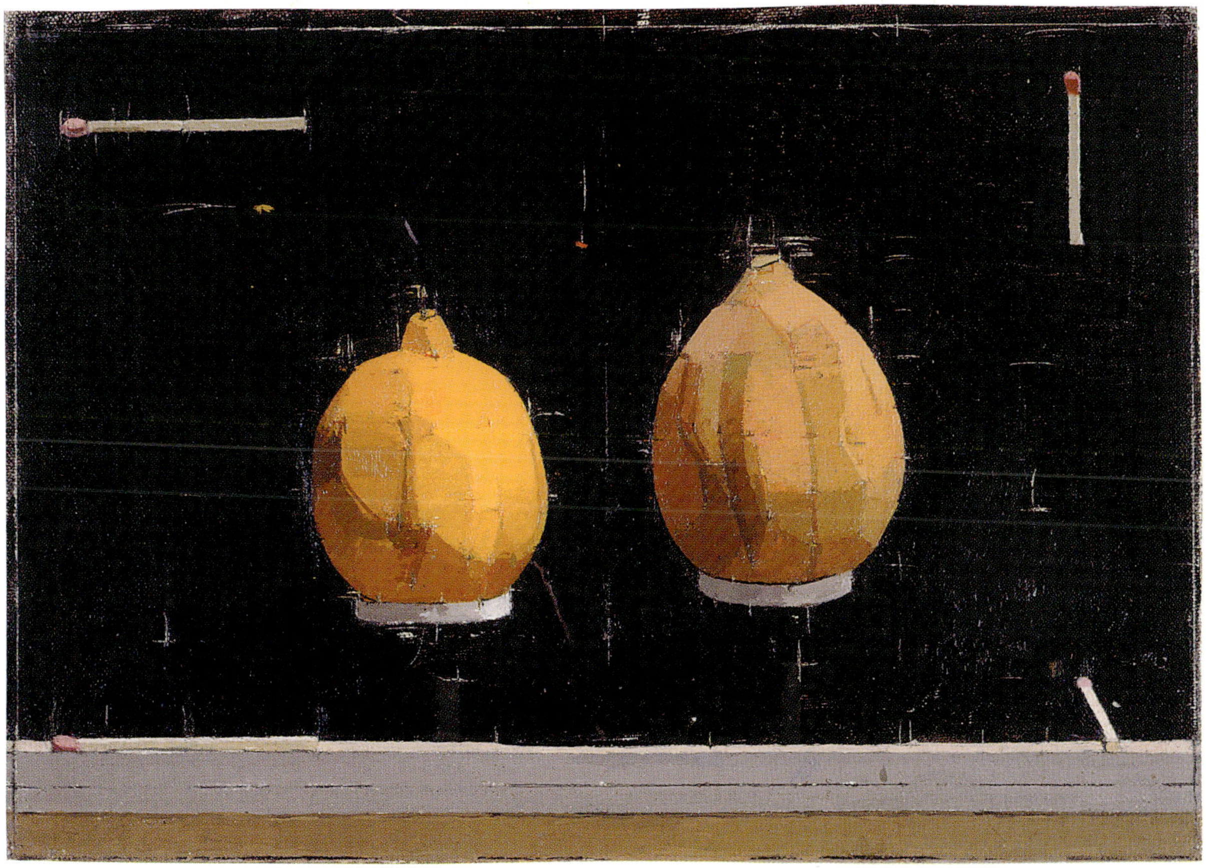

Lemons, 1975
oil on canvas, laid on panel 8 x 11¼ inches

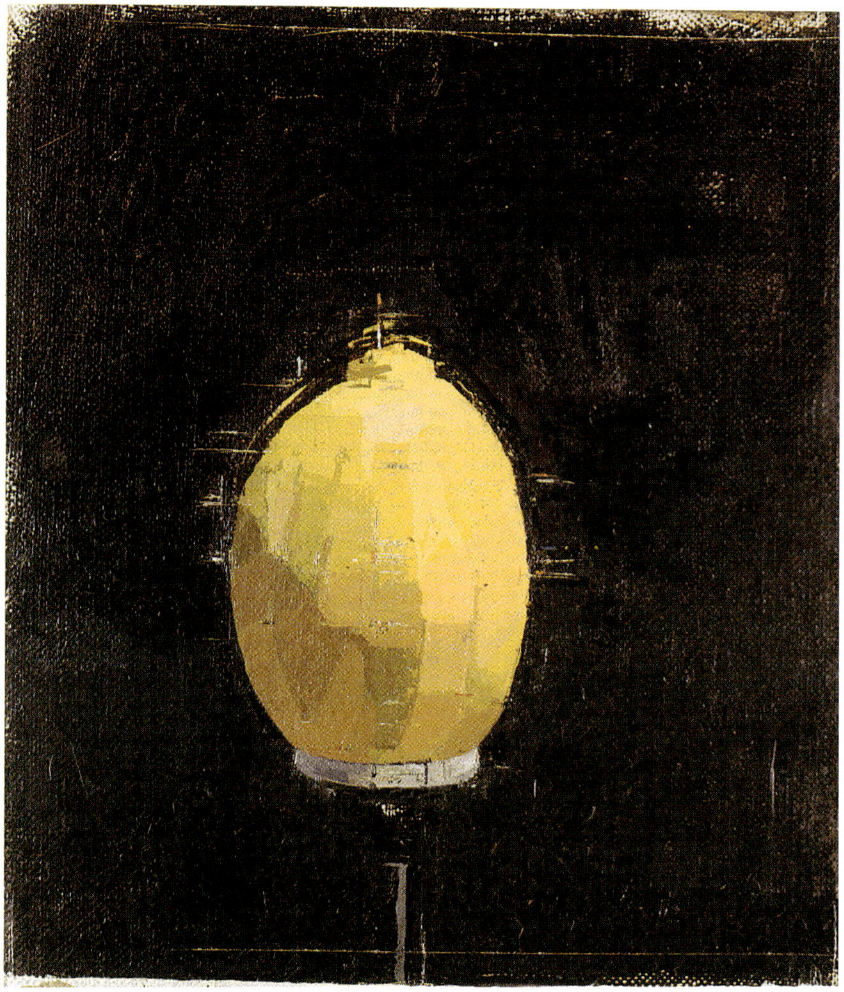

Lemon, 1975

oil on canvas, laid on panel 7¾ x 6¼ inches

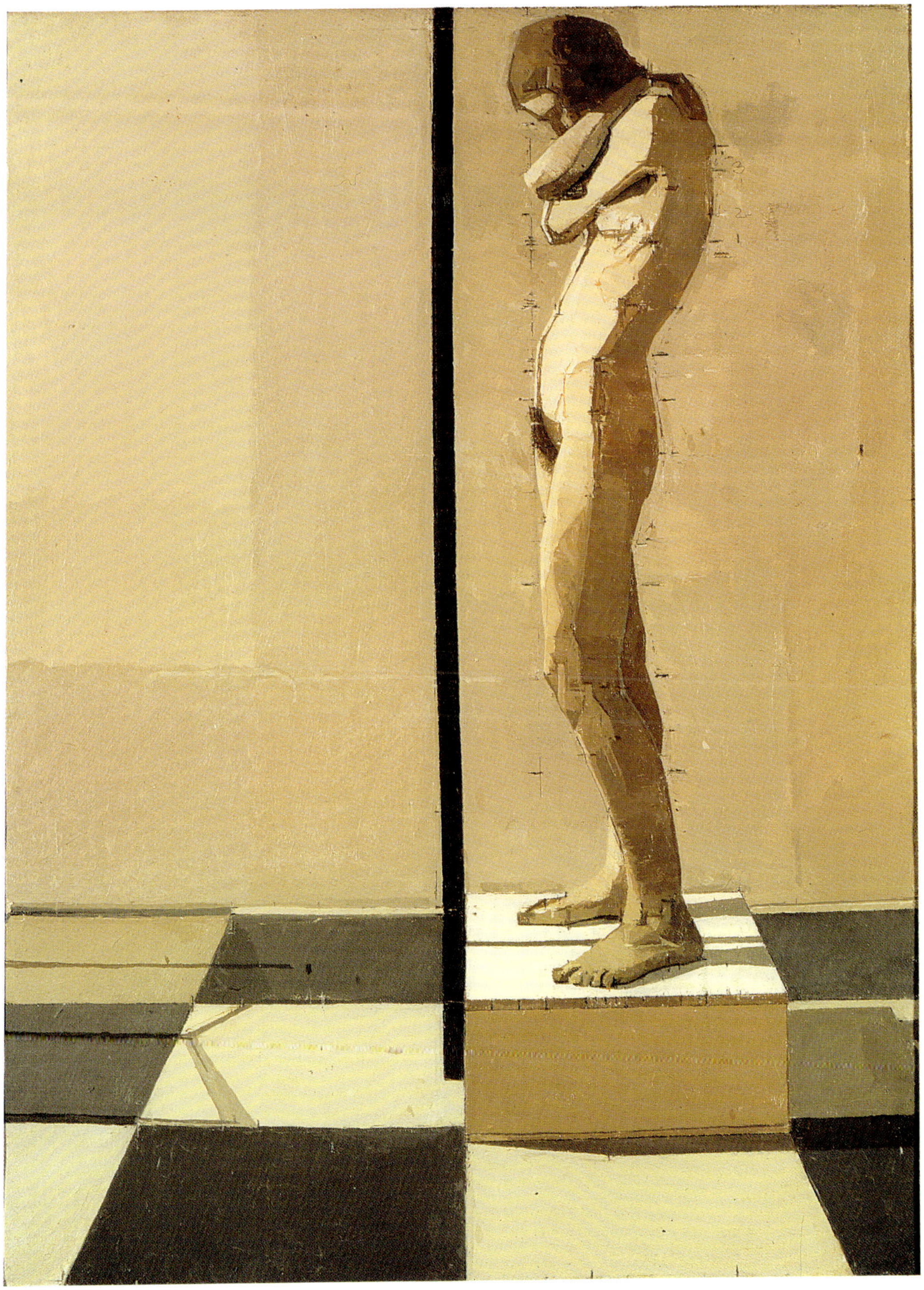

Snake, 1975

oil on canvas 19½ x 13¾ inches

The Arts Council of Great Britain, Hayward Gallery

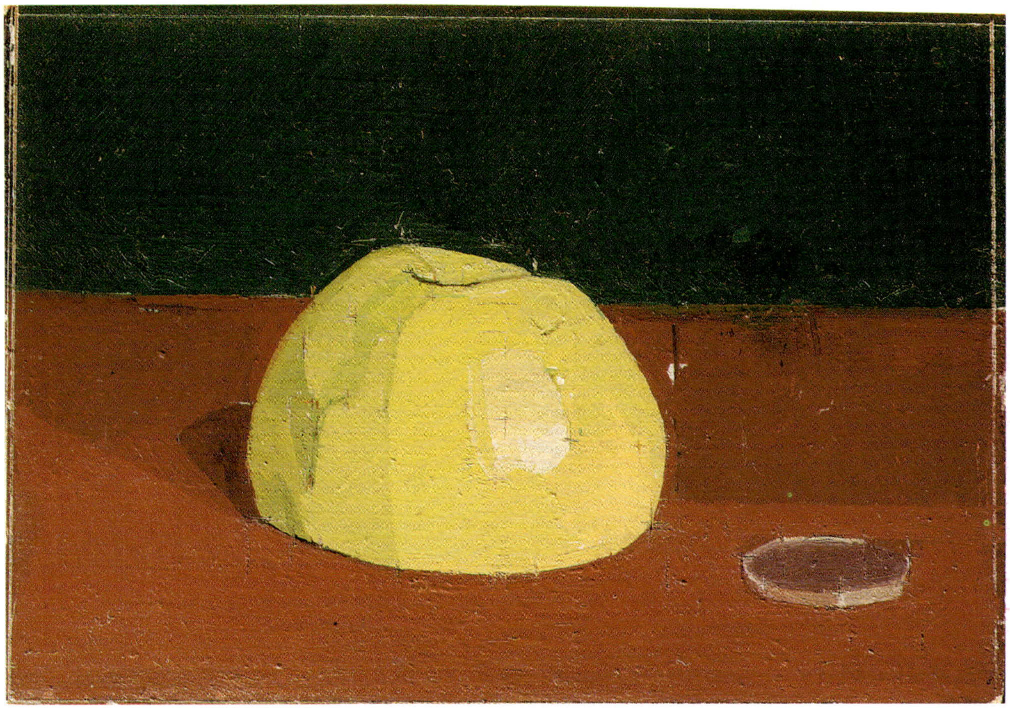

Half an apple, 1976
oil on canvas, laid on panel   5½ x 7½ inches

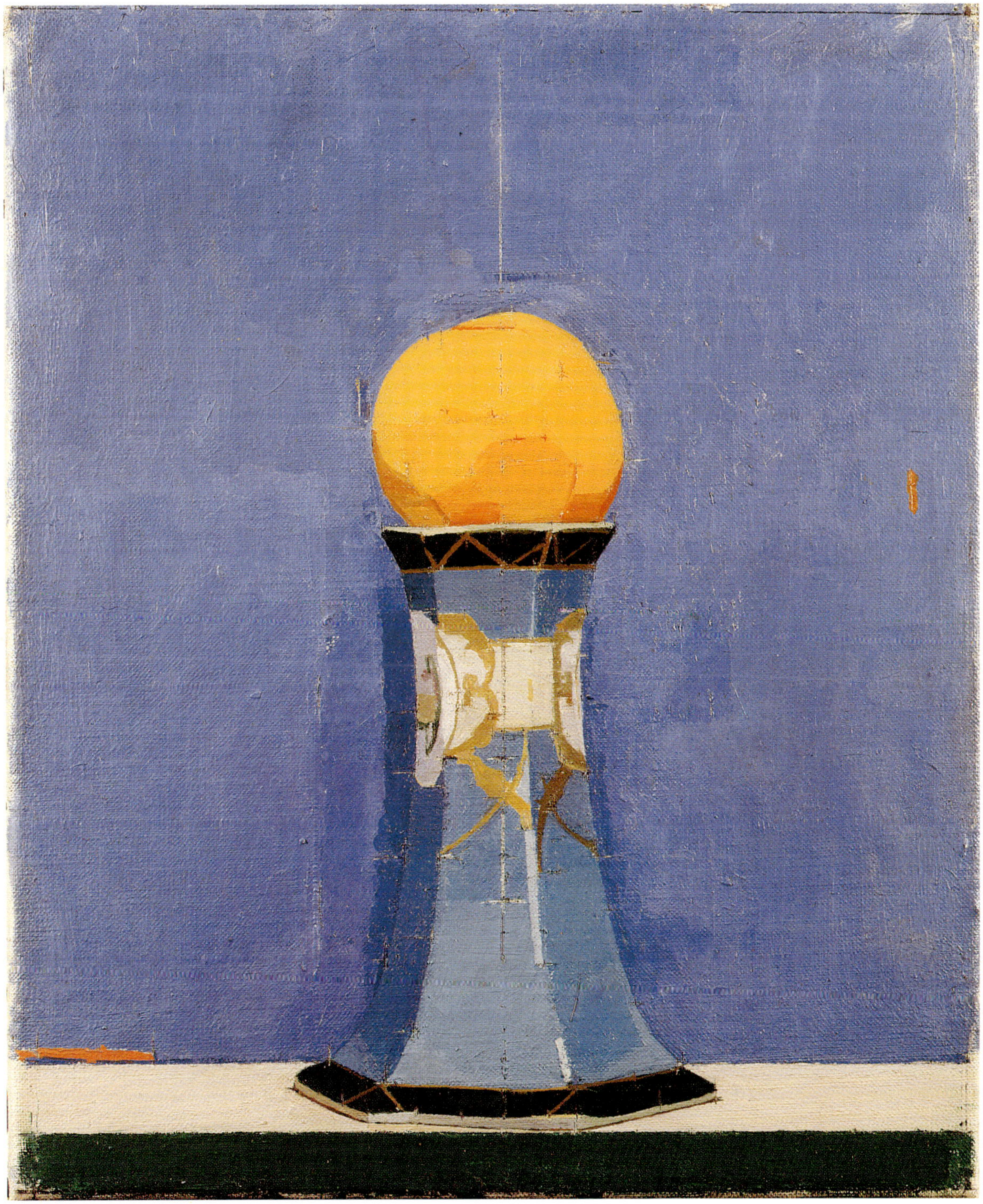

Peach with blue vase, 1976
oil on canvas, laid on panel   12 x 9¾ inches

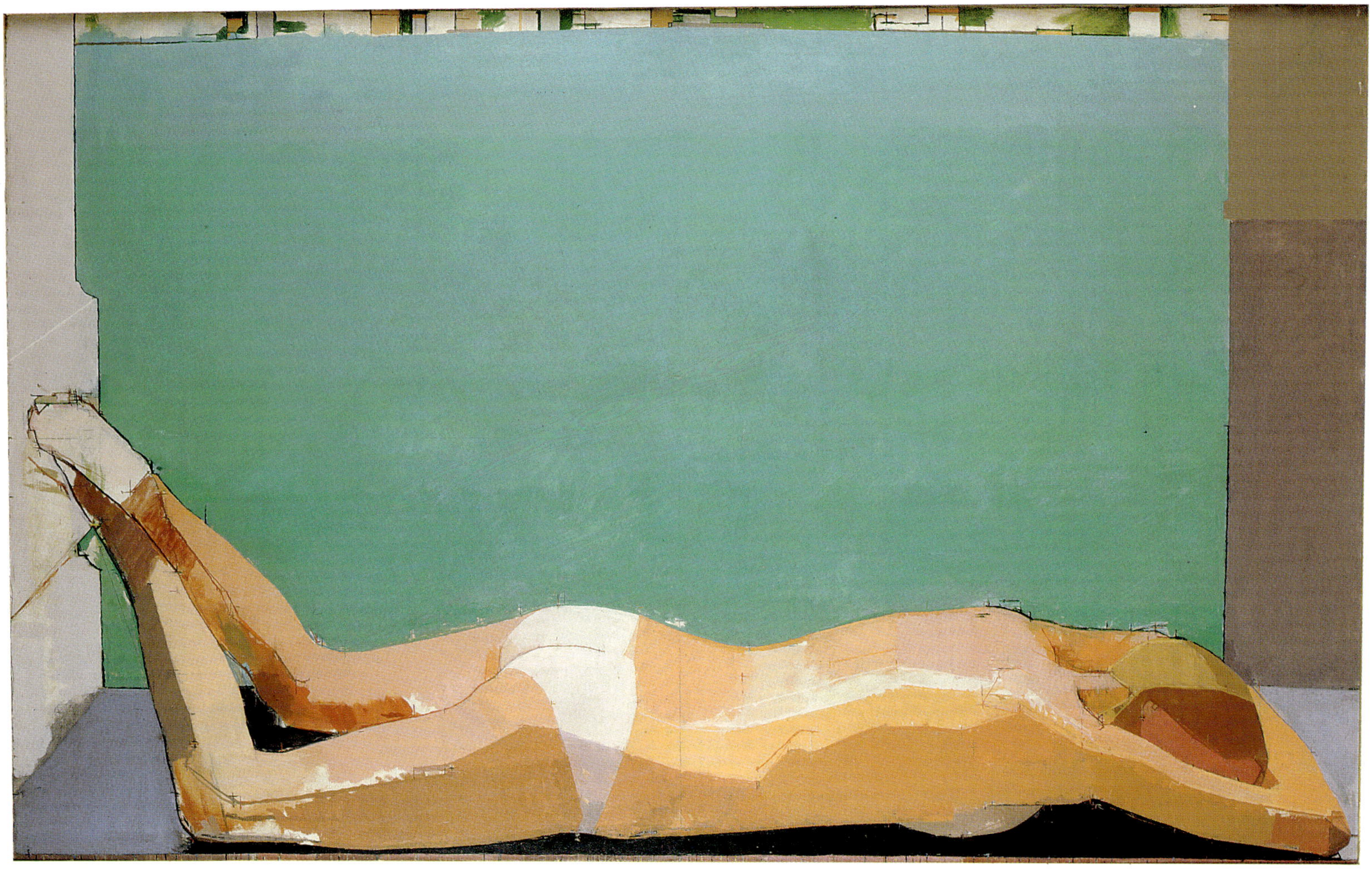

Nude with Lake Lugano, 1976
oil on canvas $34^1/_2$ x $54^1/_2$ inches

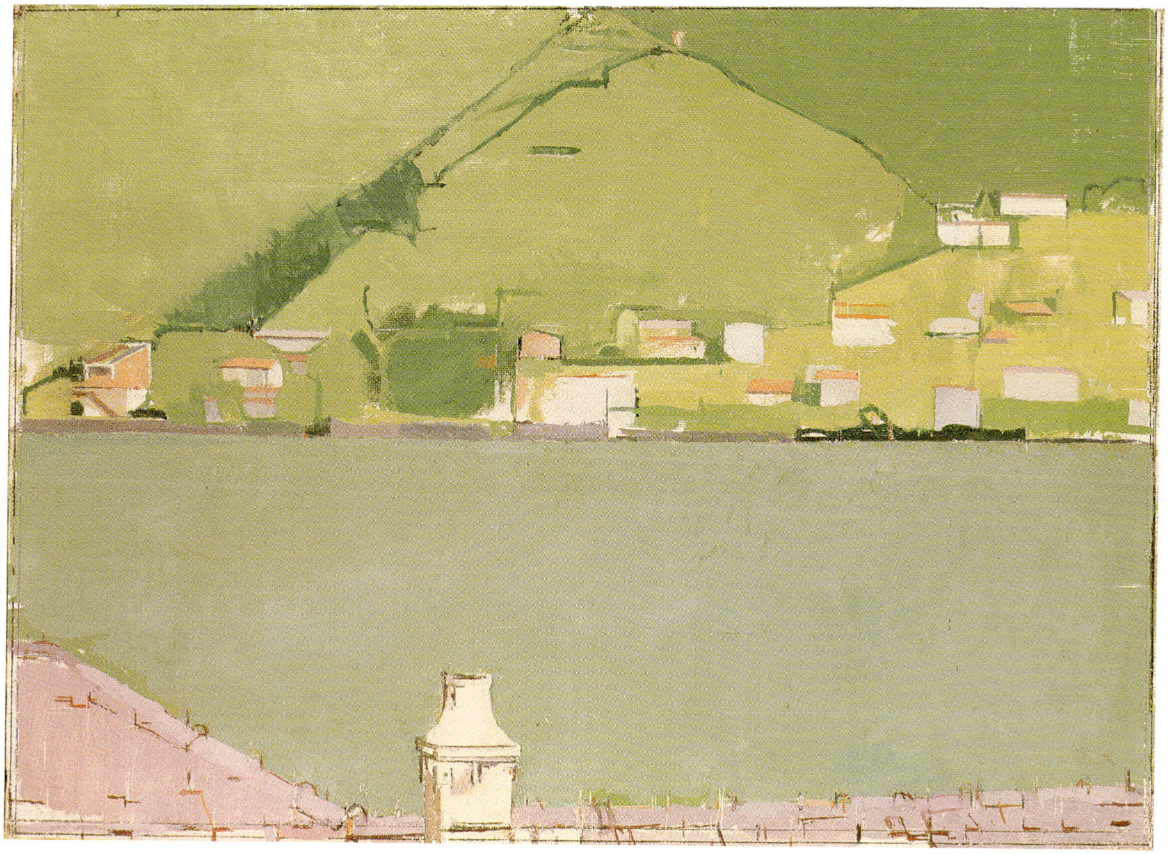

Lake Lugano, 1976
oil on canvas, laid on panel   9 5/8 x 12 7/8 inches

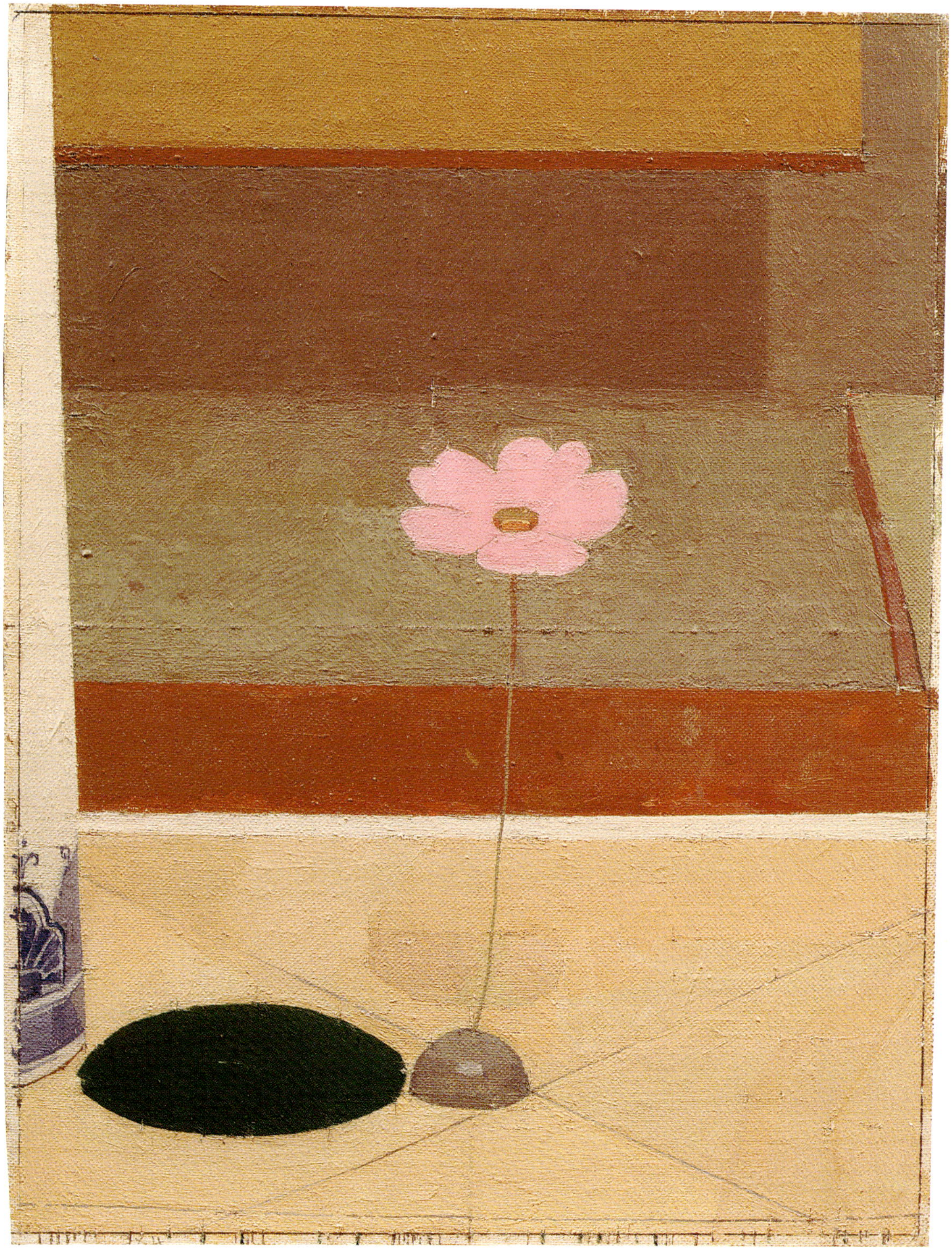

Alexandra rose, 1977
oil on canvas, laid on panel 12 x 9 inches

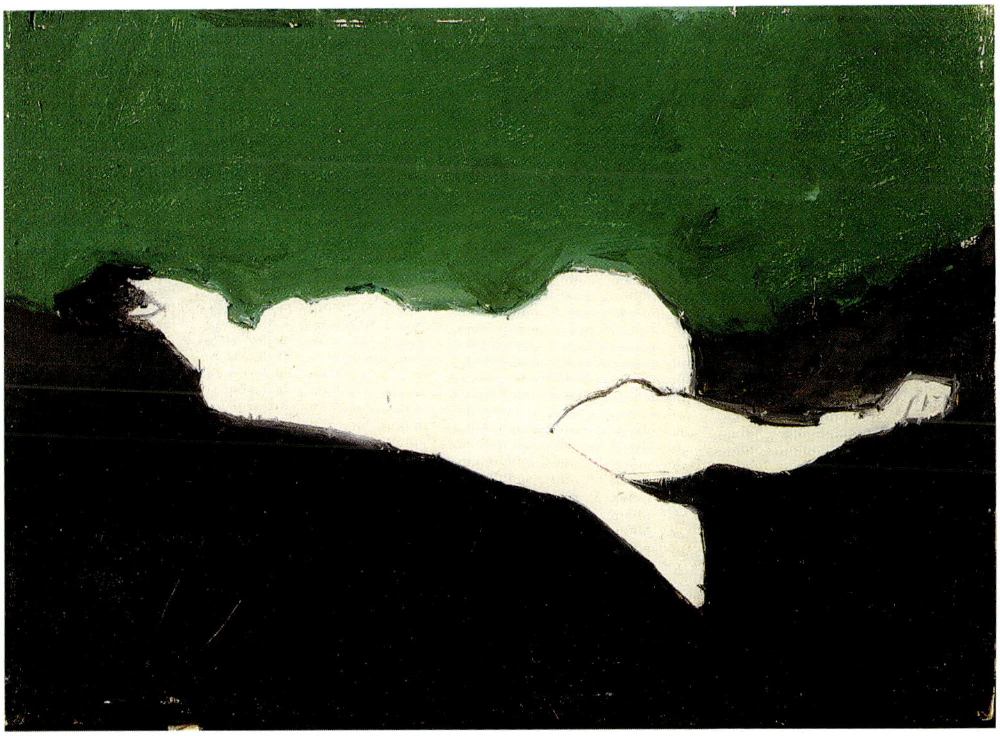

Pat's nude, 1976
oil on panel 7½ x 10½ inches

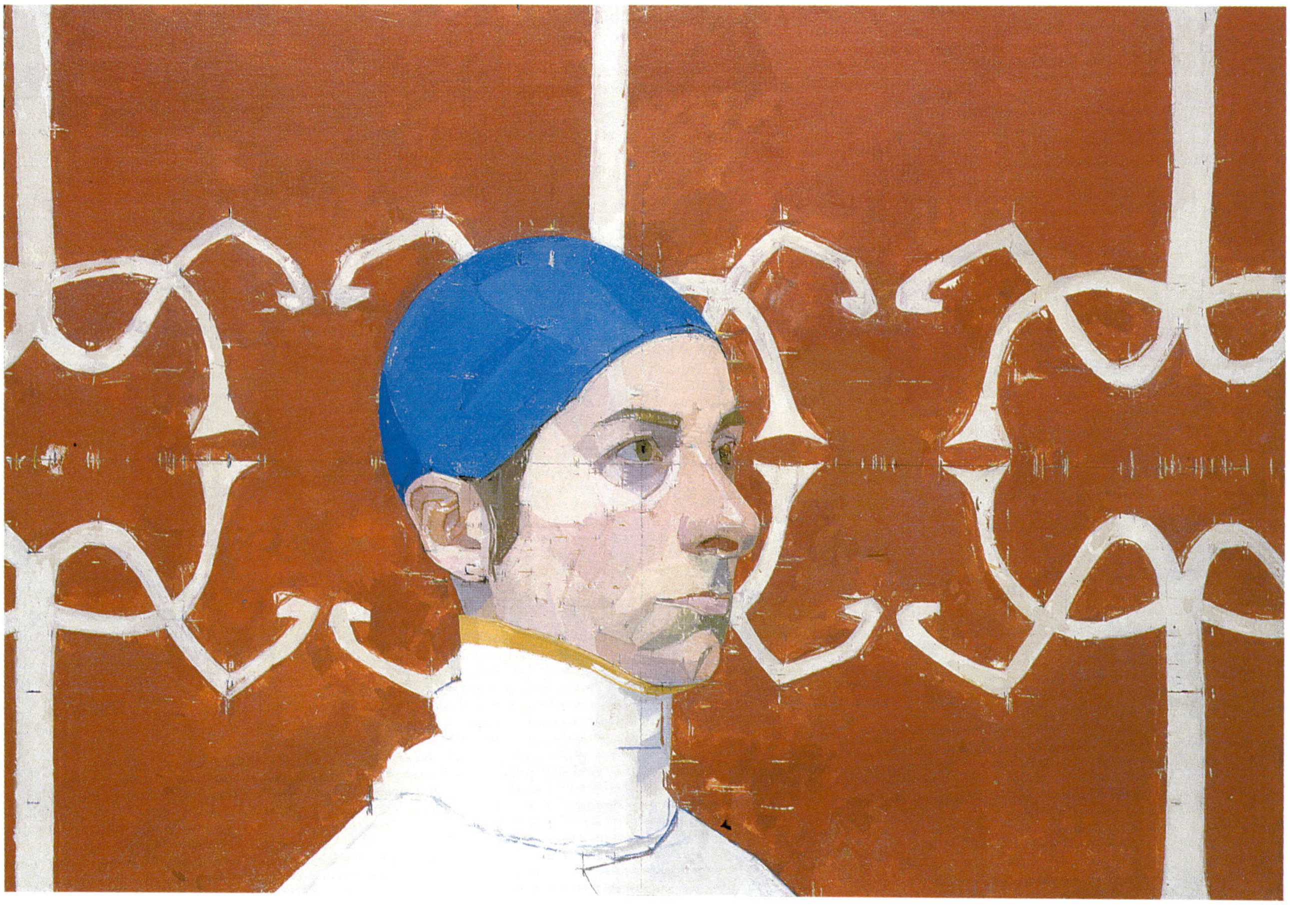

Sue wearing a blue swimming cap, 1978-80
oil on canvas 19½ x 27½ inches

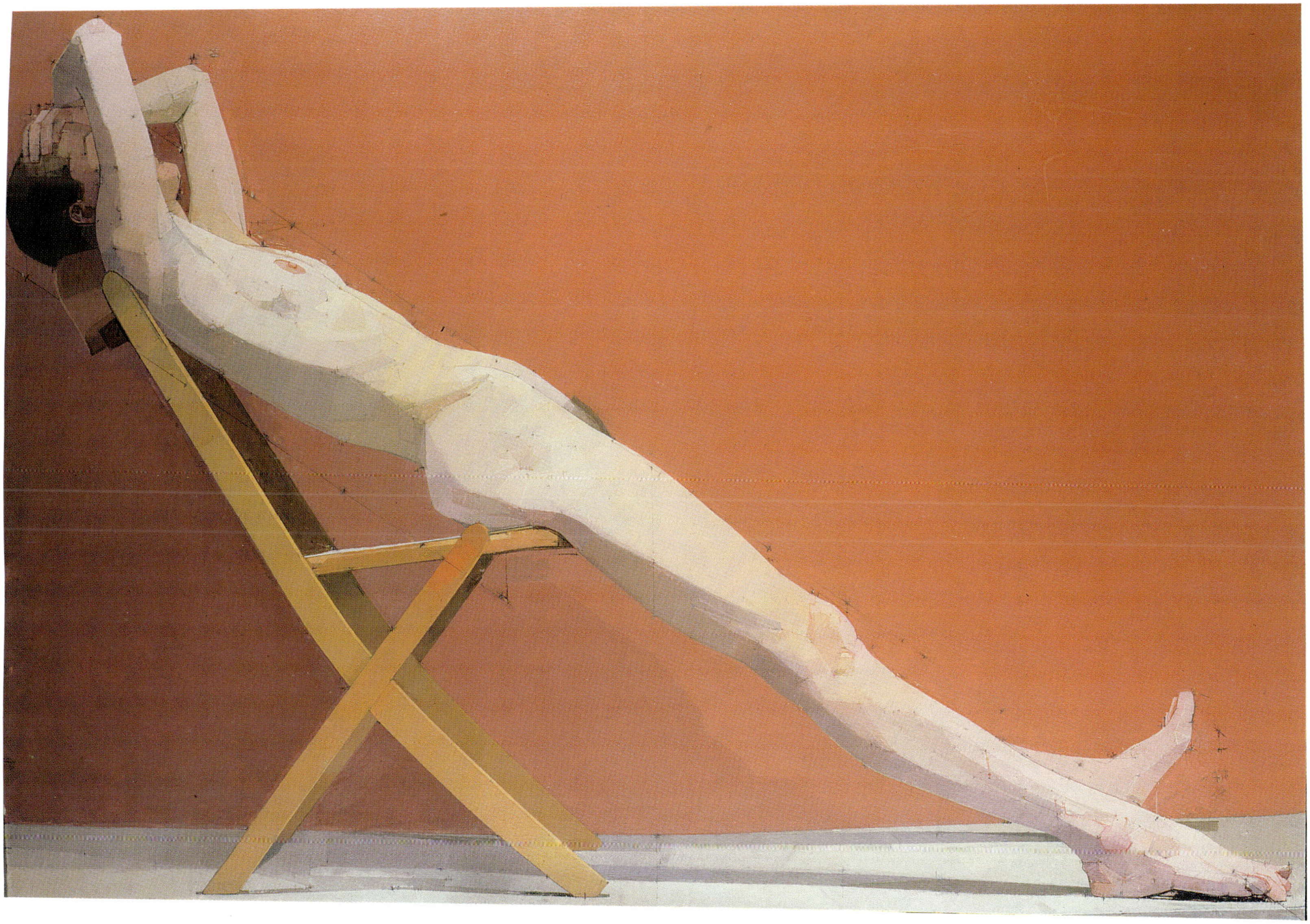

The diagonal, 1971-77
oil on canvas   46½ x 65¾ inches

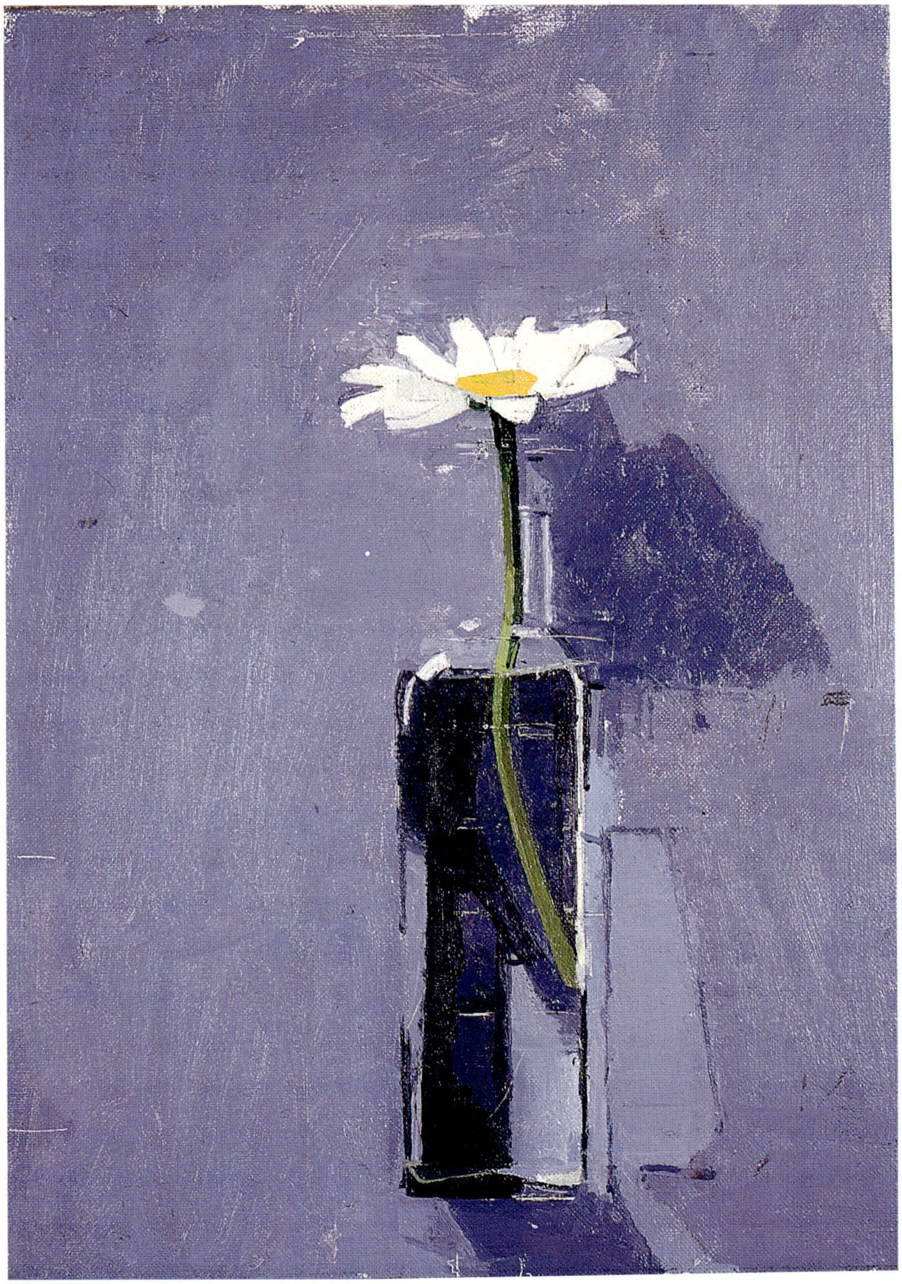

Daisy, 1976
oil on canvas, $13^{3}/_{4}$ x 10 inches

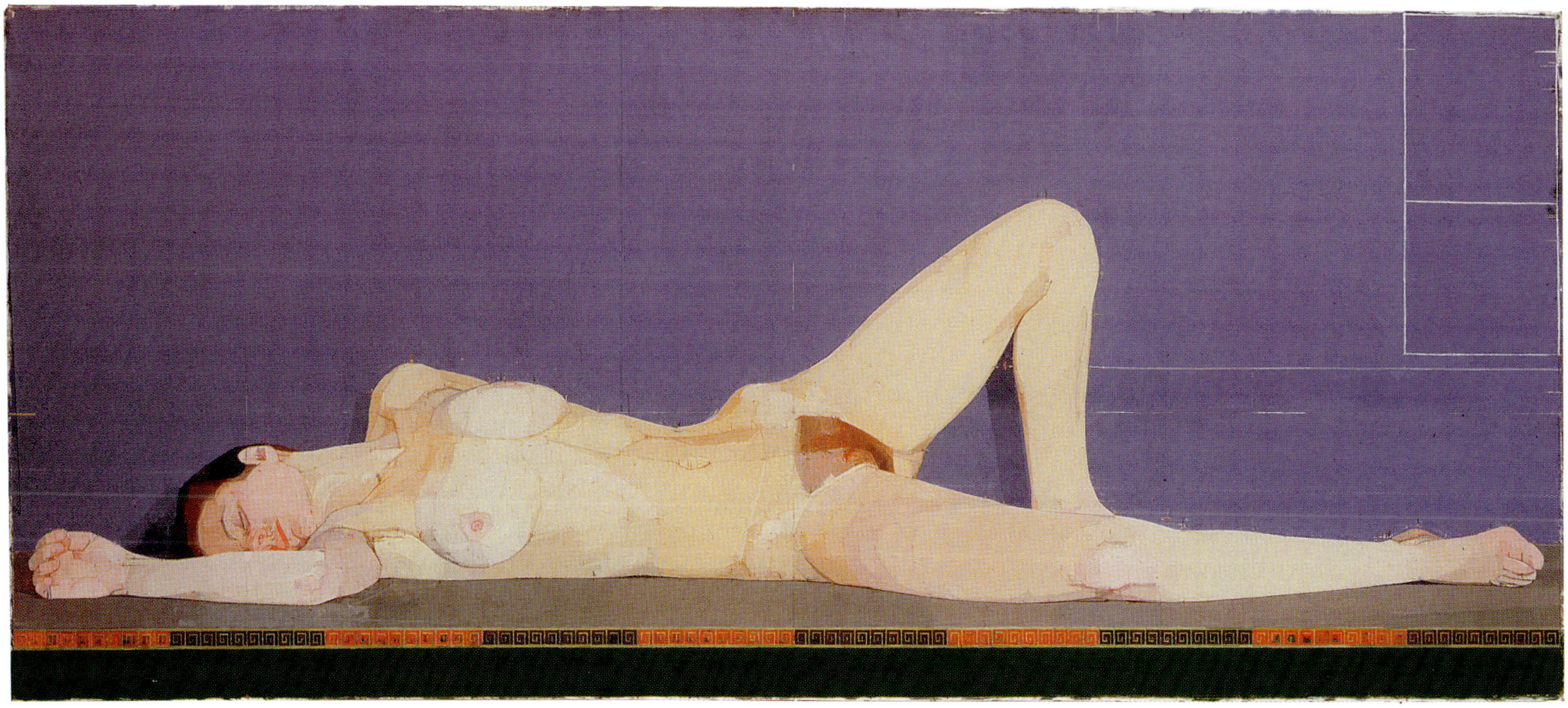

Root five nude, 1976
oil on canvas 30.25 x 67.639 inches

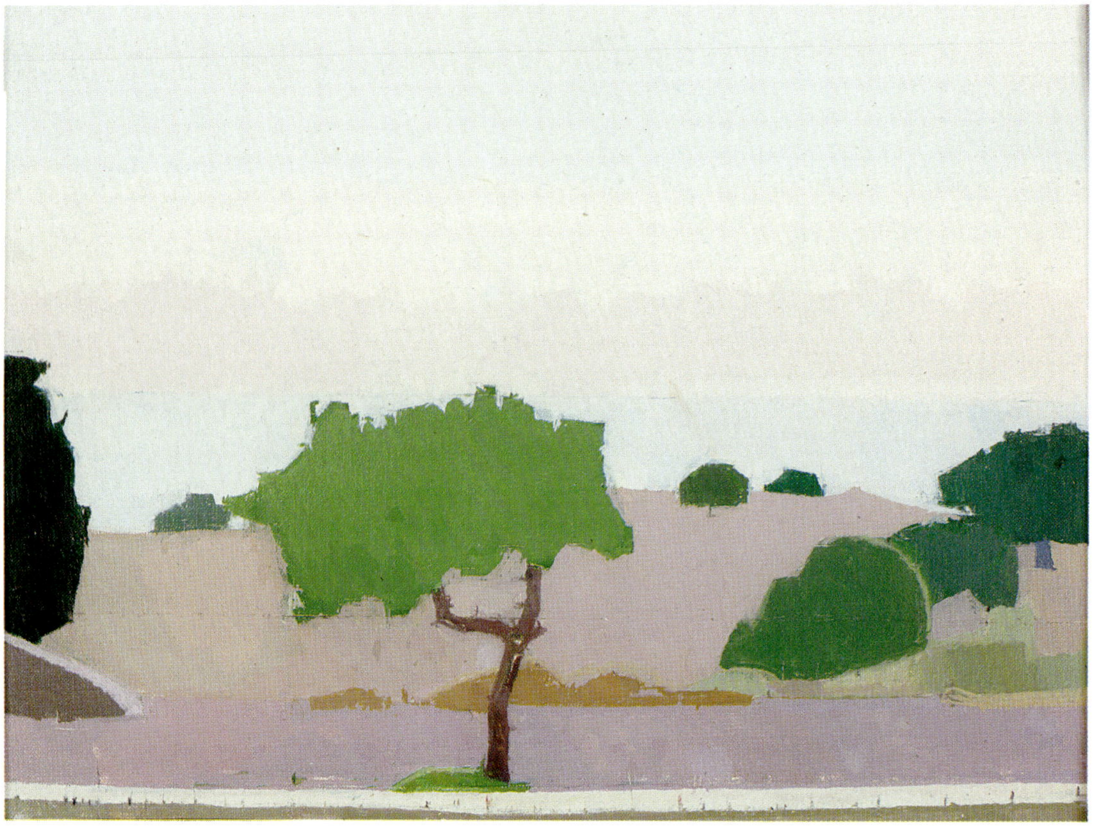

Sunset, Lemba, Cyprus, 1980

oil on canvas, laid on panel   12 1/8 x 16 1/4 inches

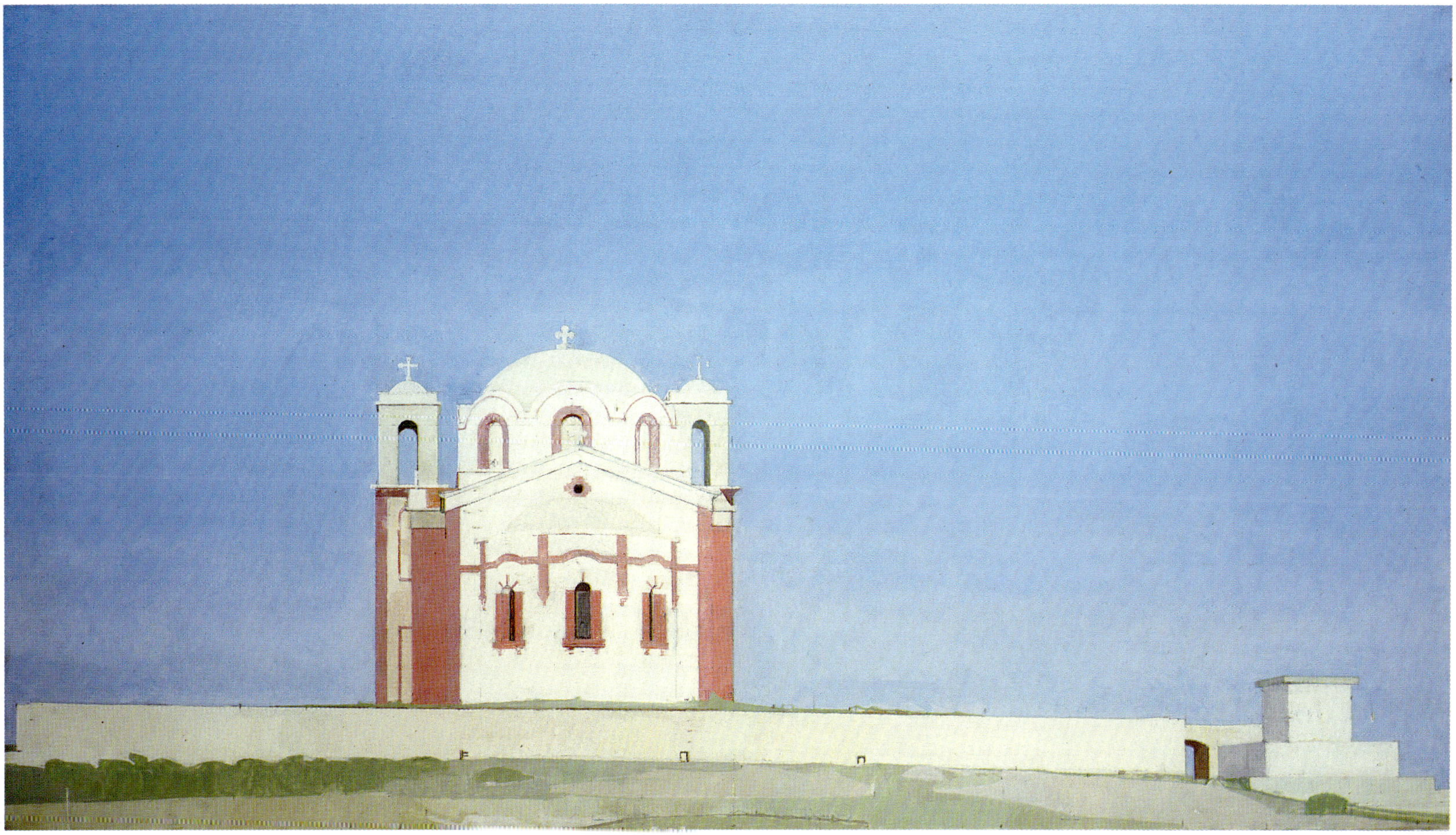

The Church by the sea, Khlorakas, Cyprus, 1980
oil on canvas $28\frac{1}{2}$ x $49\frac{3}{4}$ inches

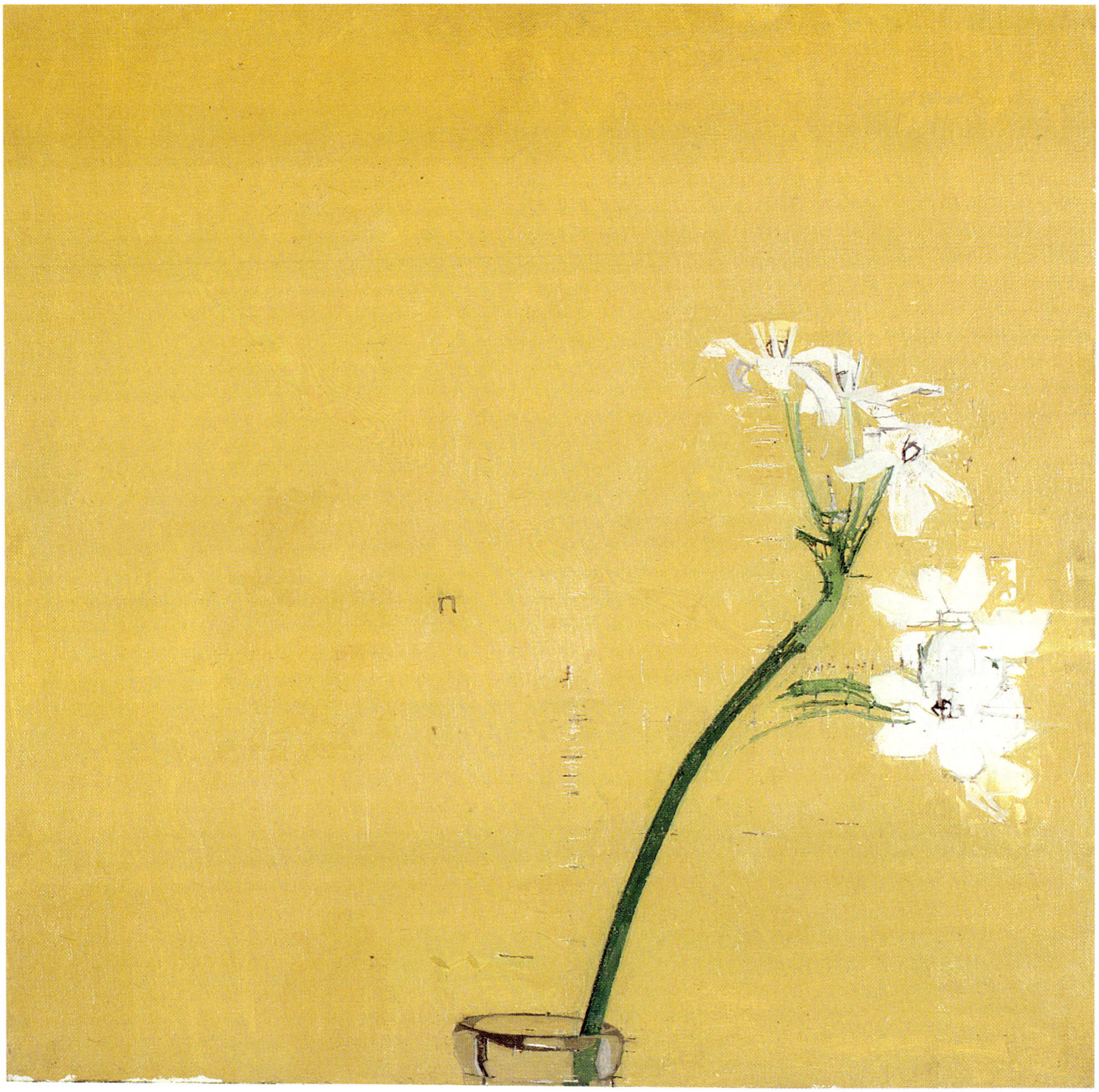

Narcissus on yellow ground, 1979
oil on canvas, laid on panel   15¼ x 15¼ inches

The De Beers' Central Selling Organization Collection

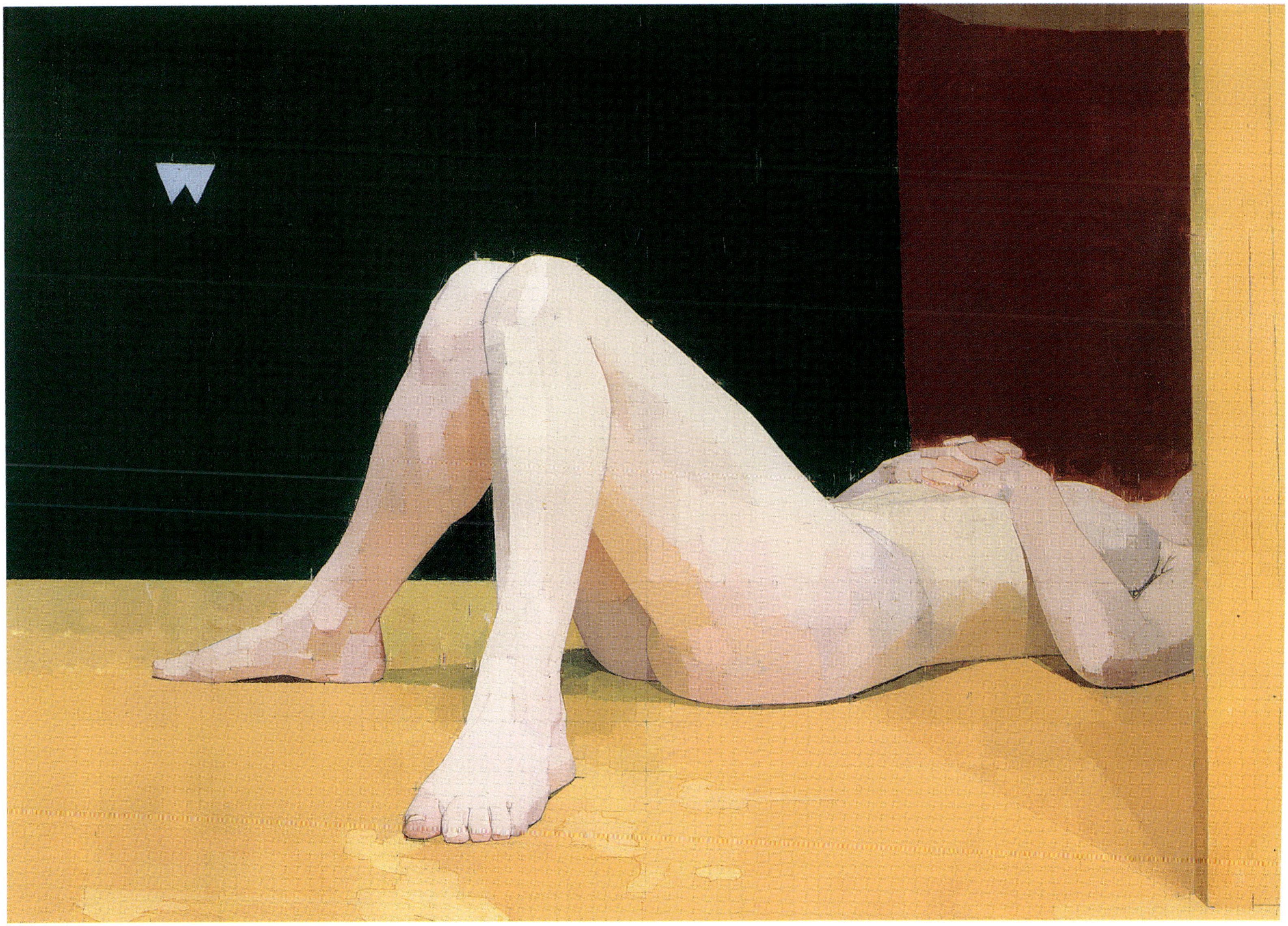

The Quarry Pignano, 1979-80
oil on canvas 31½ x 44½ inches

The Arts Council of Great Britain, Hayward Gallery

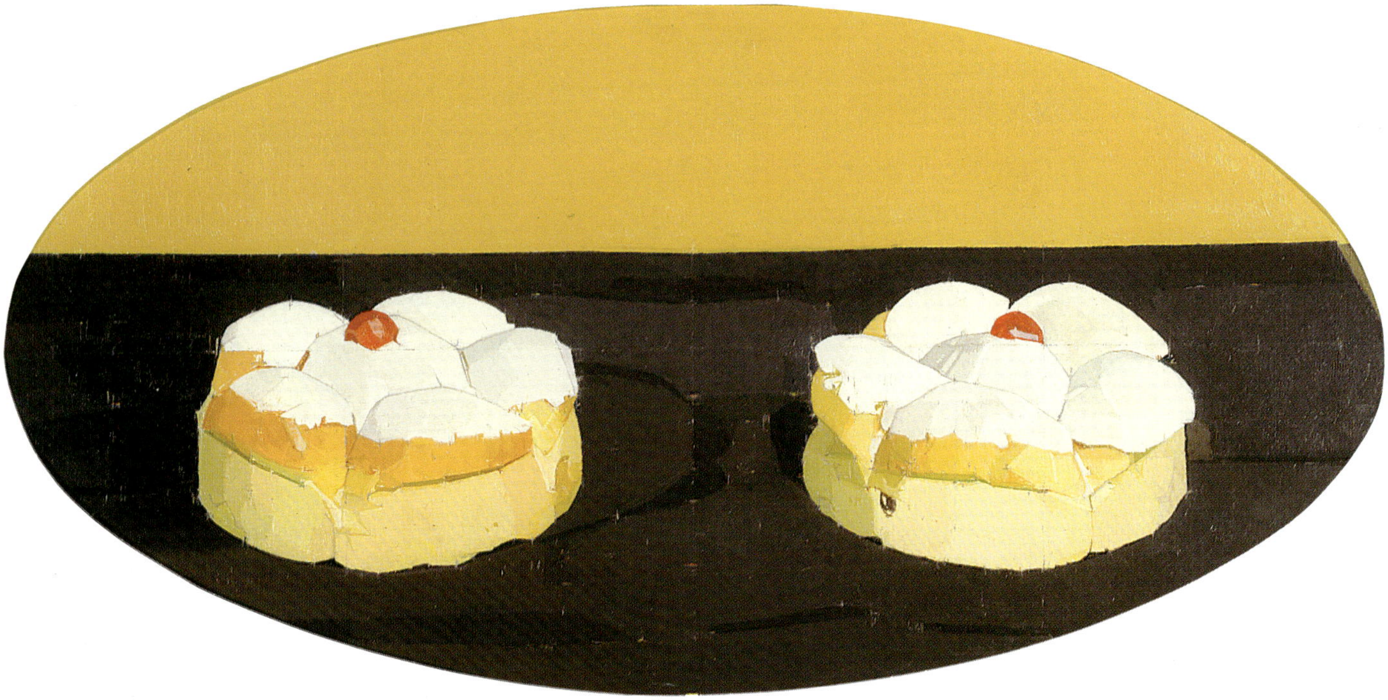

Buns, 1979
oil on canvas, laid on panel 13½ x 27 inches

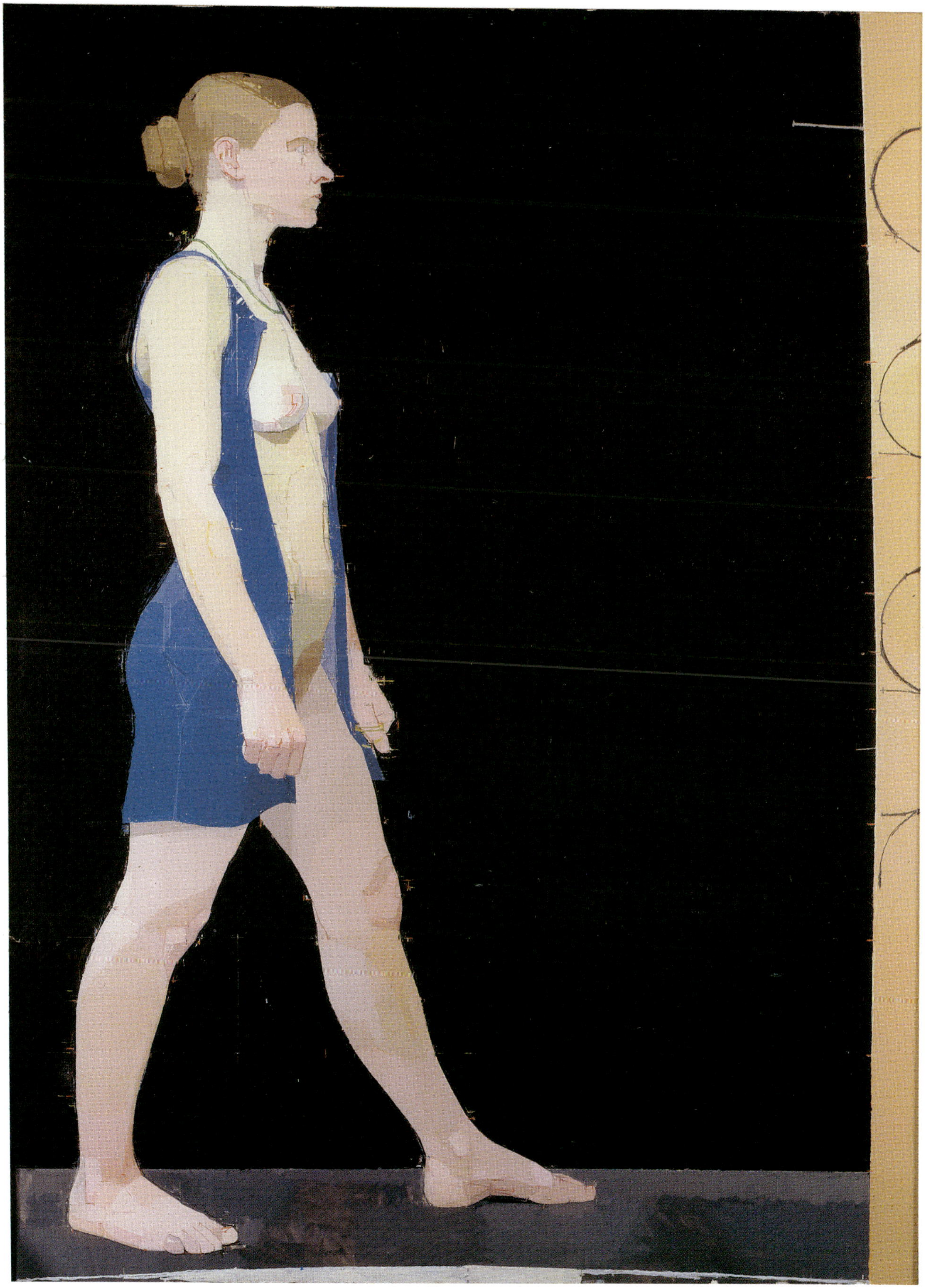

Striding nude, blue dress, II   1978-81
oil on canvas   59¾ x 43½ inches

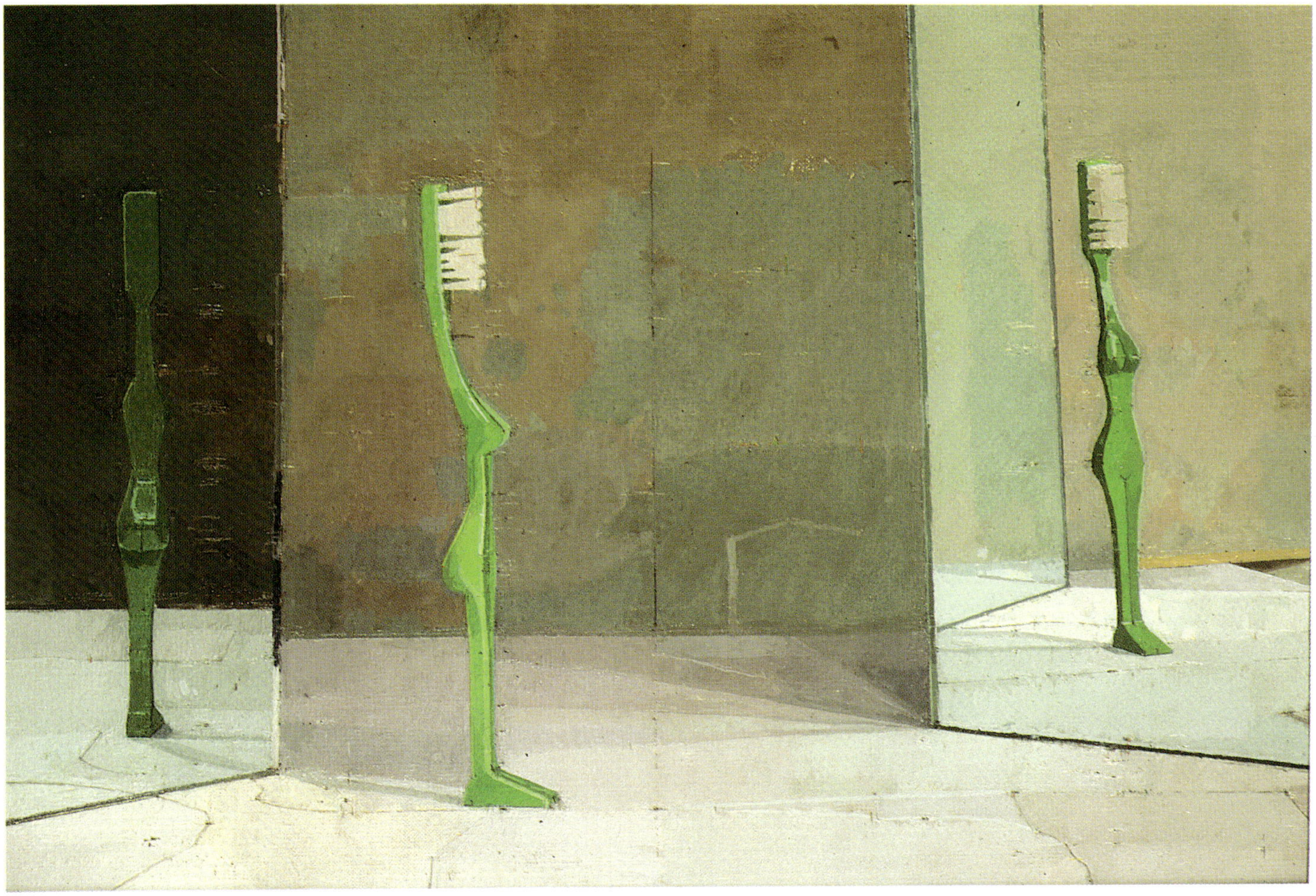

The three Graces, 1979-81
oil on canvas, laid on panel 12¾ x 18 inches

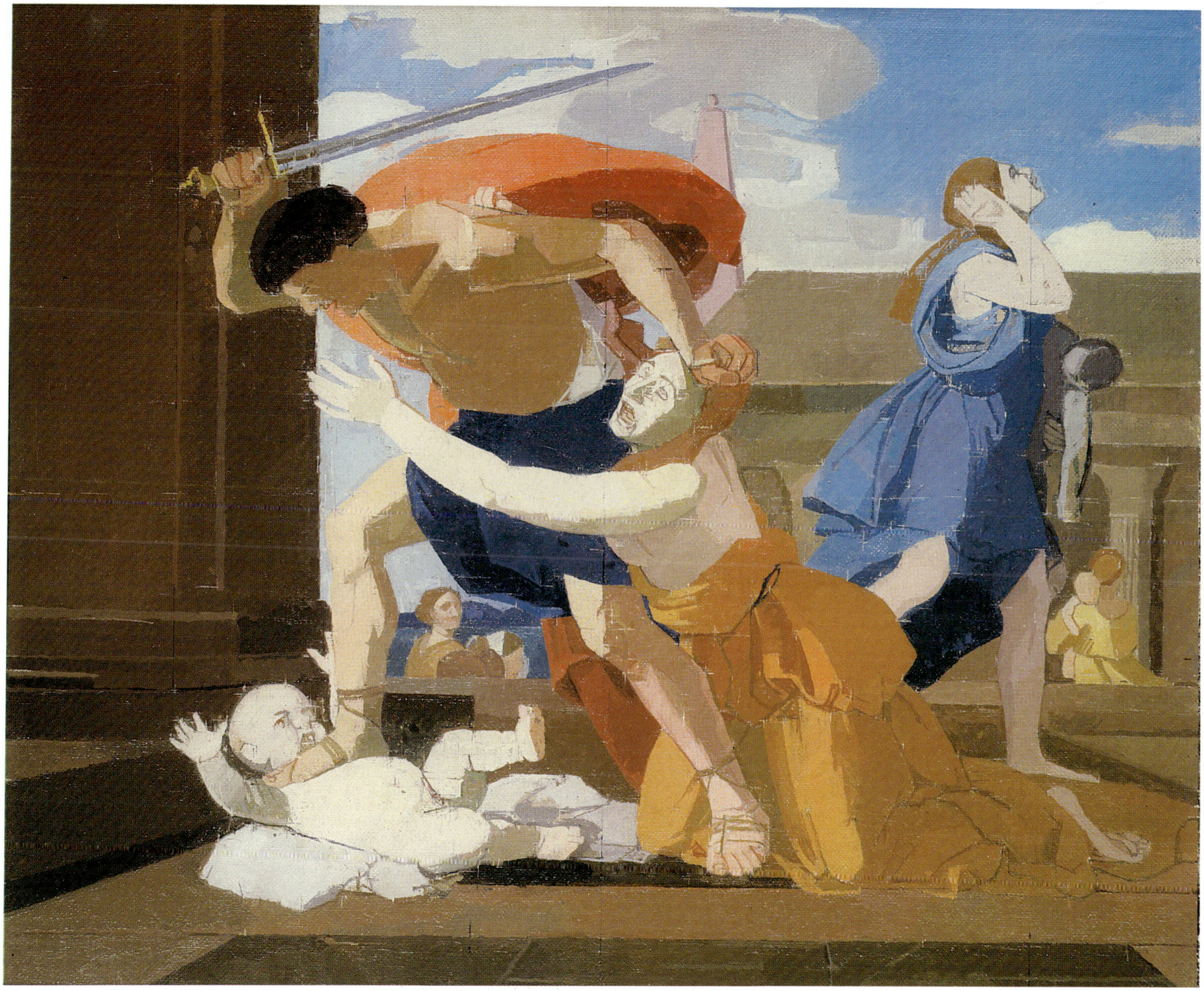

The Massacre of the Innocents (after Poussin), 1979-81
oil on canvas, laid on panel   16¼ x 19¼ inches

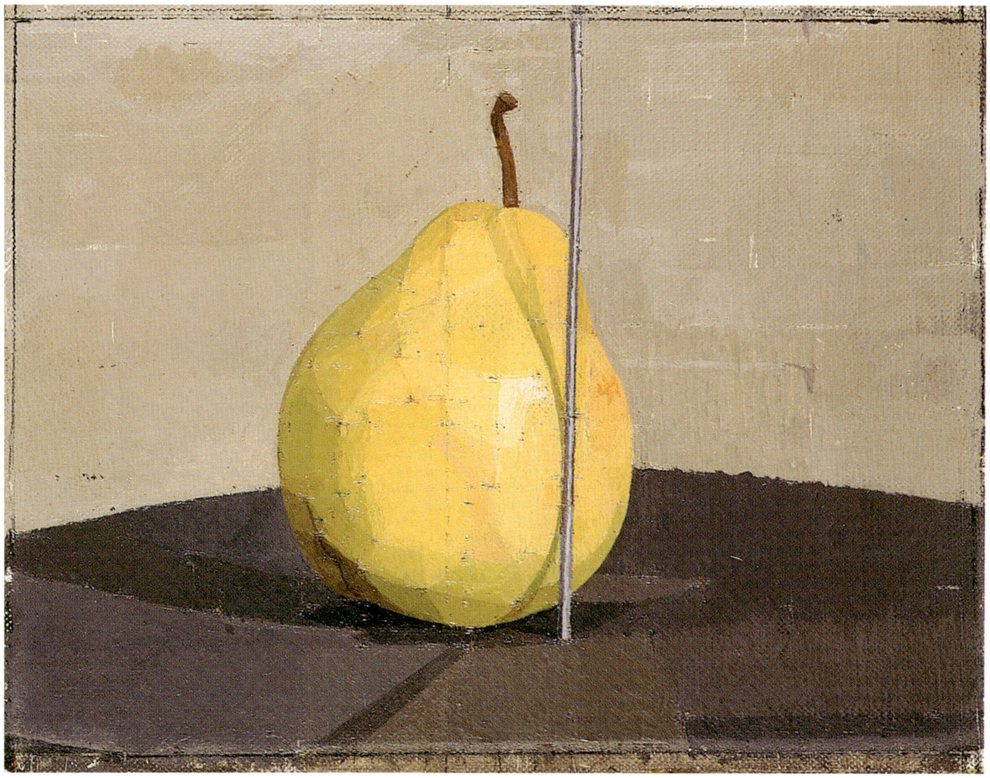

Pear, 1982
oil on canvas, laid on panel $6\frac{1}{2}$ x $8\frac{1}{4}$ inches

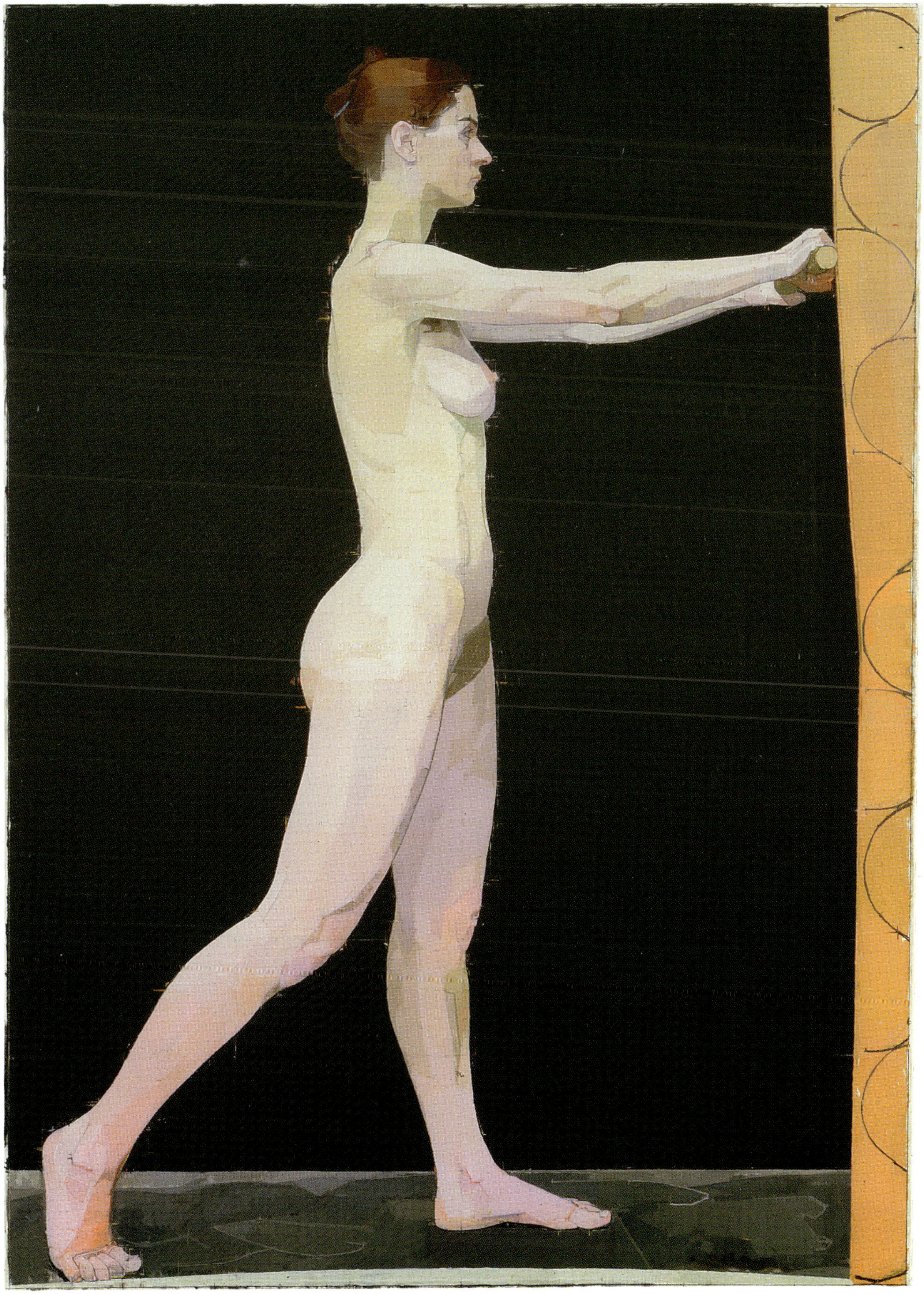

Zagi, 1981-82
oil on canvas 58¾ x 41½ inches

The Trustees of the Tate Gallery, London

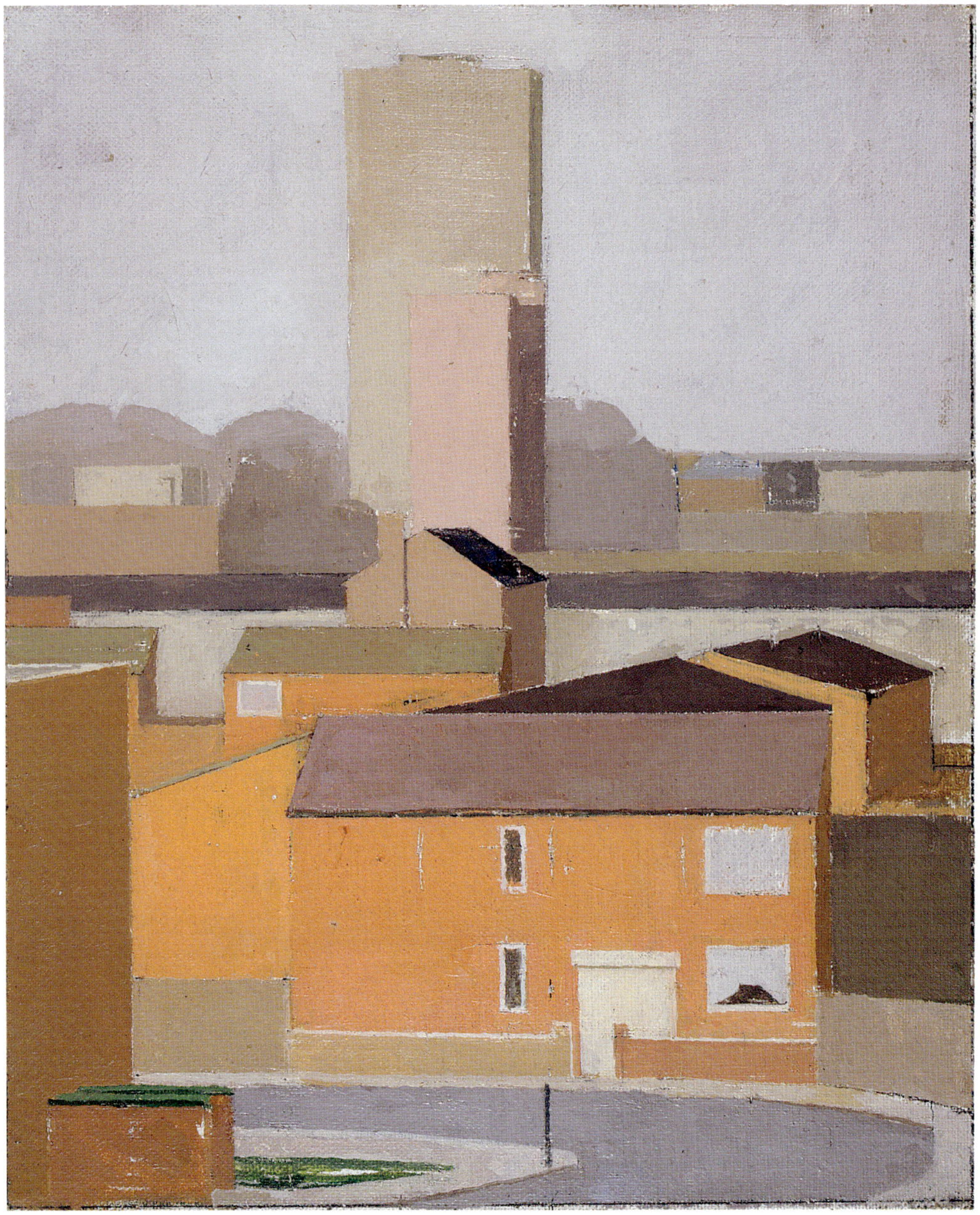

Winter sun, 1980-83
oil on canvas, laid on panel $9^{3}/_{4}$ x 8 inches

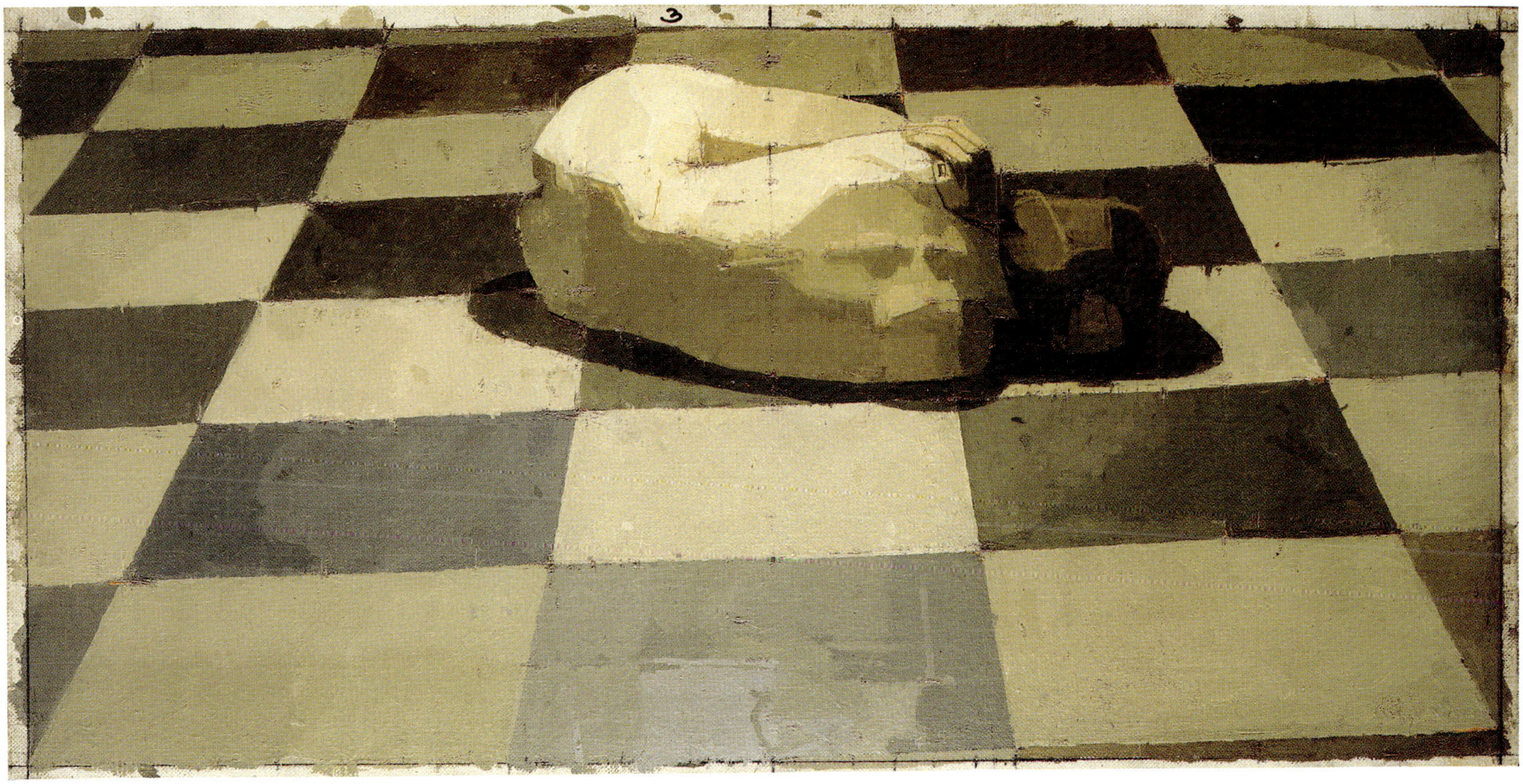

Double square, double square, 1980-83
oil on canvas, laid on panel 9¼ x 18½ inches

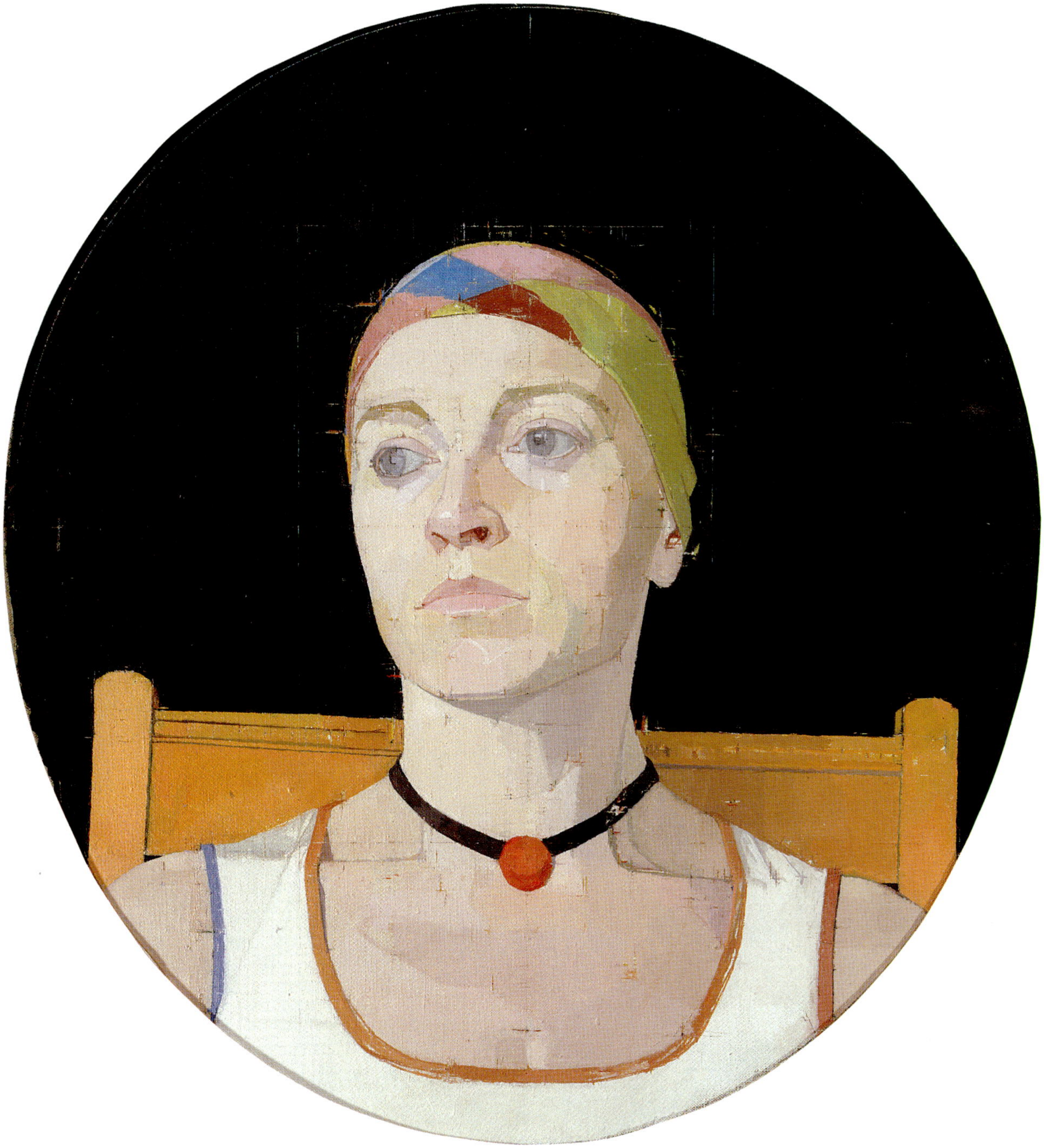

Head of Pat, 1978-83
oil on canvas, laid on panel   ovoid 19½ x 21½ inches

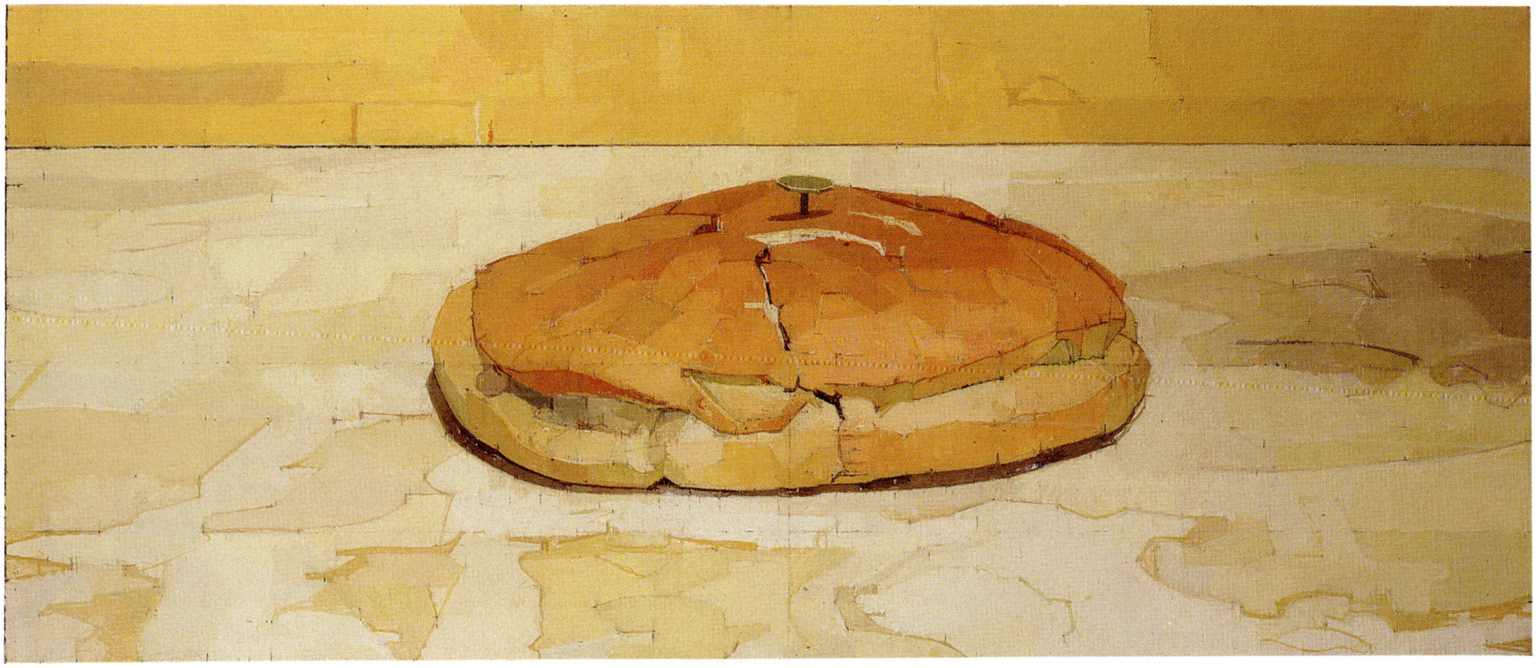

Loaf, 1979-83

oil on canvas 13^3/4 x 31^1/8 inches

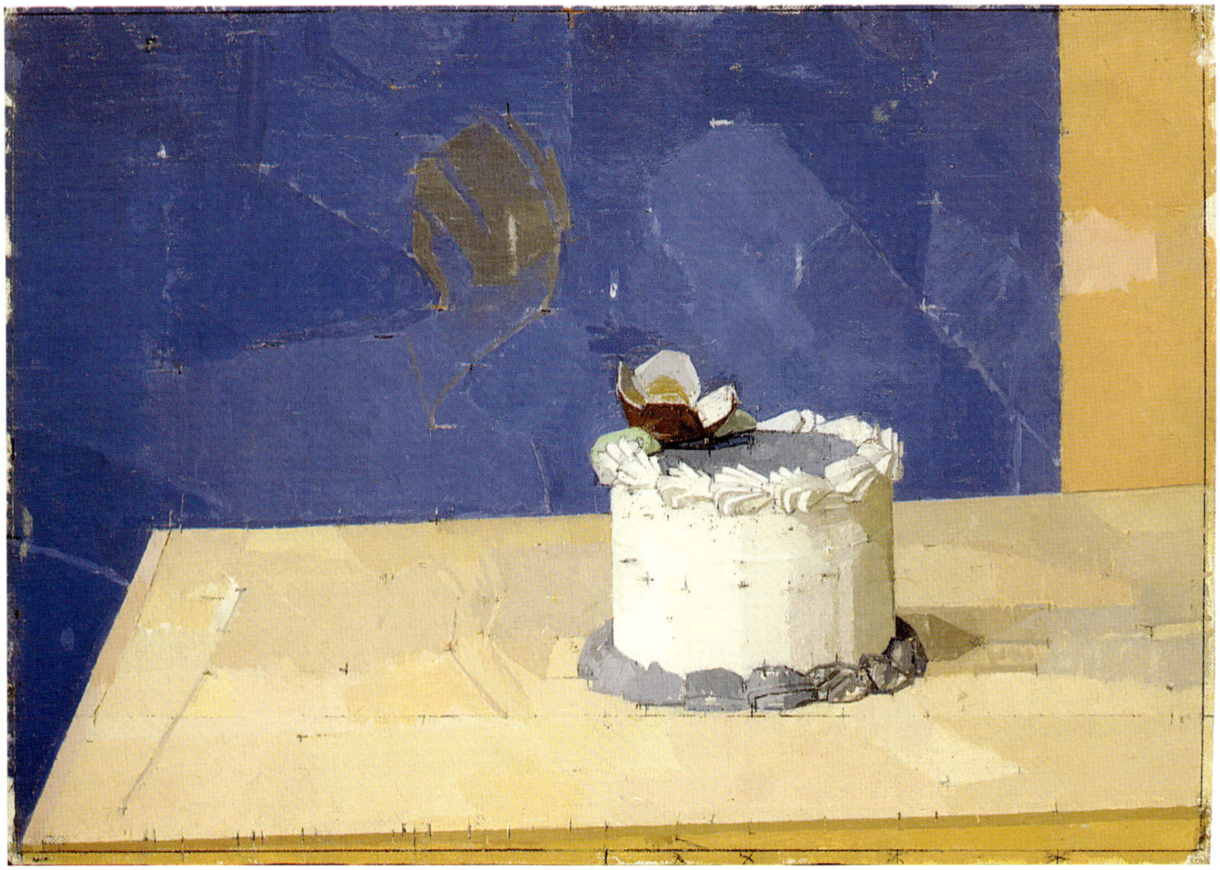

Craigie's birthday cake, 1984-85
oil on canvas, laid on panel 10¼ x 14¼ inches

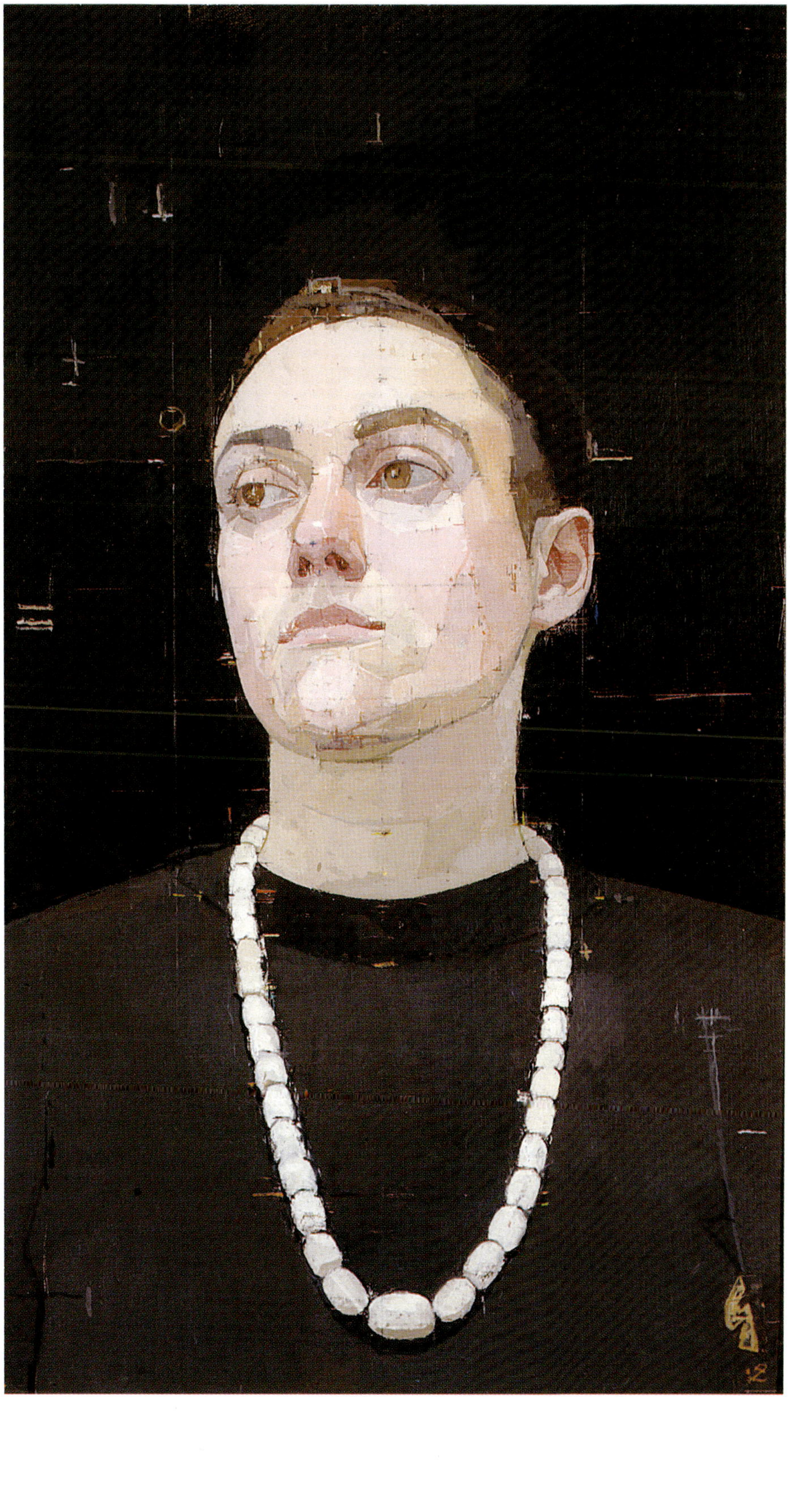

Cati with a string of beads, 1986
oil on canvas, laid on panel 22¼ x 12¾ inches

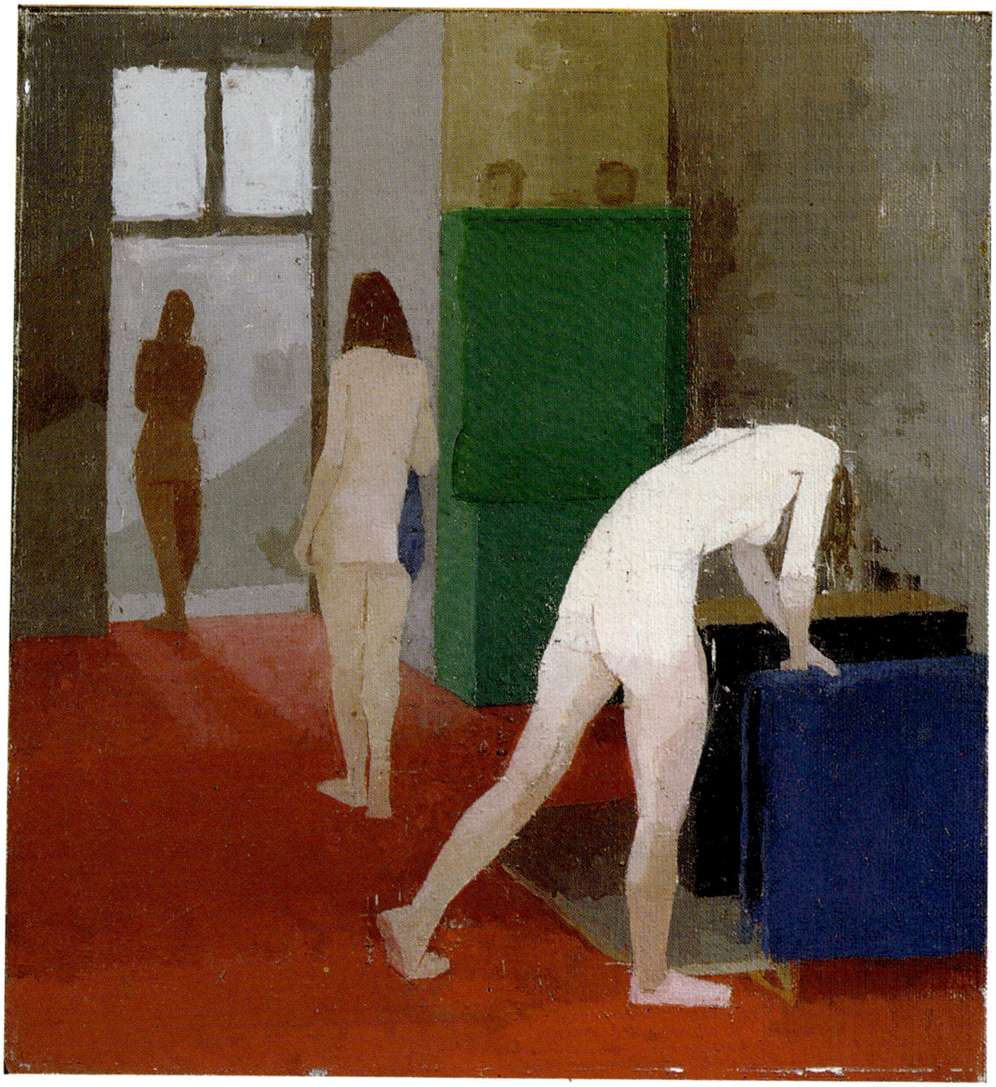

The blue towel, 1982-83
oil on canvas, laid on panel 9⅝ x 9⅞ inches

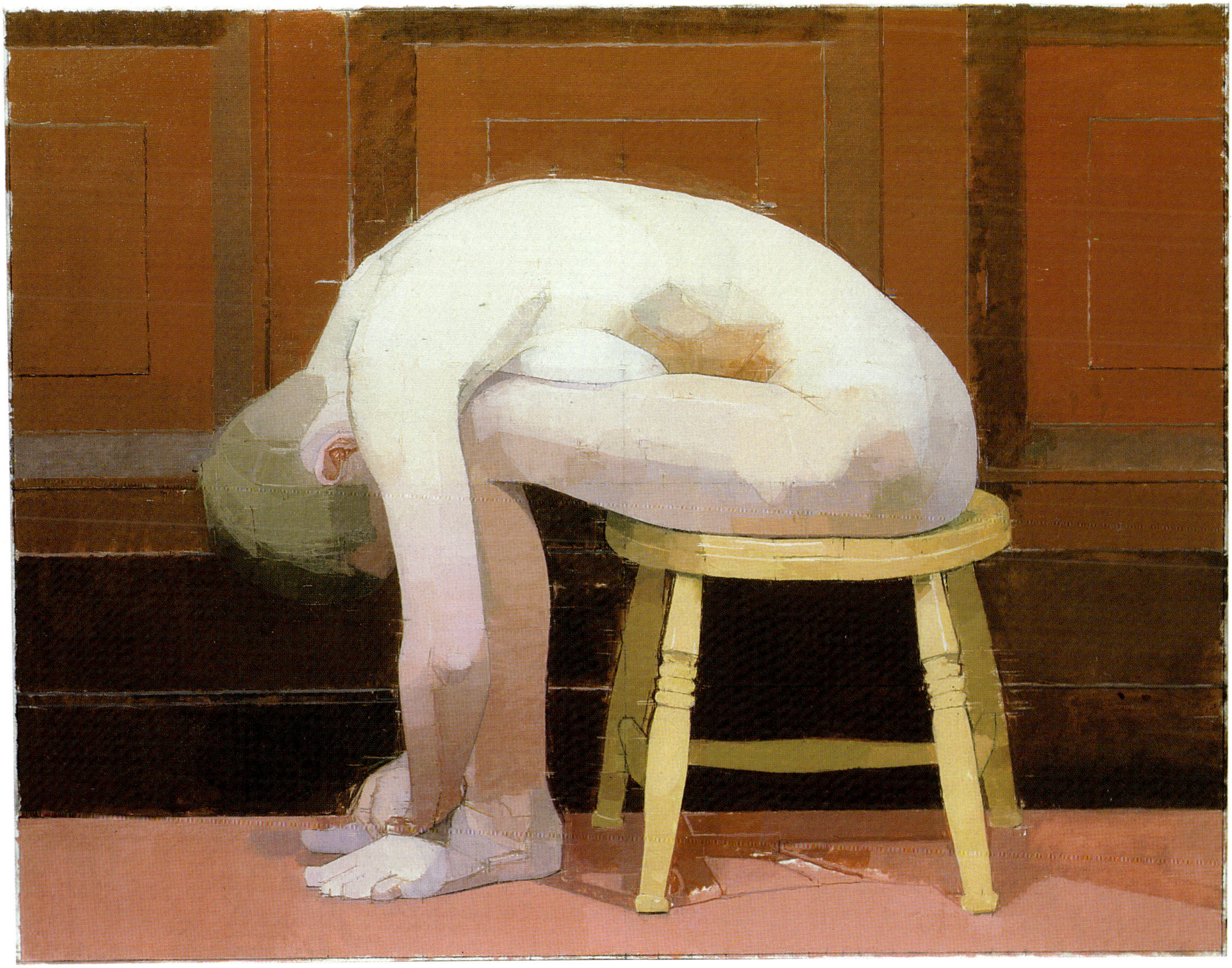

Curled nude on a stool, 1982-83
oil on canvas 30¾ x 39½ inches

The Ferens Art Gallery, Hull

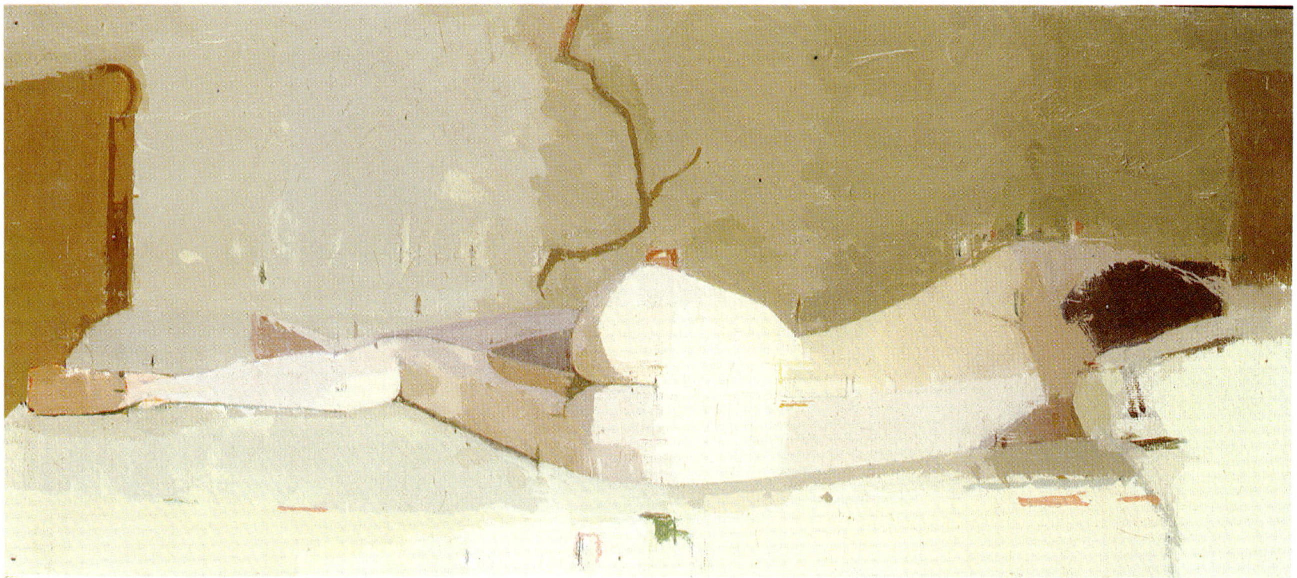

In the shadow of the cypress, 1984
oil on canvas, laid on panel   7¾ x 17¾ inches

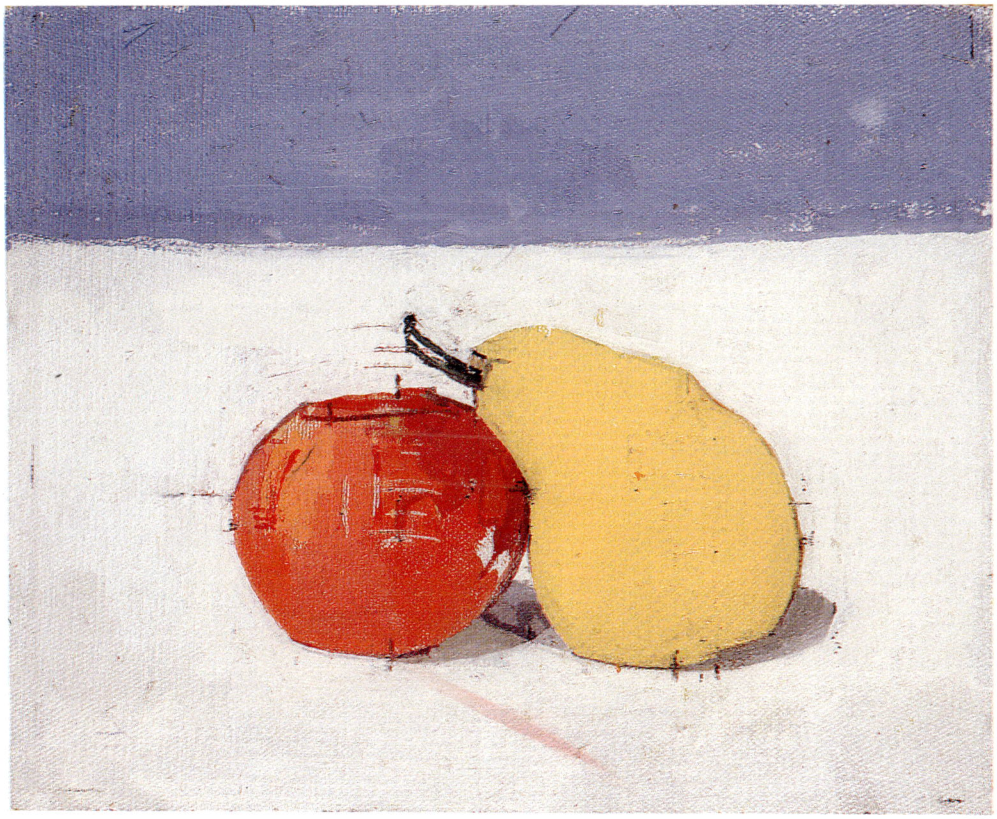

Apple and pear, 1985
oil on canvas, laid on panel $7^{1}/_{8}$ x $8^{3}/_{4}$ inches

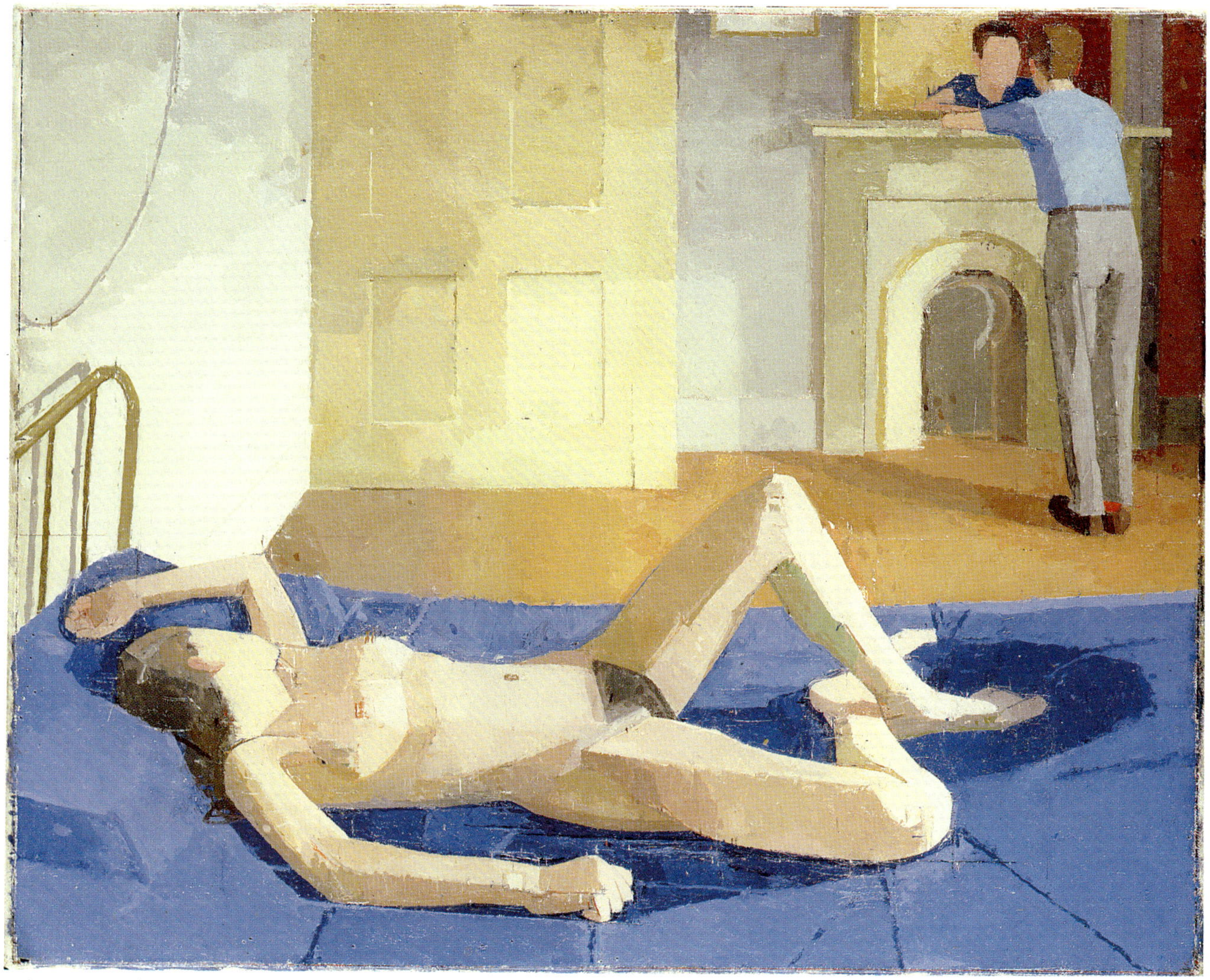

Narcissus, 1986
oil on canvas   17¾ x 21½ inches

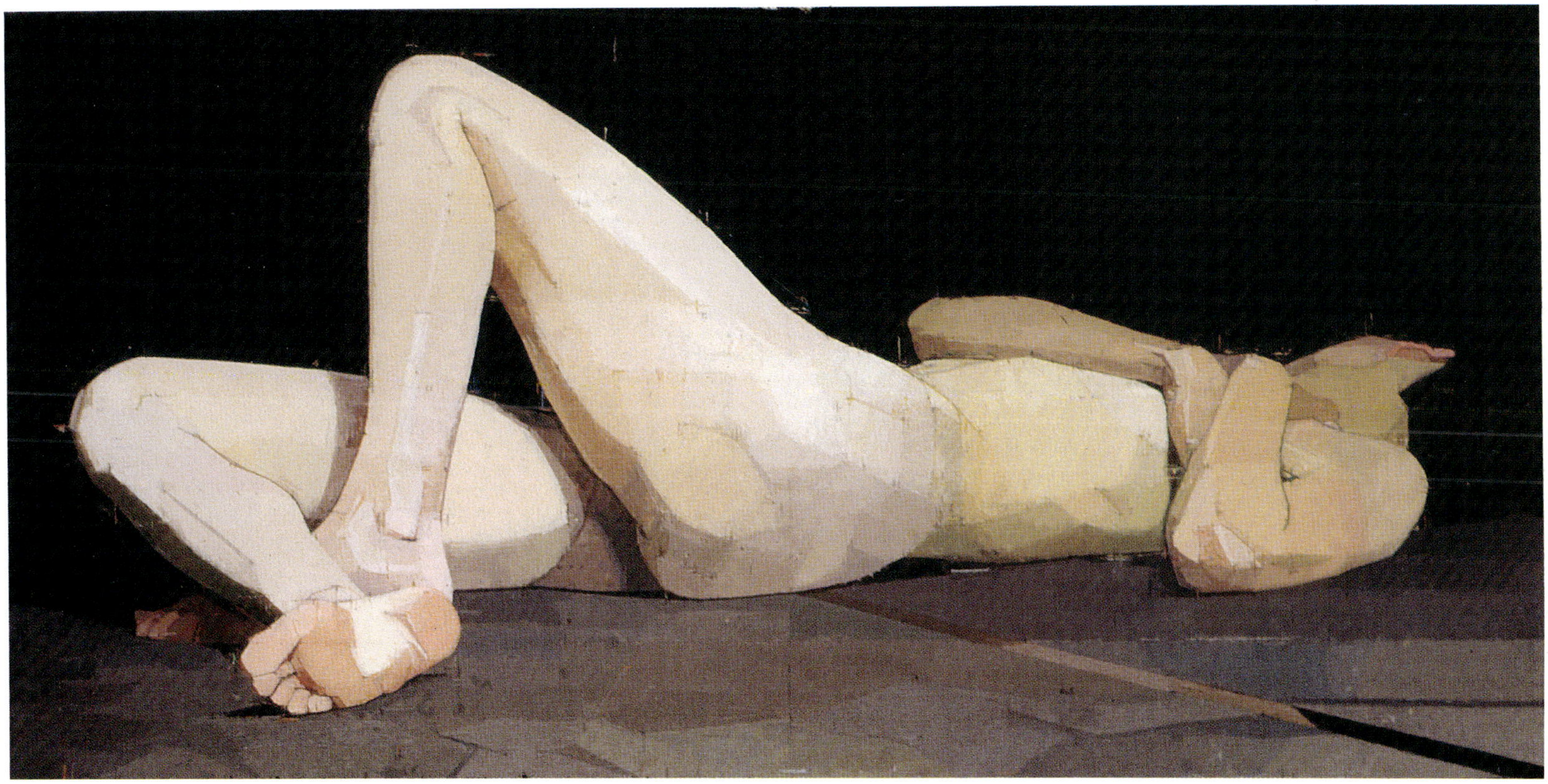

Pepe's painting, 1984-85
oil on canvas 17¾ x 35½ inches

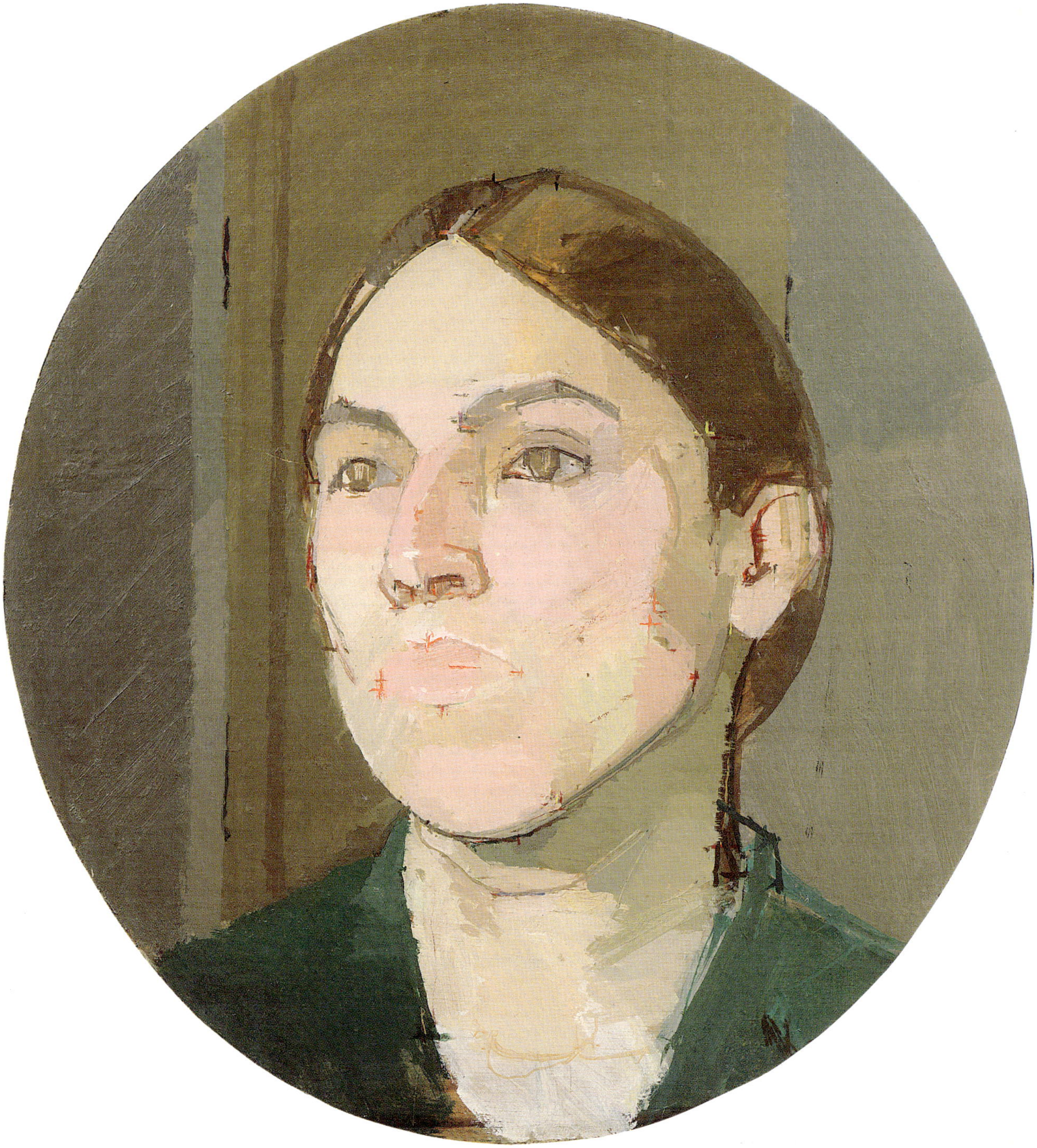

Oval portrait, 1964
oil on panel   17¾ x 16 inches

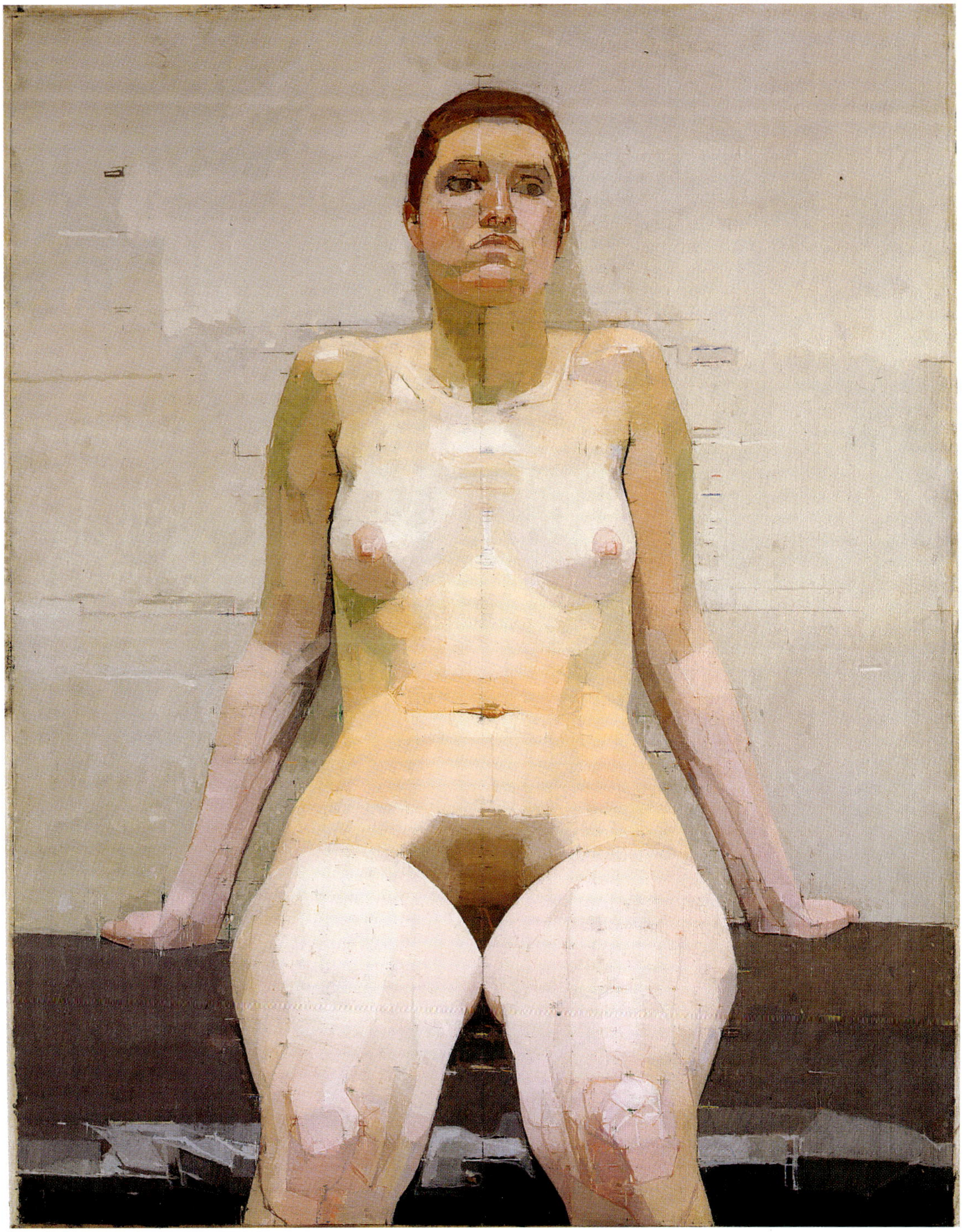

Celebration of a new skylight, 1986-87
oil on canvas   35½ x 27½ inches

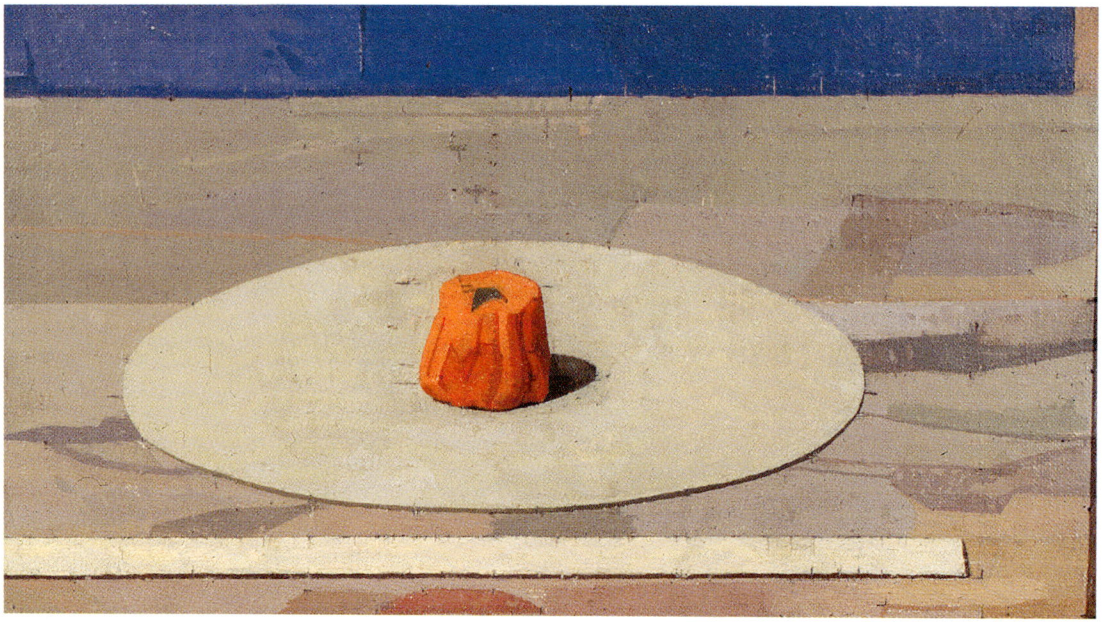

Shrunken tangerine, 1988
oil on canvas, laid on panel 6¾ x 11⅞ inches

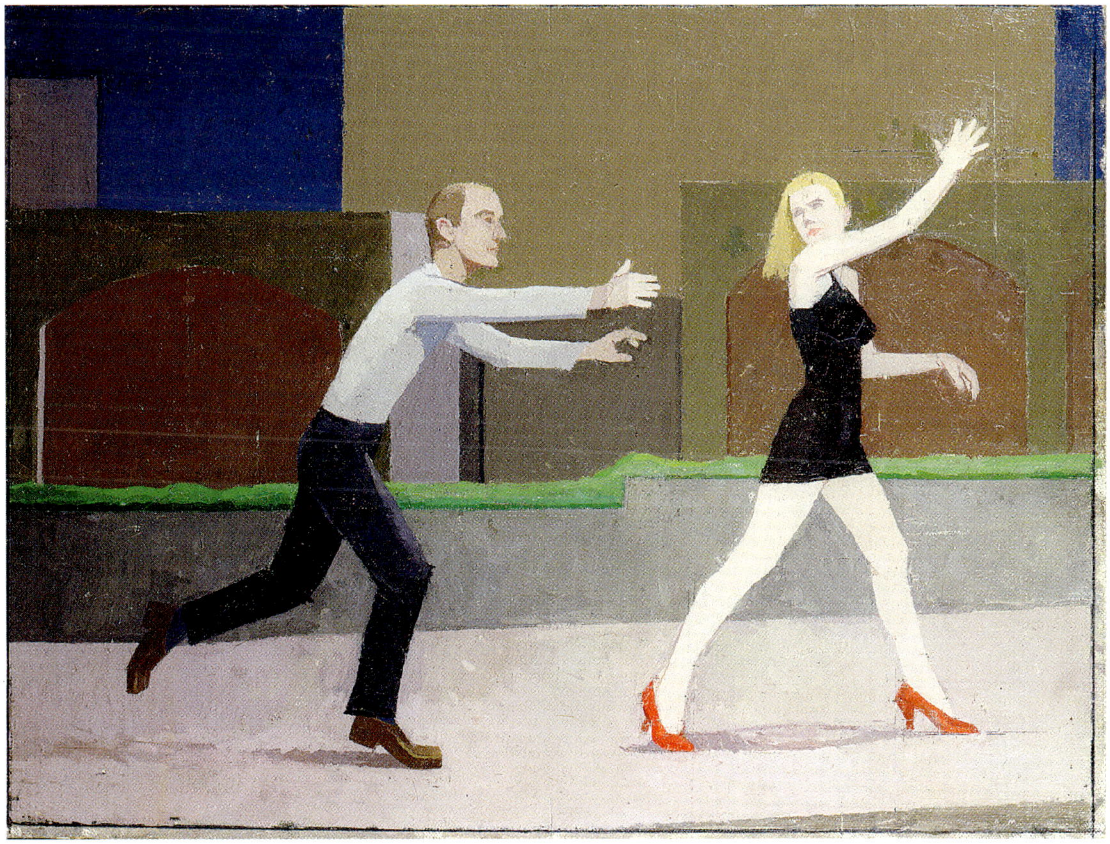

Christmas chase, 1988
oil on canvas 9¾ x 12½ inches

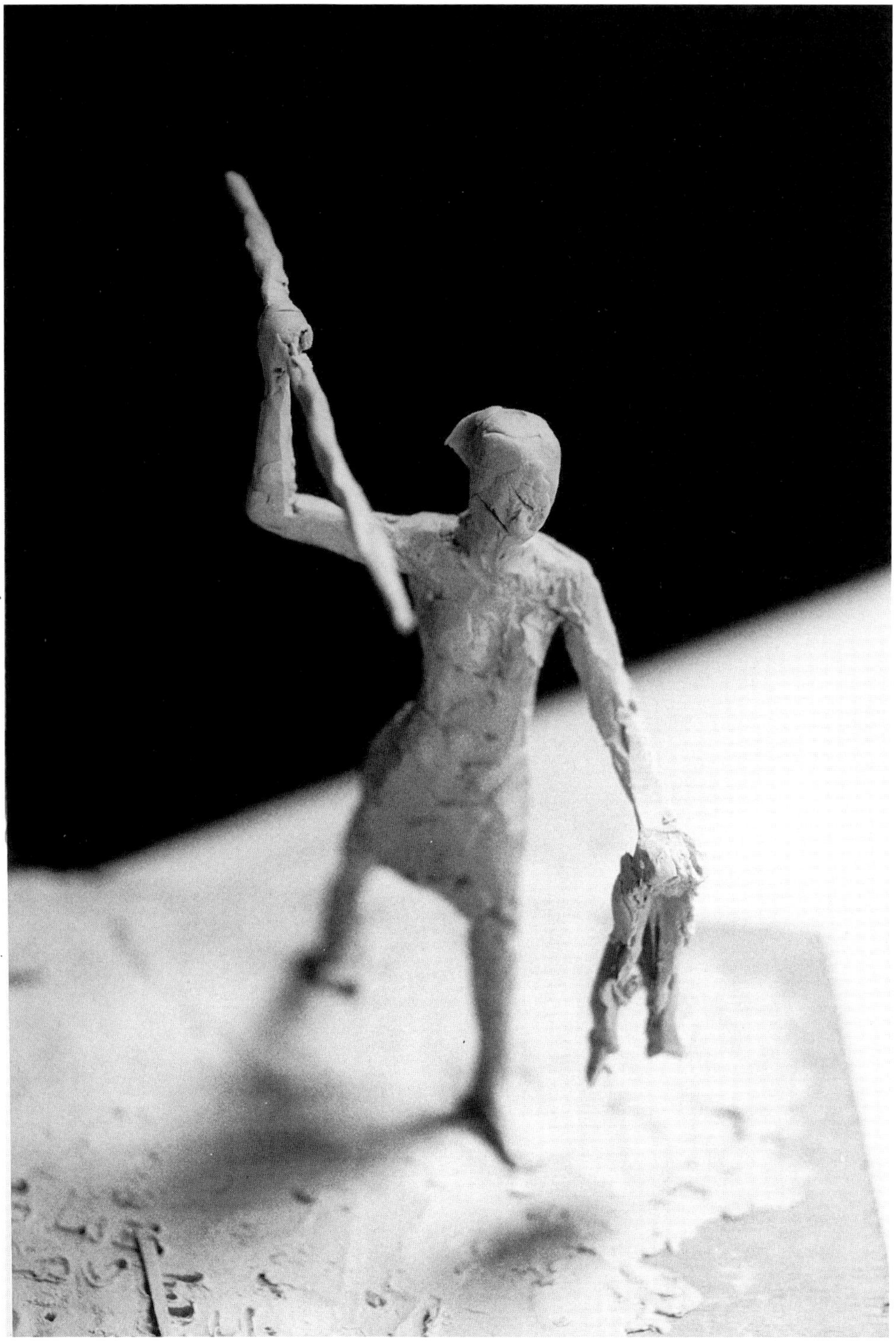

The Egyptian spearess
plasticine *photograph by Jacob Sutton*

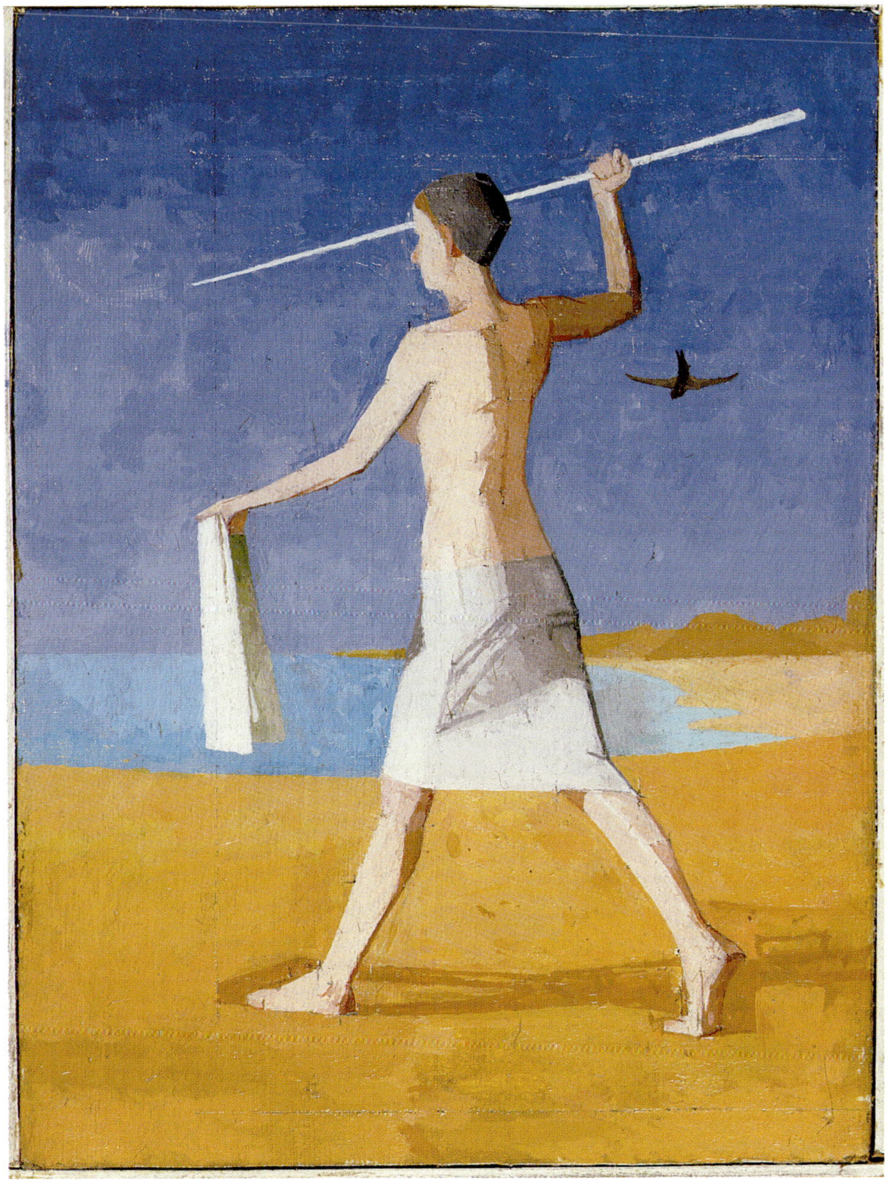

The Egyptian spearess, 1986-87
oil on canvas, laid on panel 11 x 7¾ inches

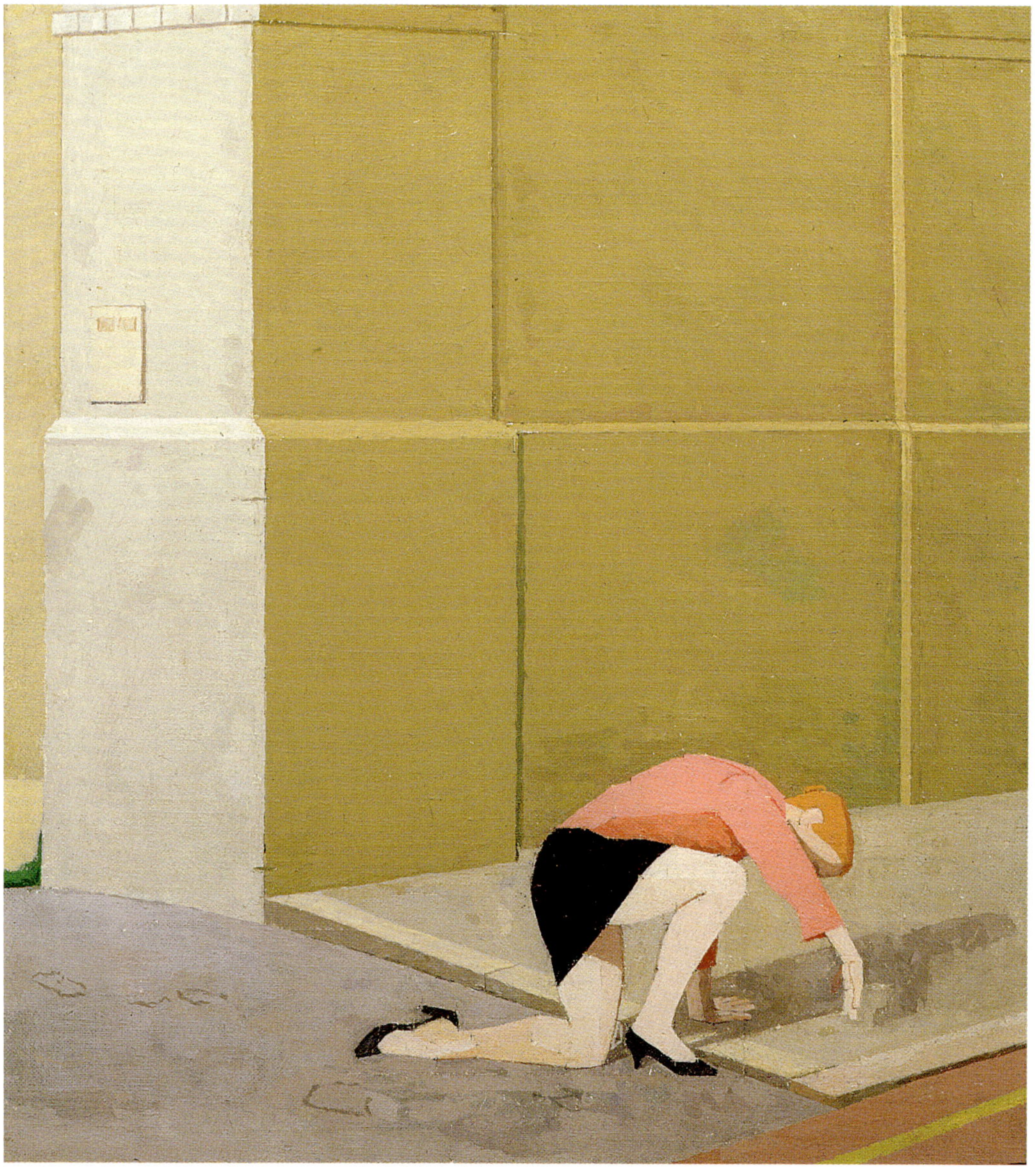

Girl tripping, 1992
oil on canvas 13 x 11 inches

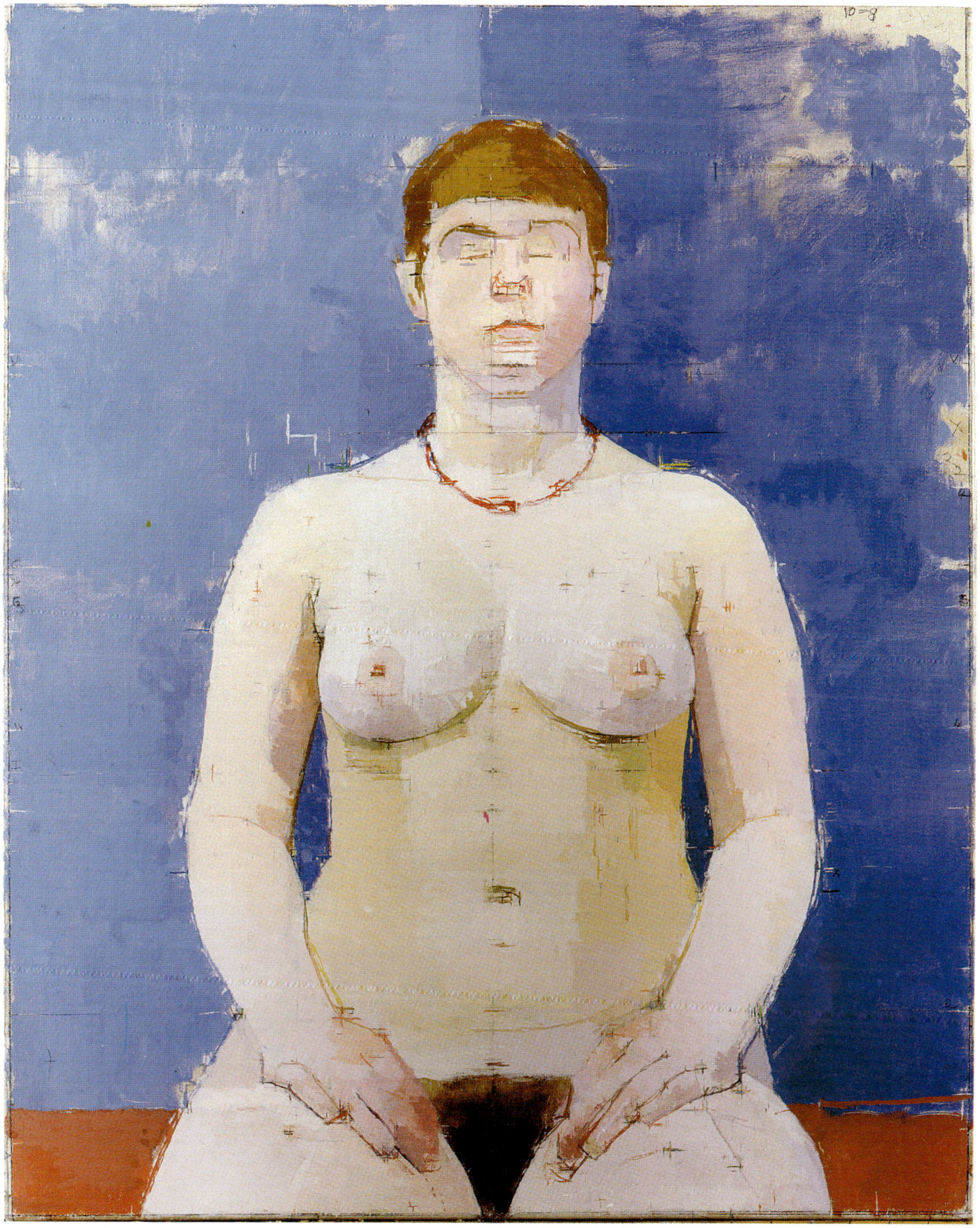

The lightest painting on Earth, 1989-93
oil on canvas 27 1/4 x 21 7/8 inches

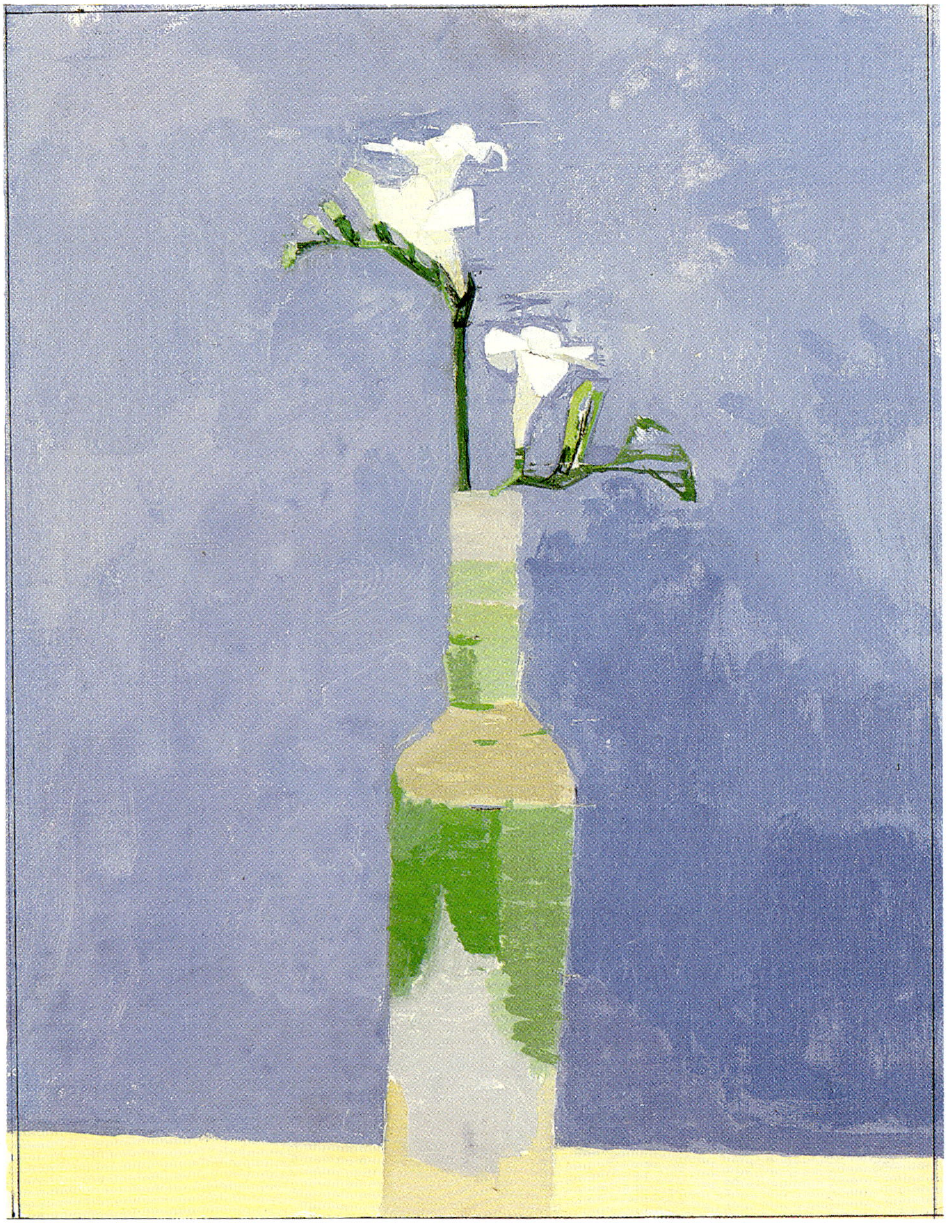

Boxing day freesias, 1988
oil on canvas, laid on panel   15 x 11 inches

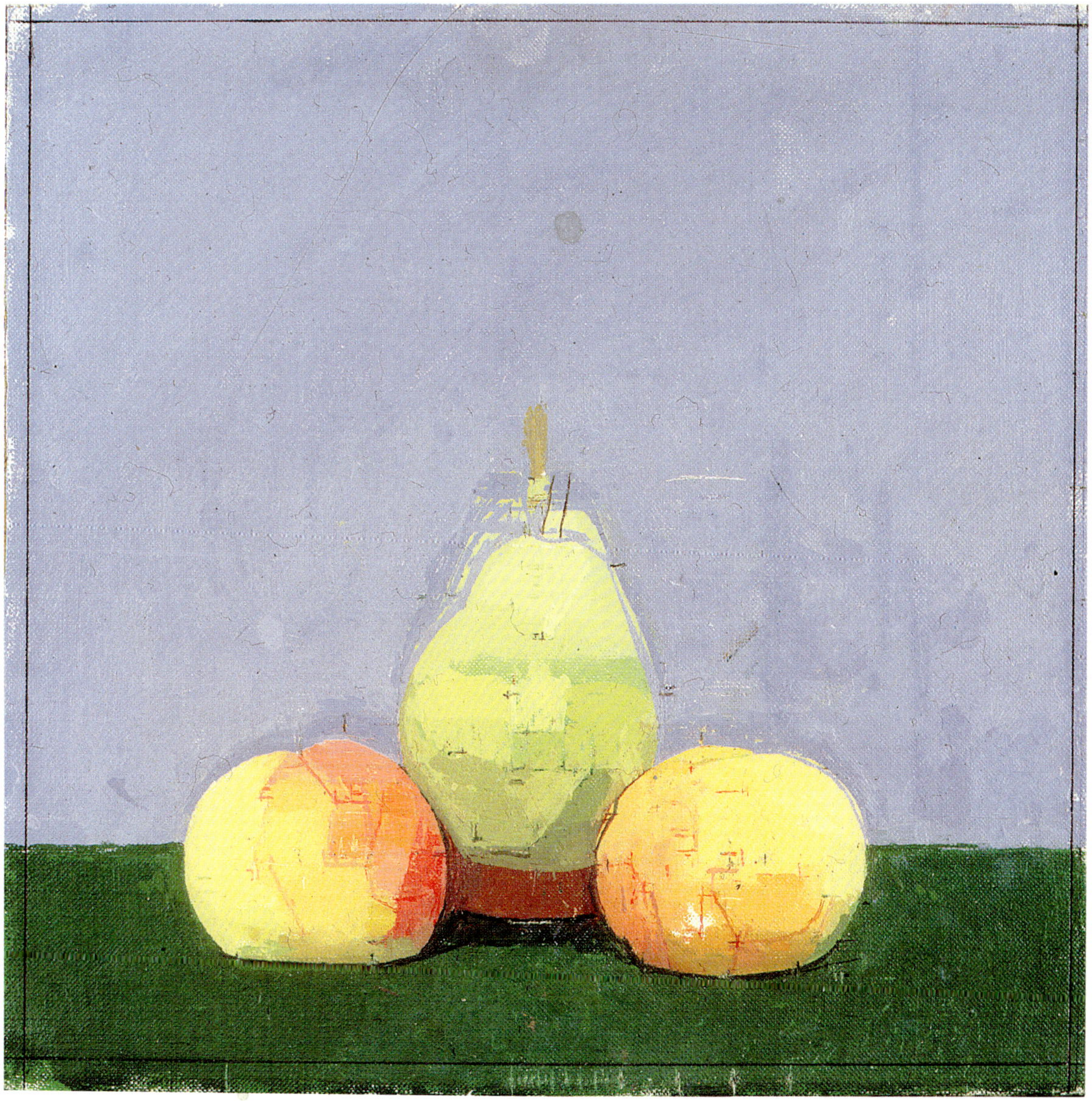

Fruit pyramid, 1988

oil on canvas, laid on panel   11 x 10¾ inches

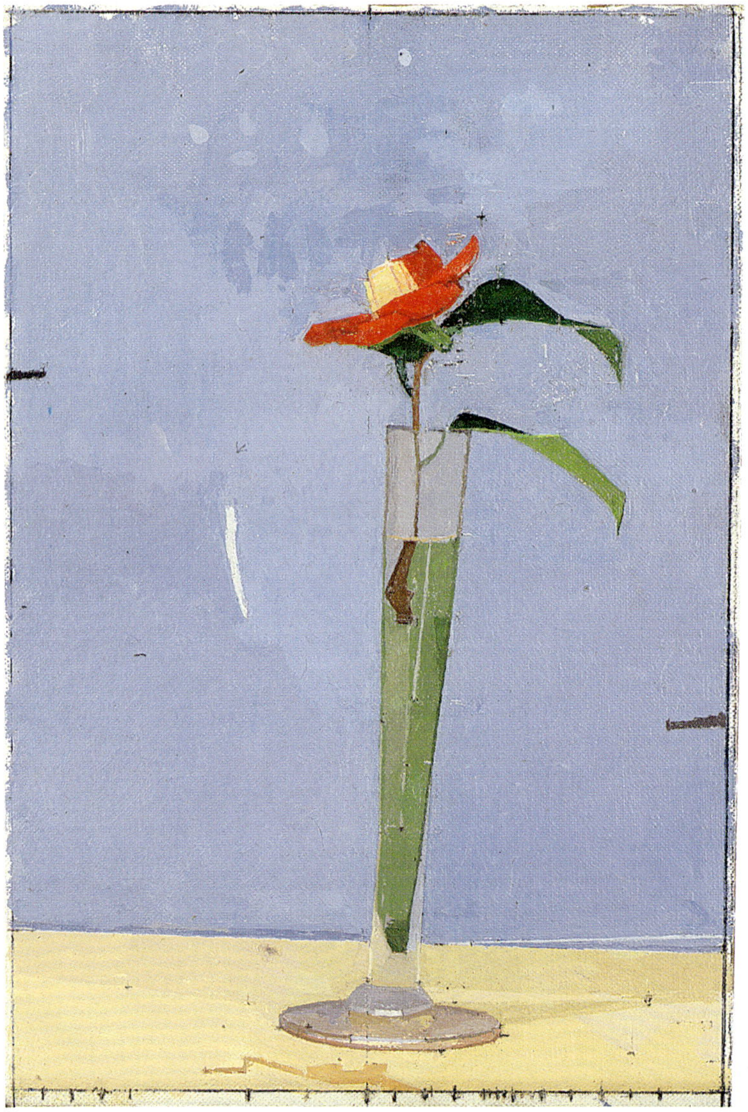

Camelia, 1989
oil on canvas, 10⅝ x 7 inches

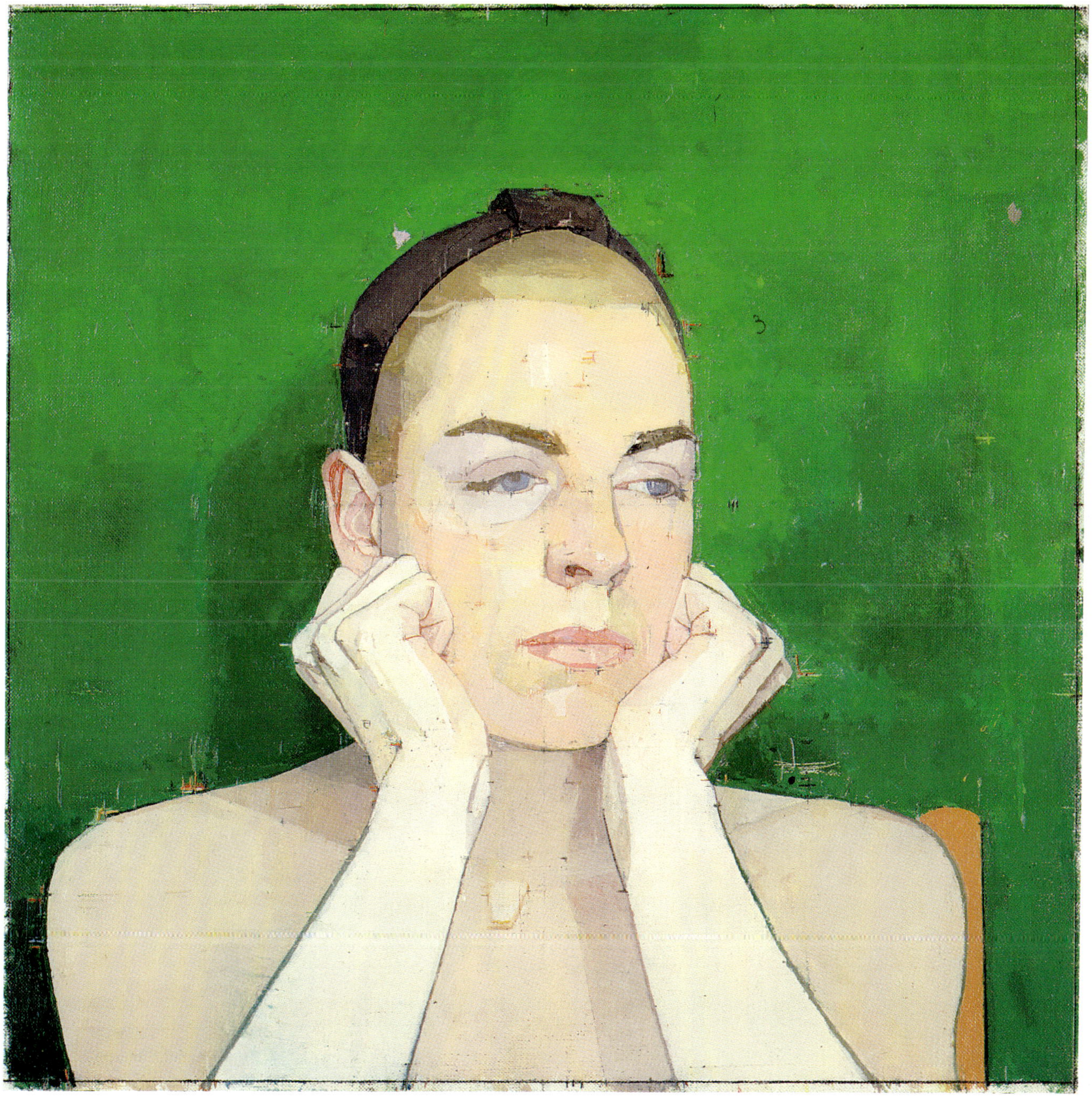

Mandi, 1985-89
oil on canvas, laid on panel   15 x 15 inches

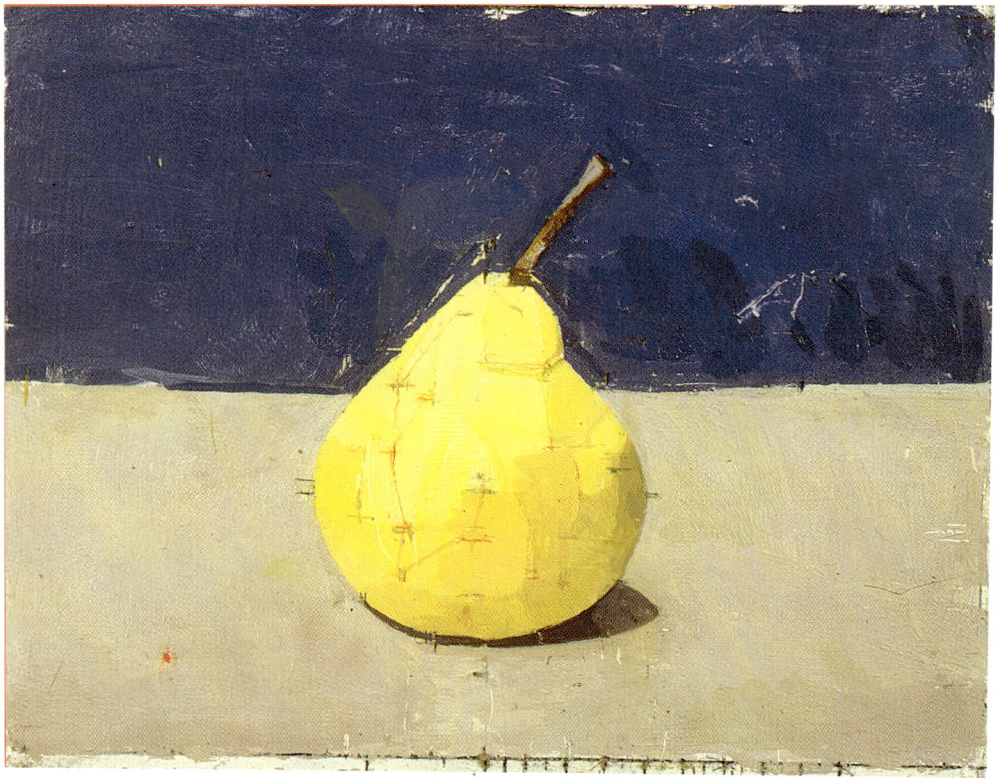

Pear, 1990
oil on board   7½ x 5¾ inches

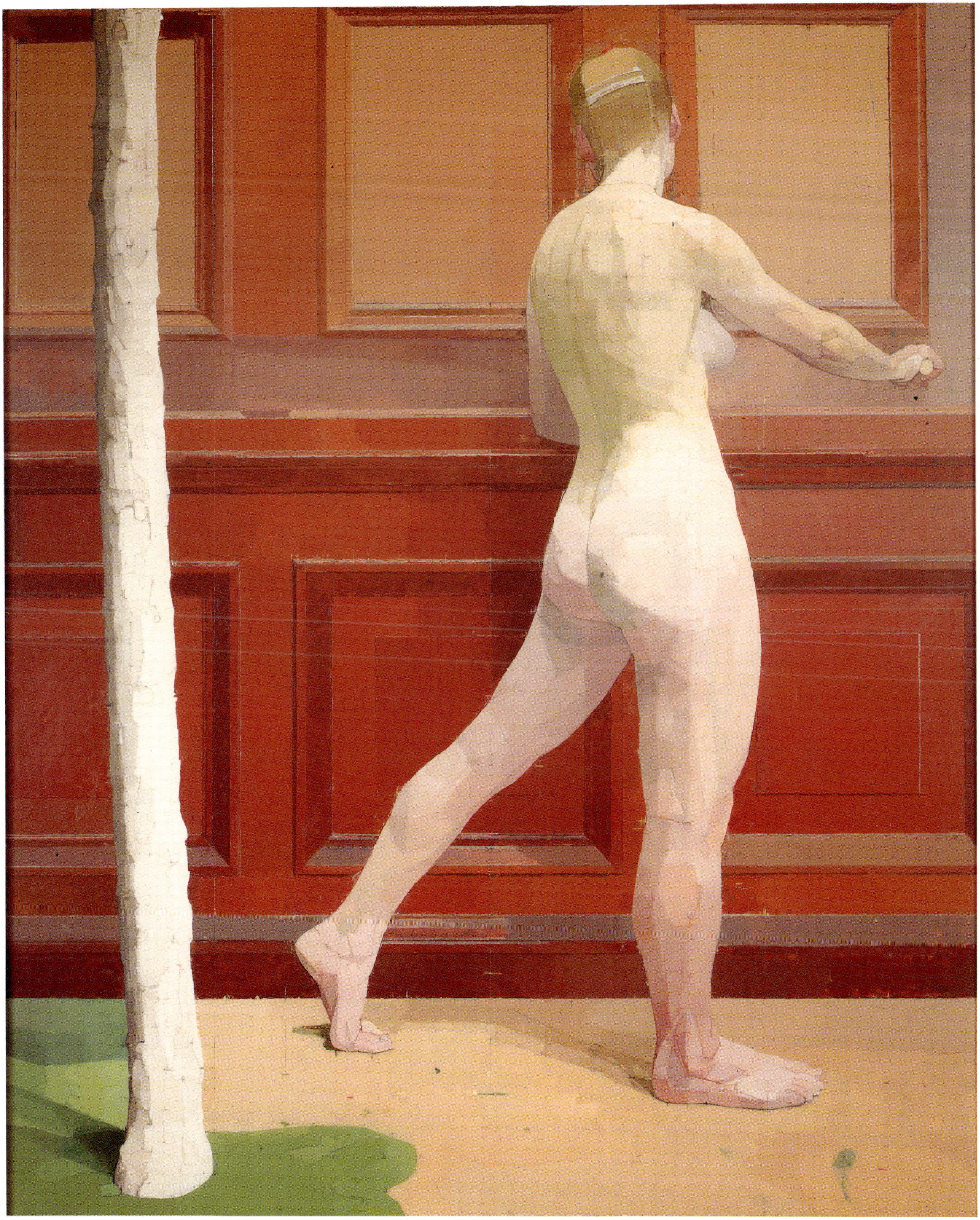

Girl tree, 1989-91
oil on canvas 59¼ x 47½ inches

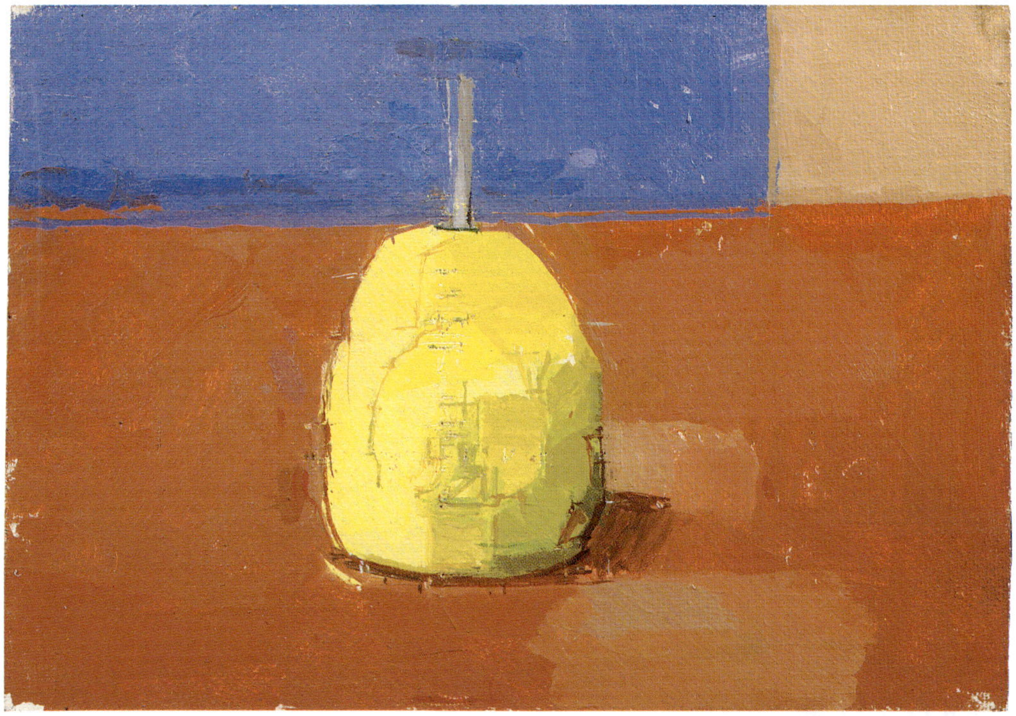

Chinese pear, 1990
oil on board 6 x 8½ inches

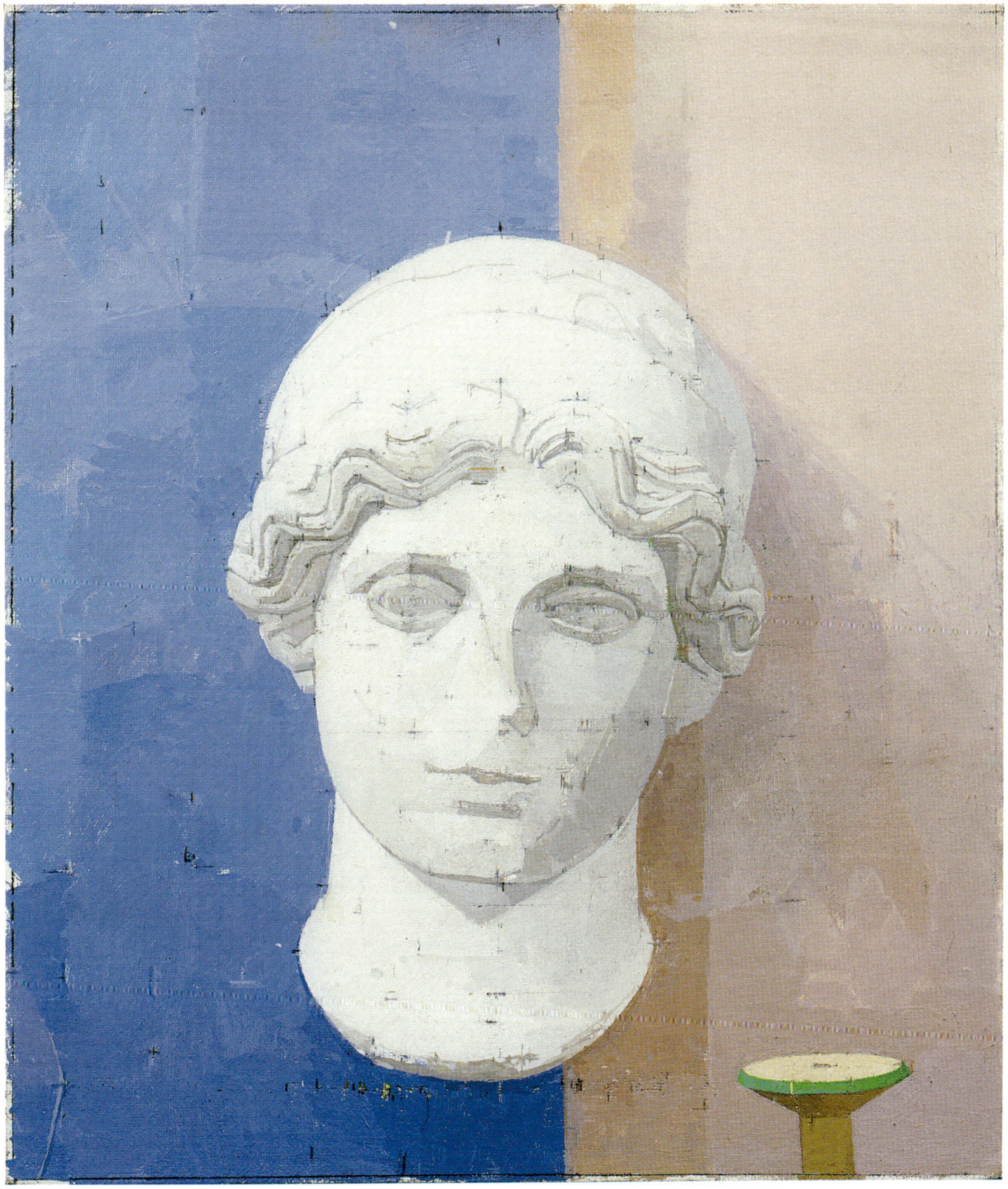

Cast, 1987-91
oil on canvas, laid on panel   13 x 11 inches

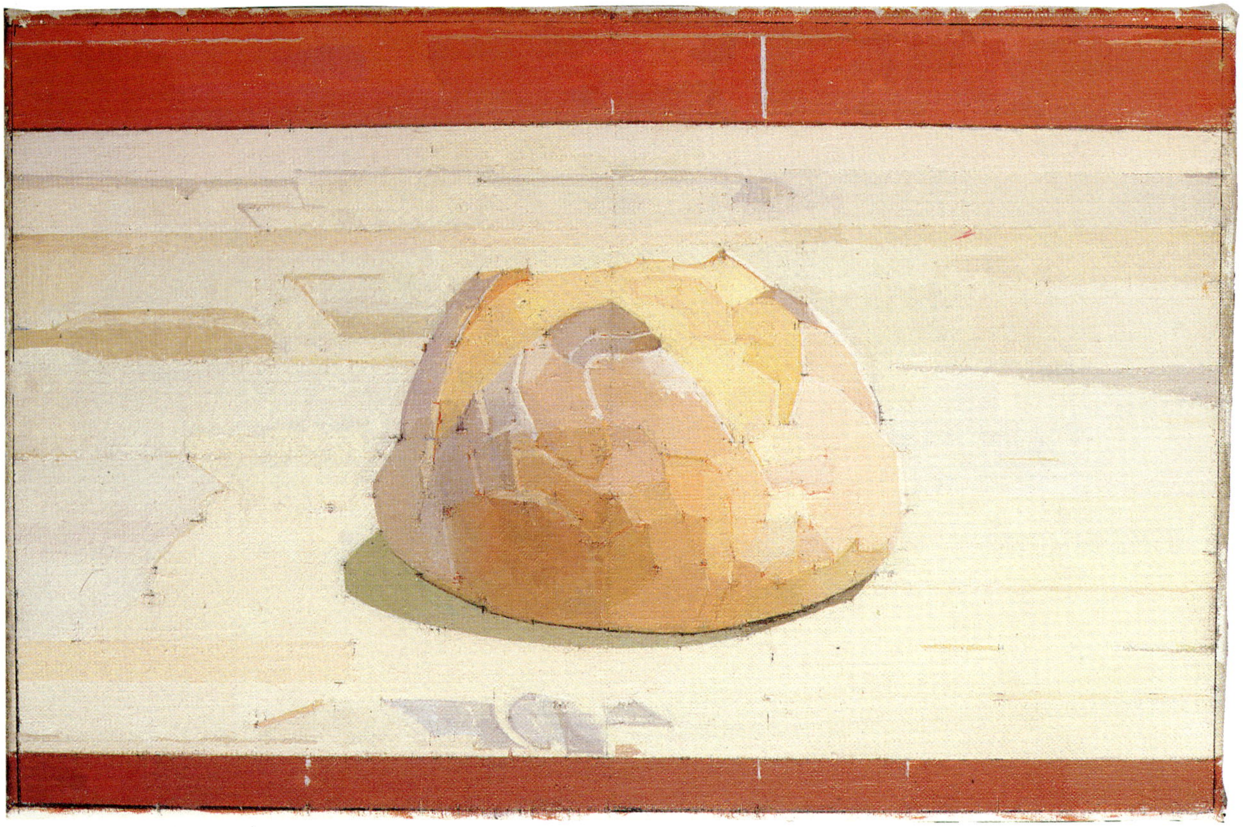

Mouse loaf, 1991-92
oil on canvas, laid on panel $9^{1}/_{2}$ x $14^{1}/_{2}$ inches

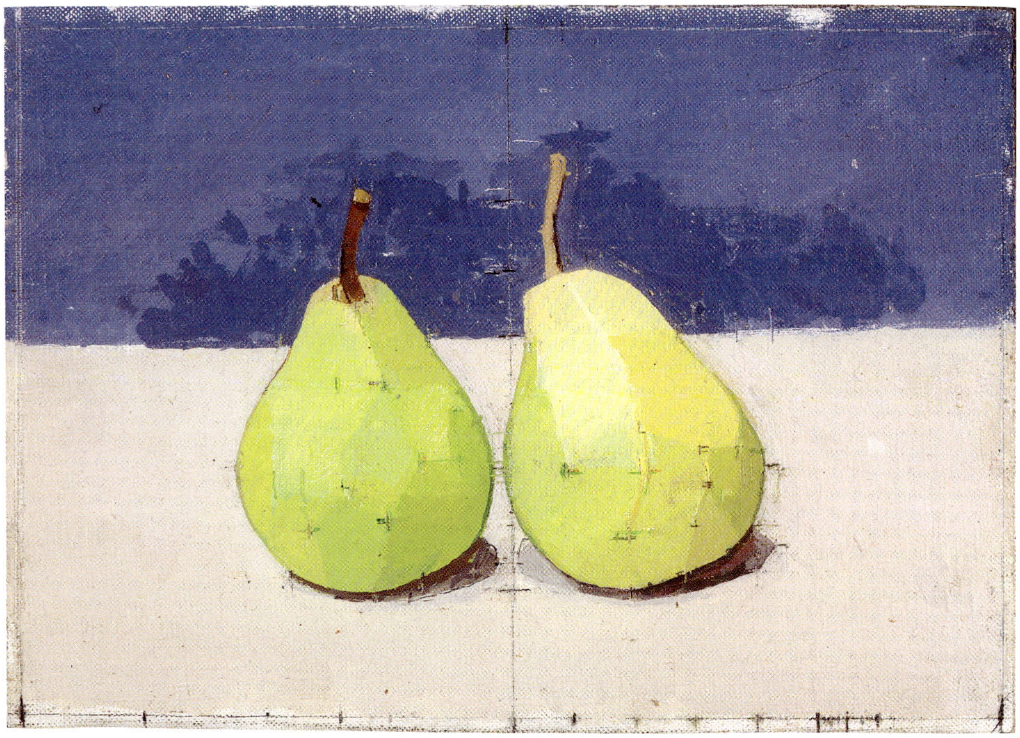

Two pears, 1990

oil on canvas, laid on panel   6¾ x 9½ inches

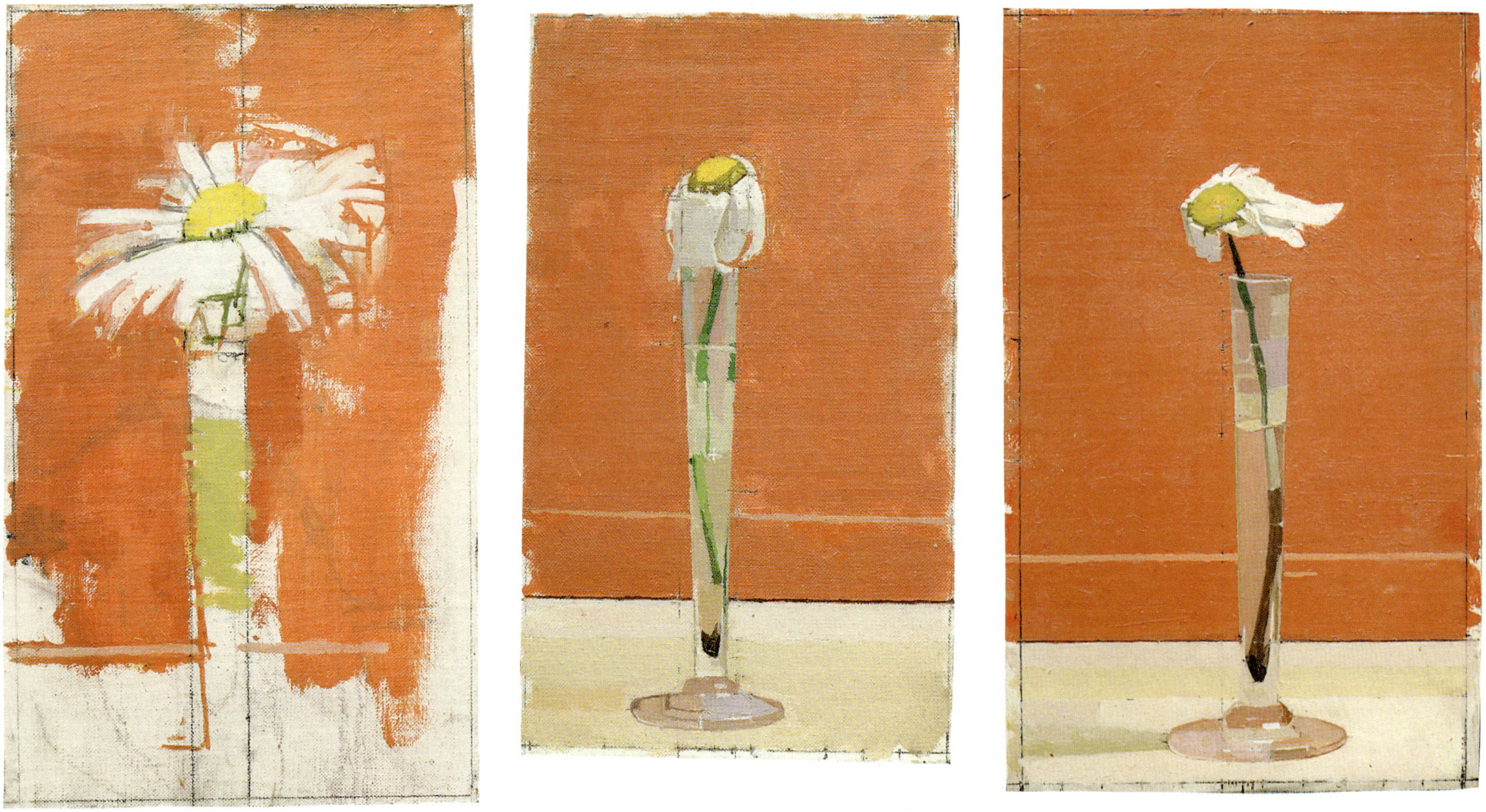

Daisy triptych, 1991
oil on canvas three each 10¾ x 8¾ inches

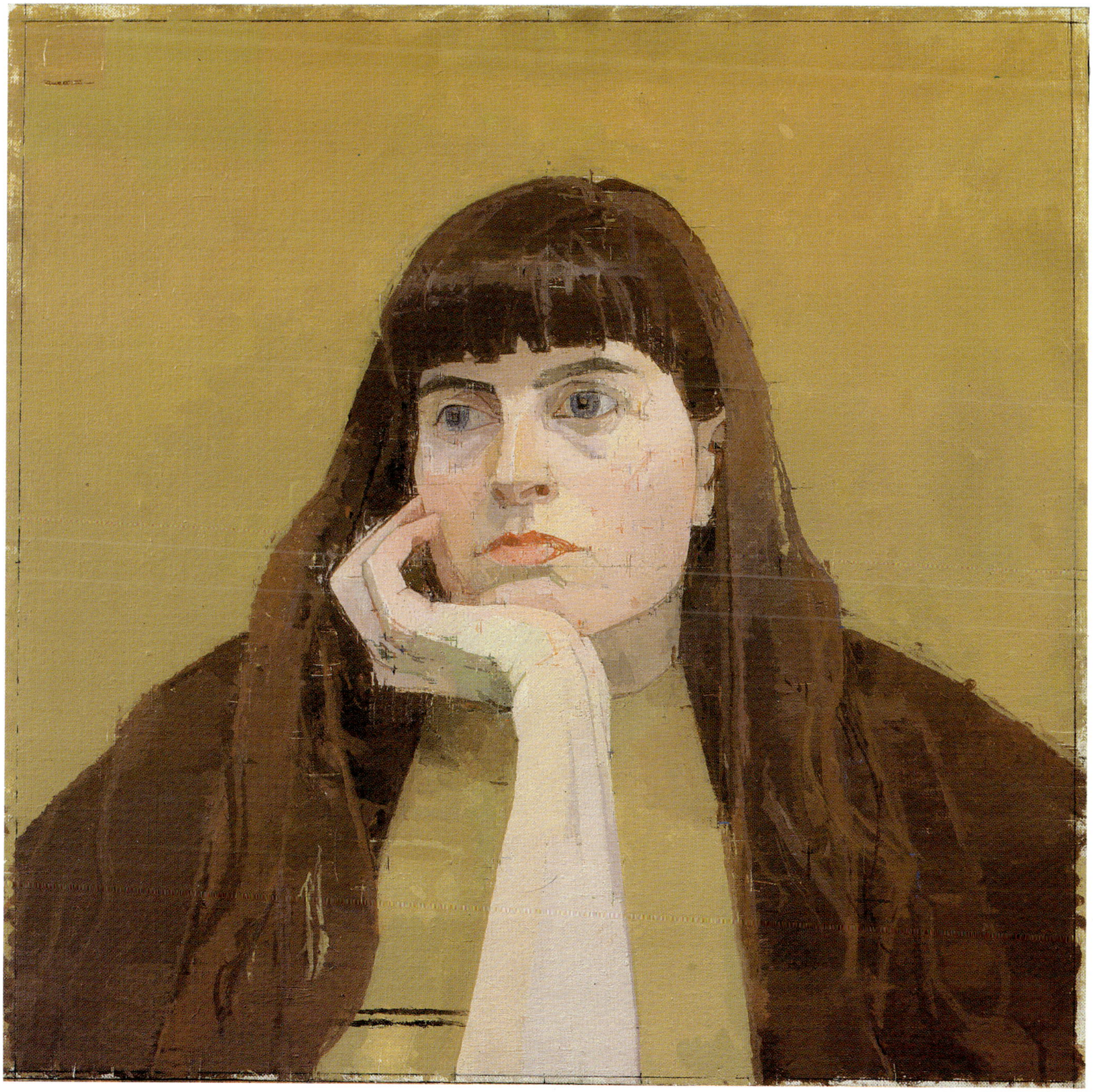

Propped head, 1989-92
oil on canvas, laid on panel 18 1/16 x 16 1/2 inches

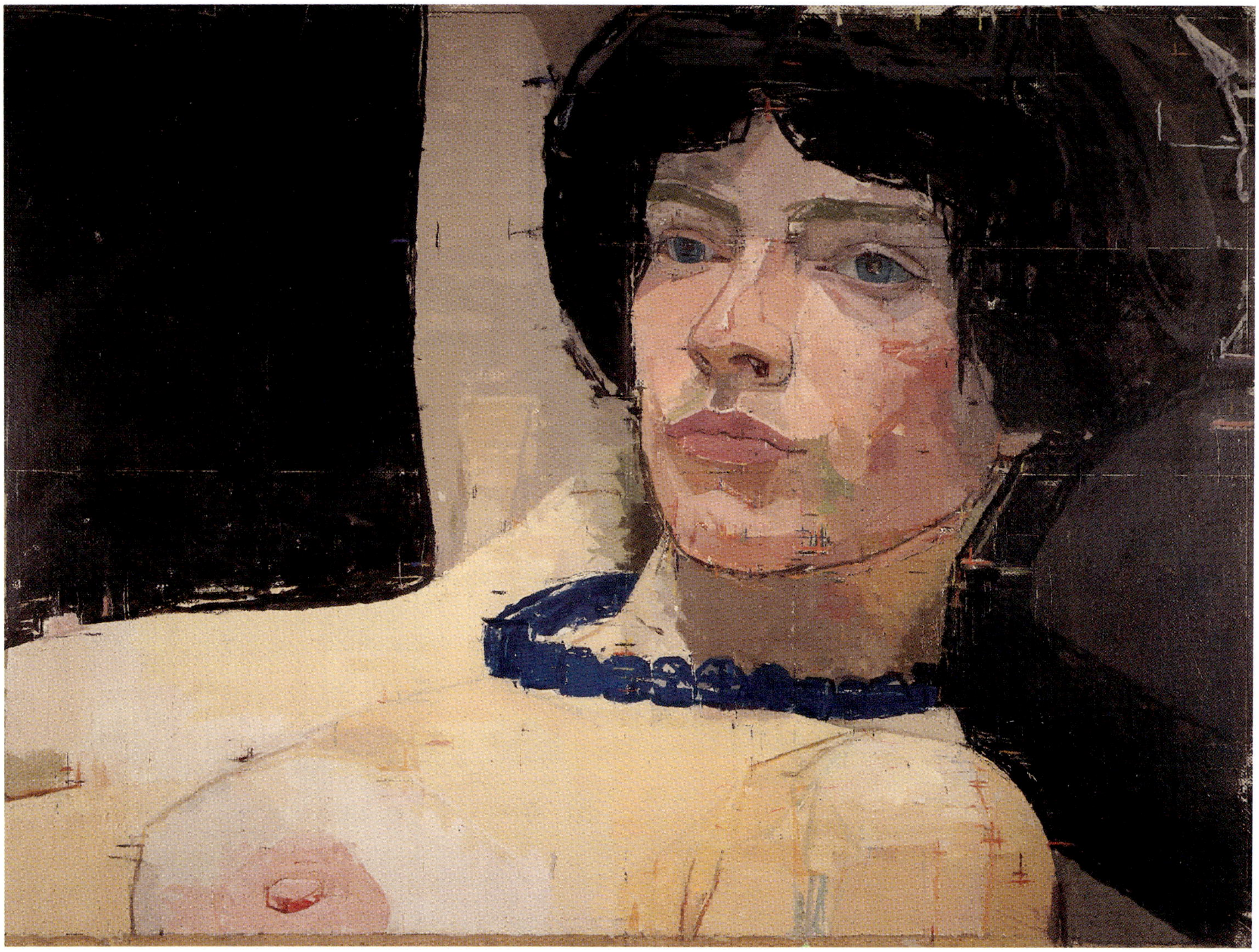

Zoë, 1987-93
oil on canvas, laid on panel 12 x 16 inches

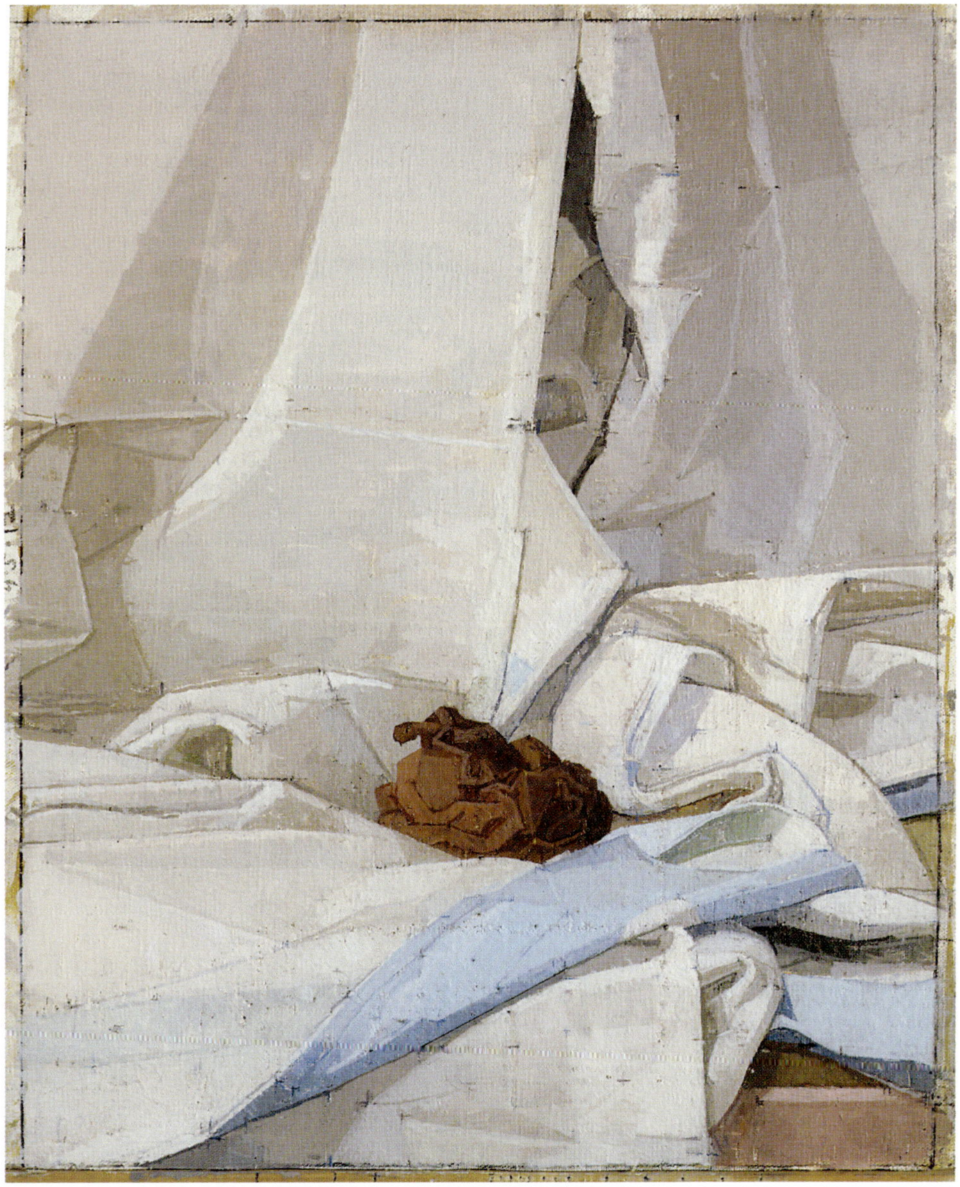

Dehydrated pear with drapery, 1993
oil on canvas, laid on panel   12 x 9½ inches

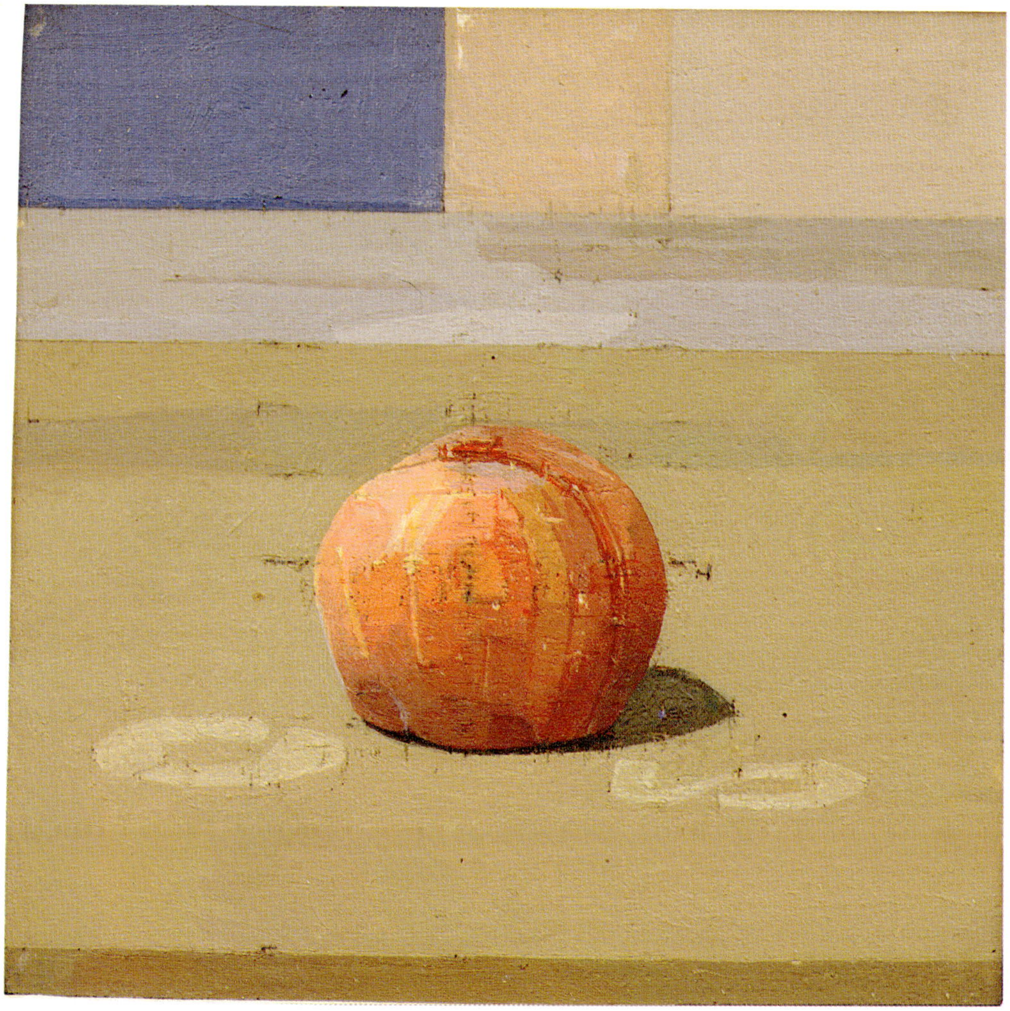

Two others have been there, 1992
oil on board 7¼ x 7 inches

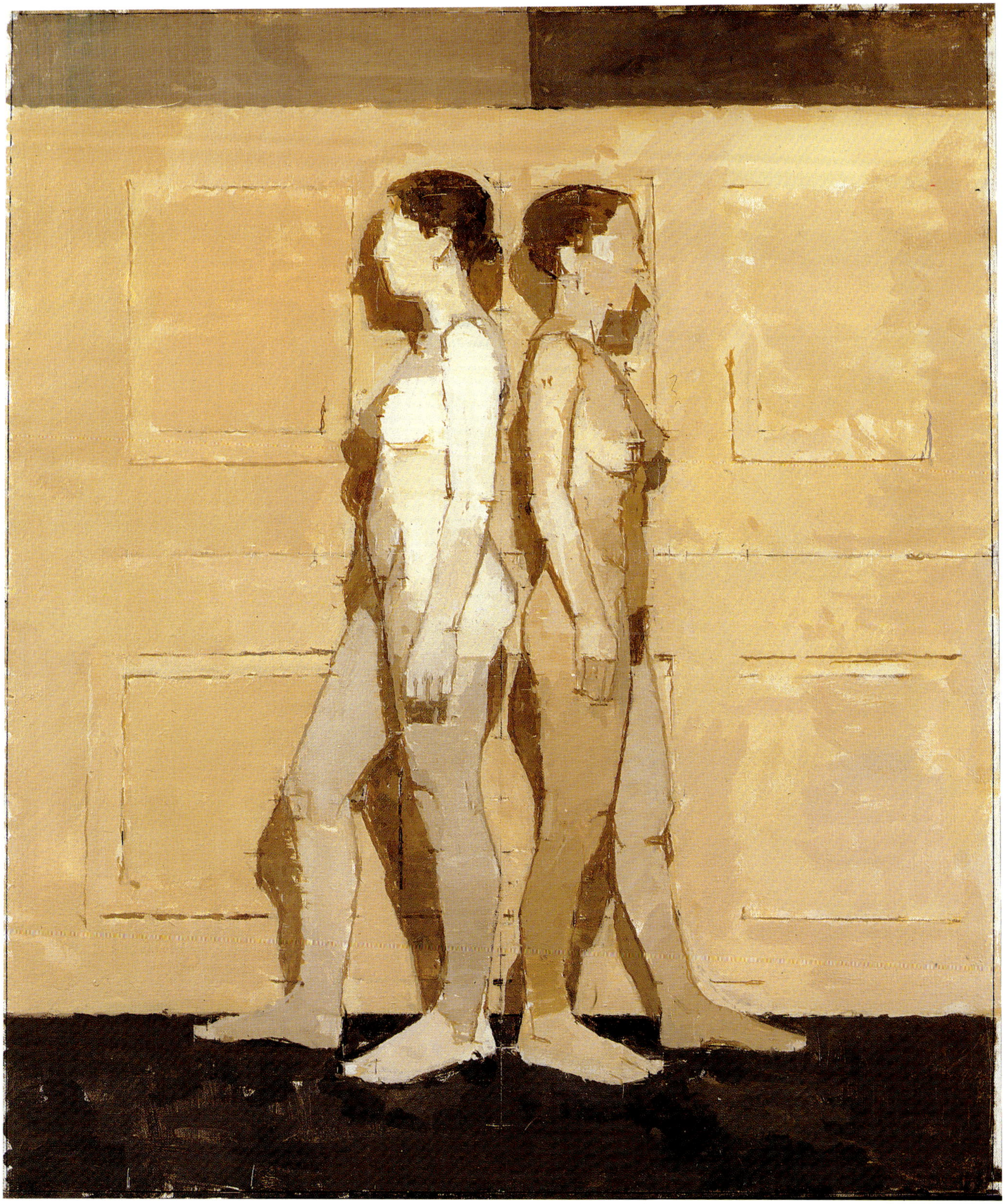

Tension, 1992-93
oil on canvas, laid on panel $22^1/_4$ x $18^5/_8$ inches

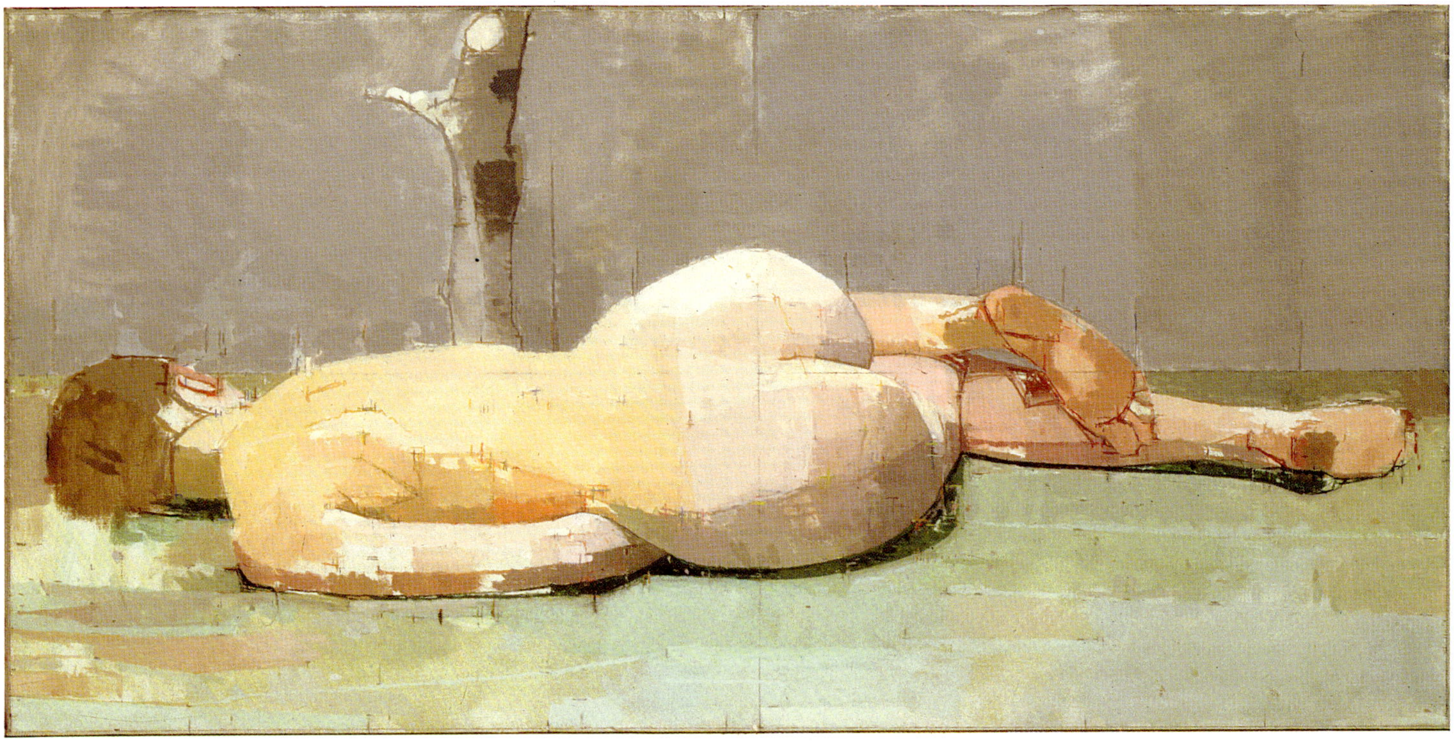

Articulation, 1993-95
oil on canvas   17¼ x 35¼ inches

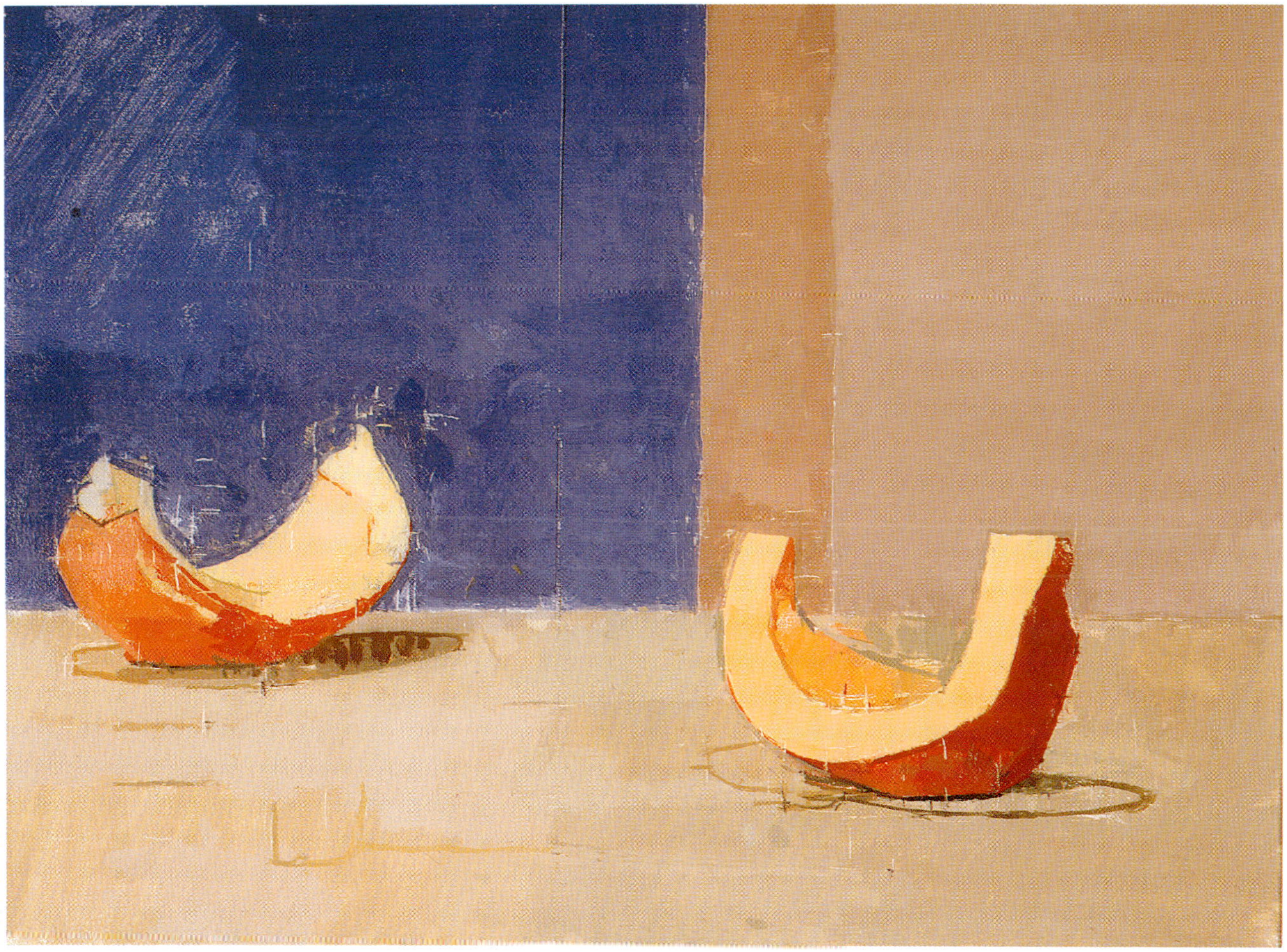

Slices of pumpkin (after Ambrogio Lorenzetti), 1993
oil on canvas 12 x 16 inches

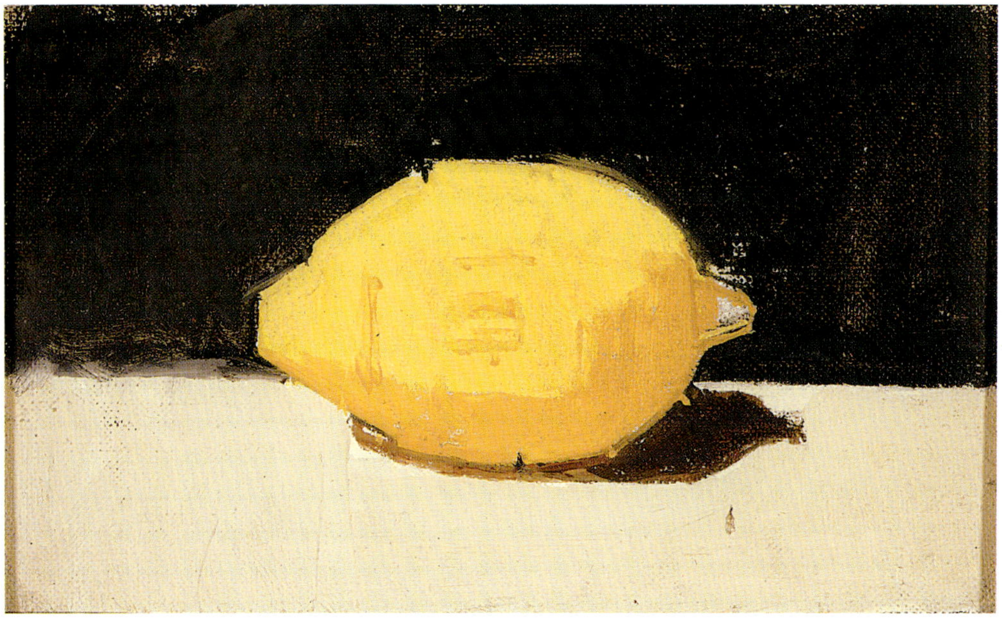

Lemon, 1996
oil on canvas, laid on panel 4¾ x 7½ inches

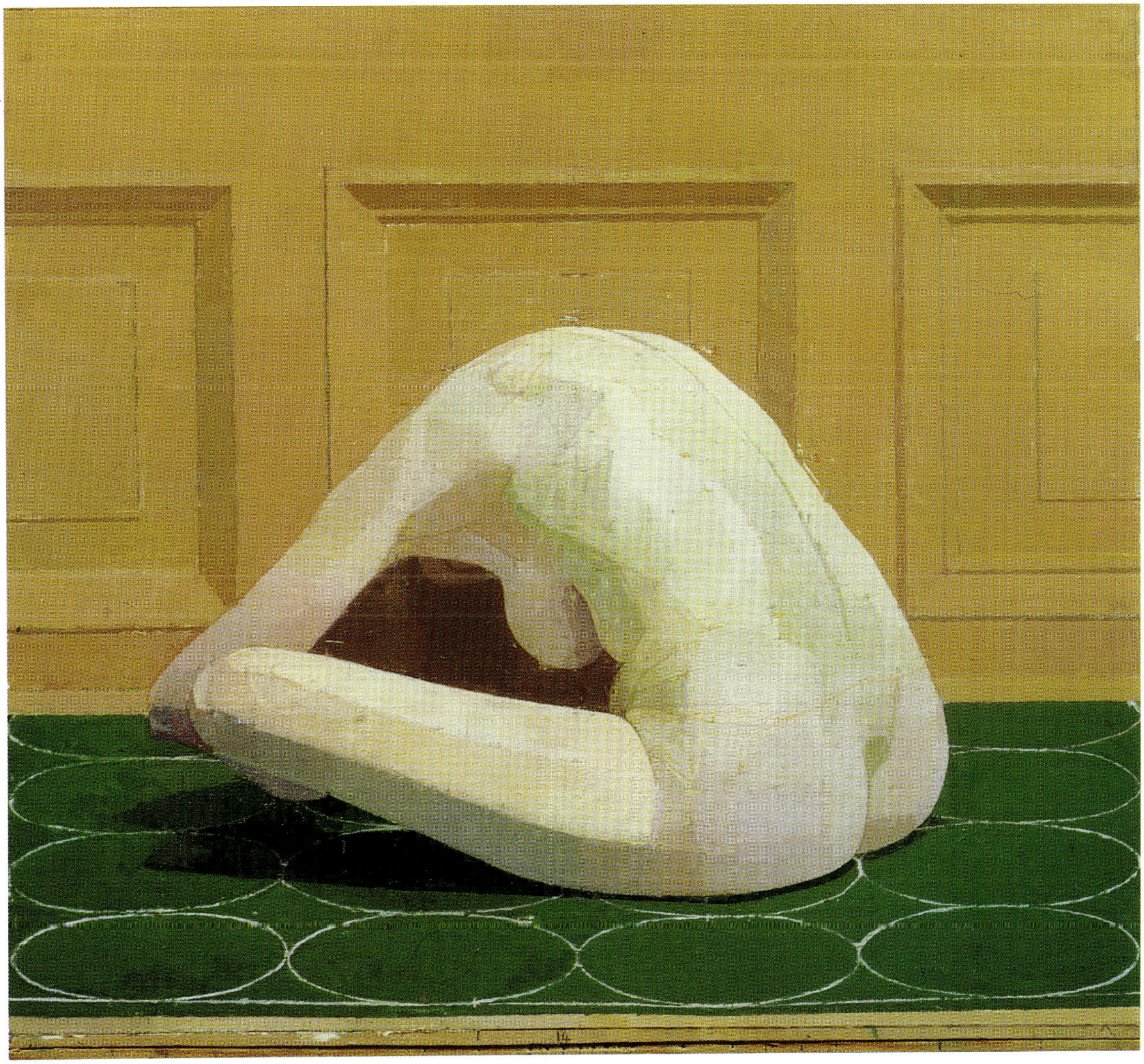

Pyramid, 1994-96
oil on canvas, laid on panel   20 x 22 inches

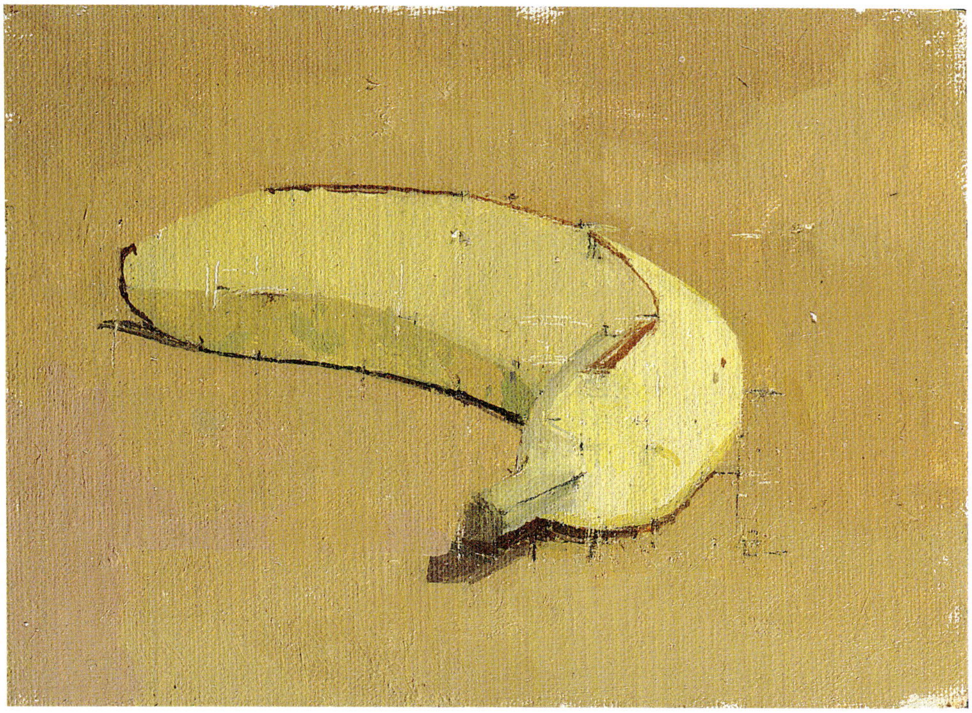

Banana, 1995
oil on canvas, laid on panel   5 x 7 inches

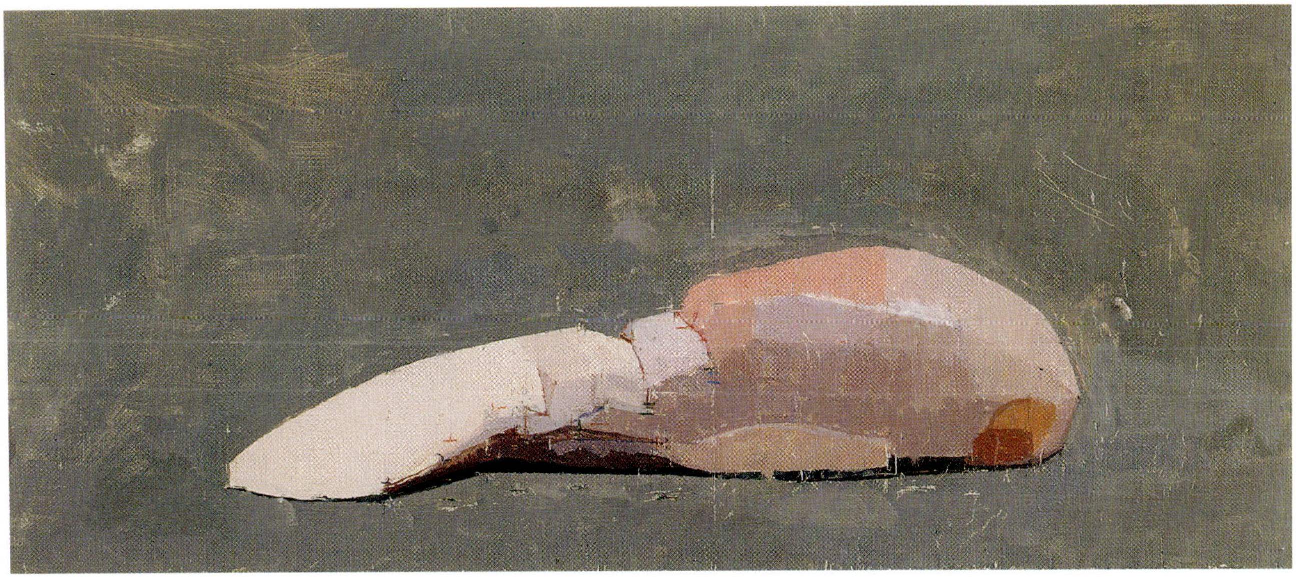

A tongue for Rudi, 1997
oil on canvas, laid on panel 7½ x 16¾ inches

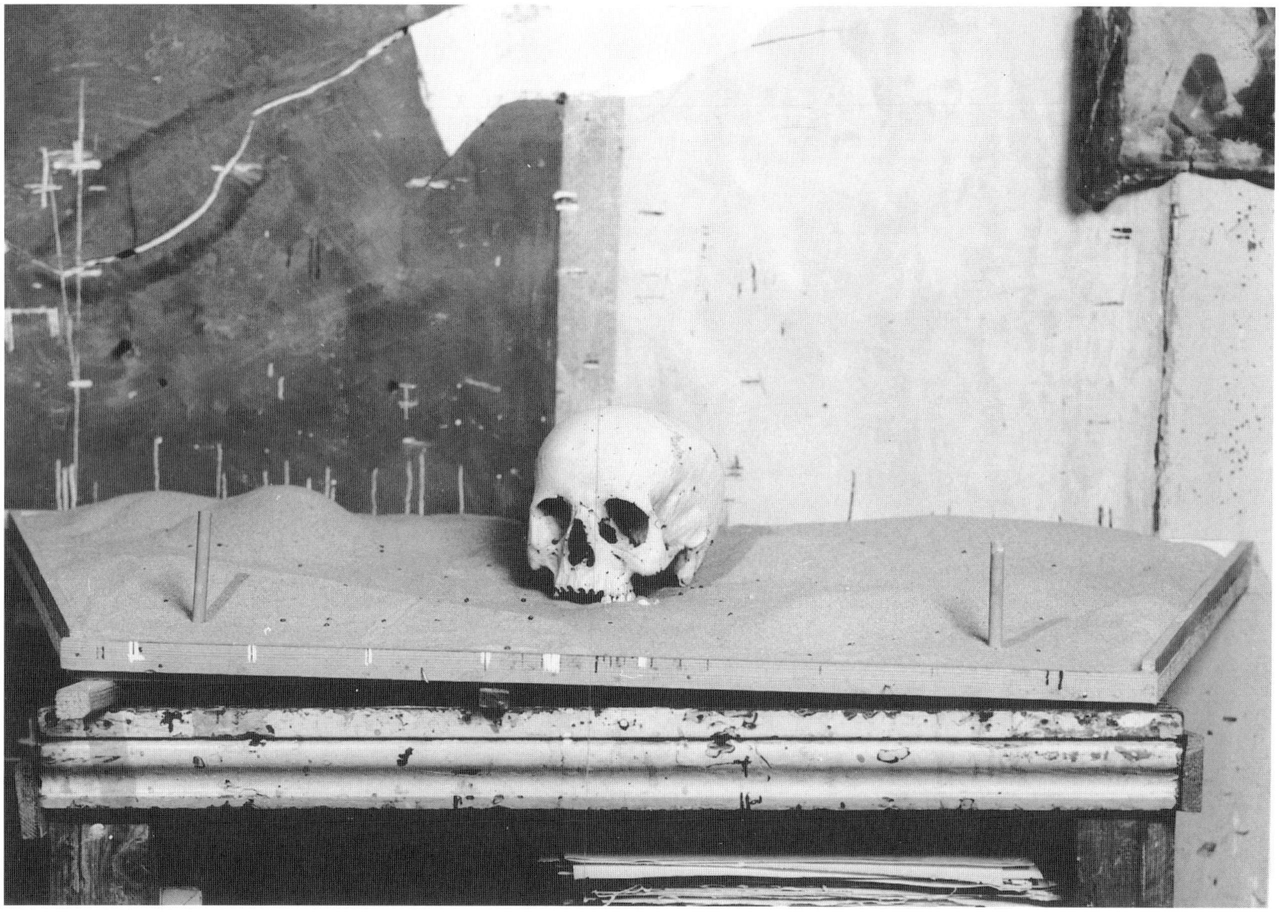

Set-up for Skull *photograph by Matt Pia*

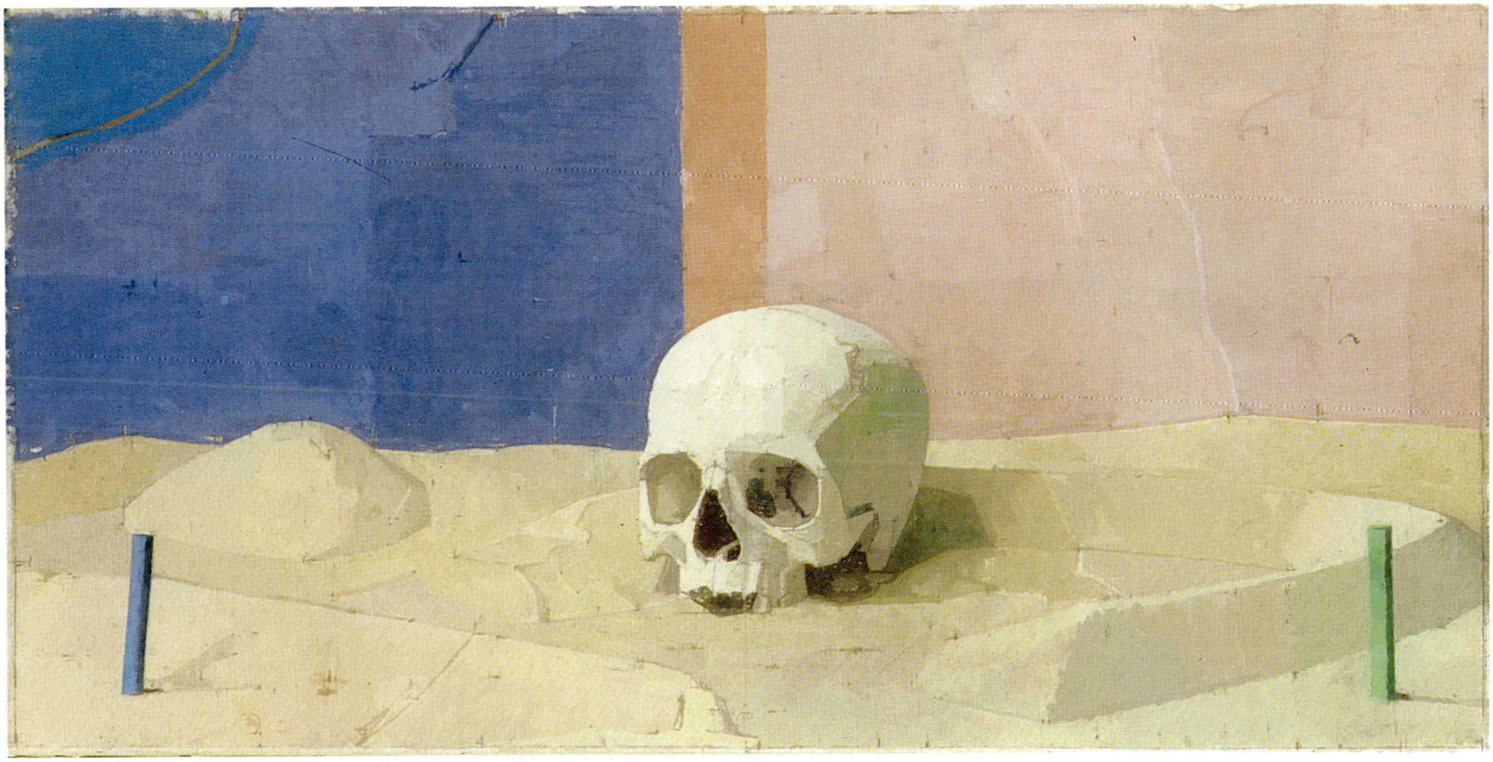

Skull, 1994-97
oil on canvas   12¾ x 25 inches

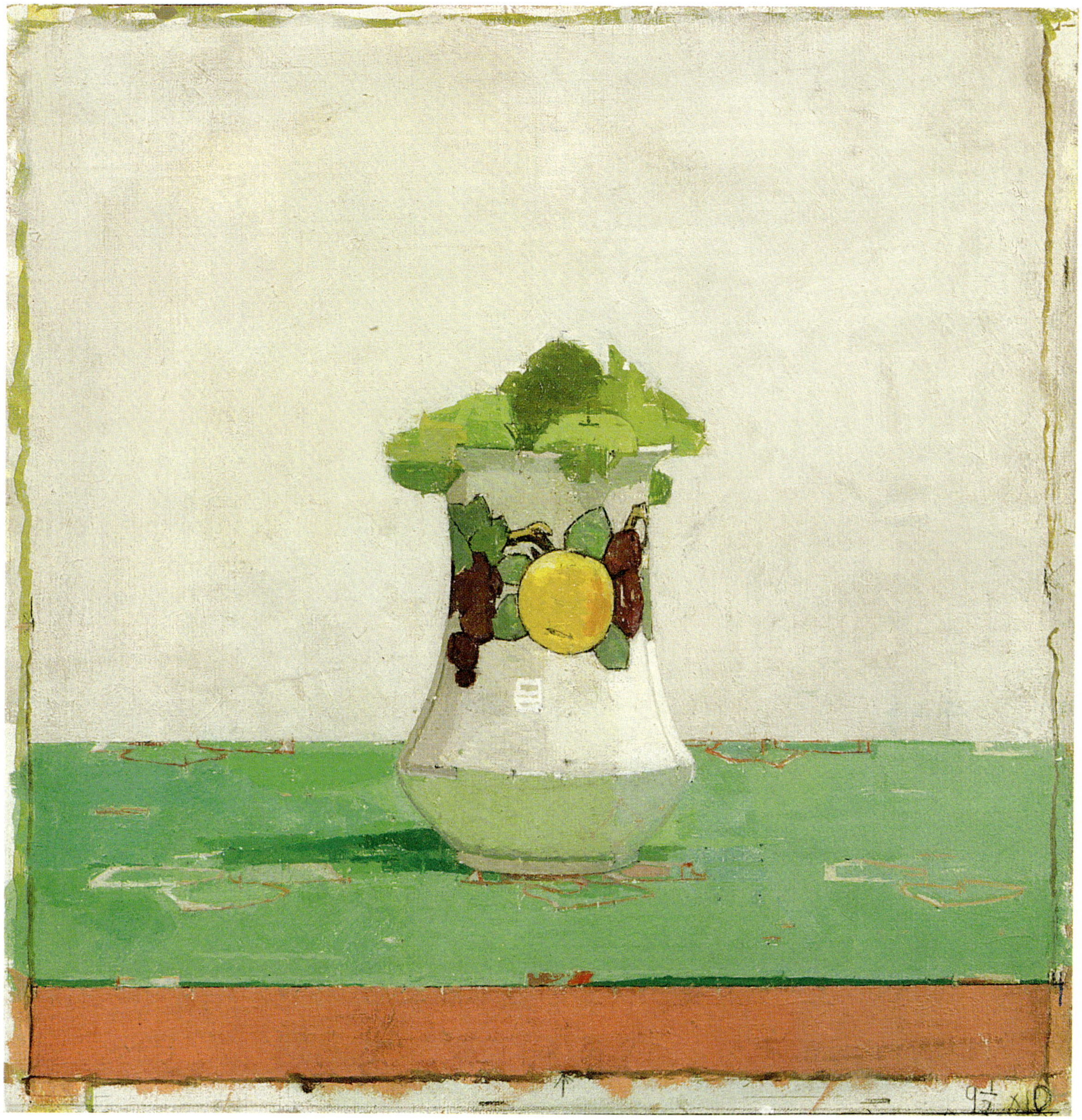

9½ x 10, 1997
oil on canvas, laid on panel   11¾ x 11⅛ inches

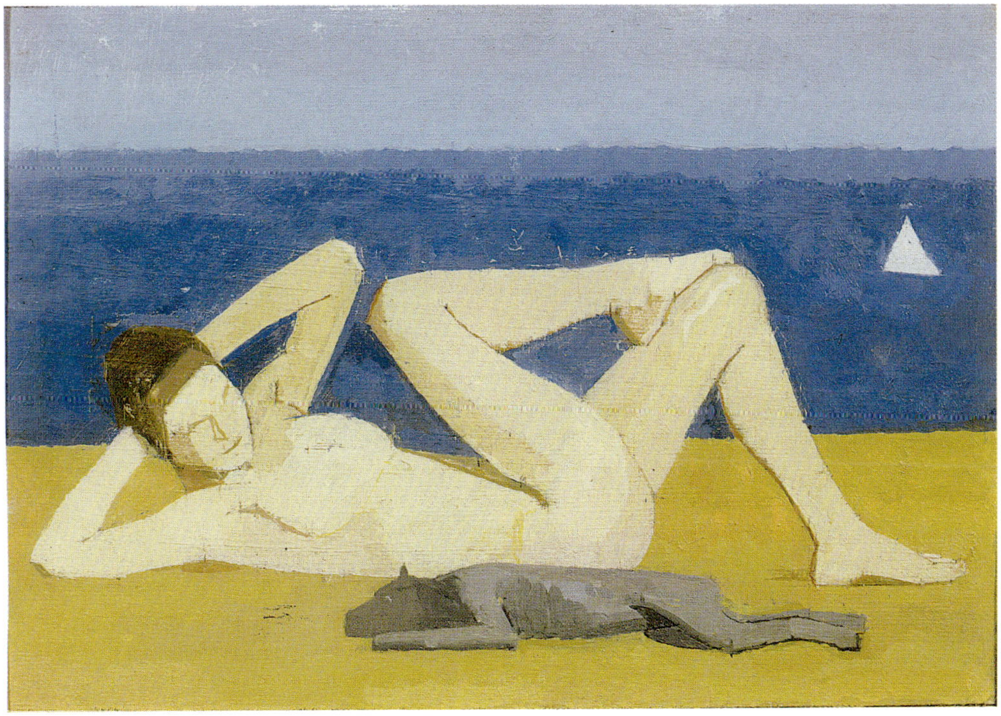

Girl with dog, 1991-97
oil on board 7¾ x 10¾ inches

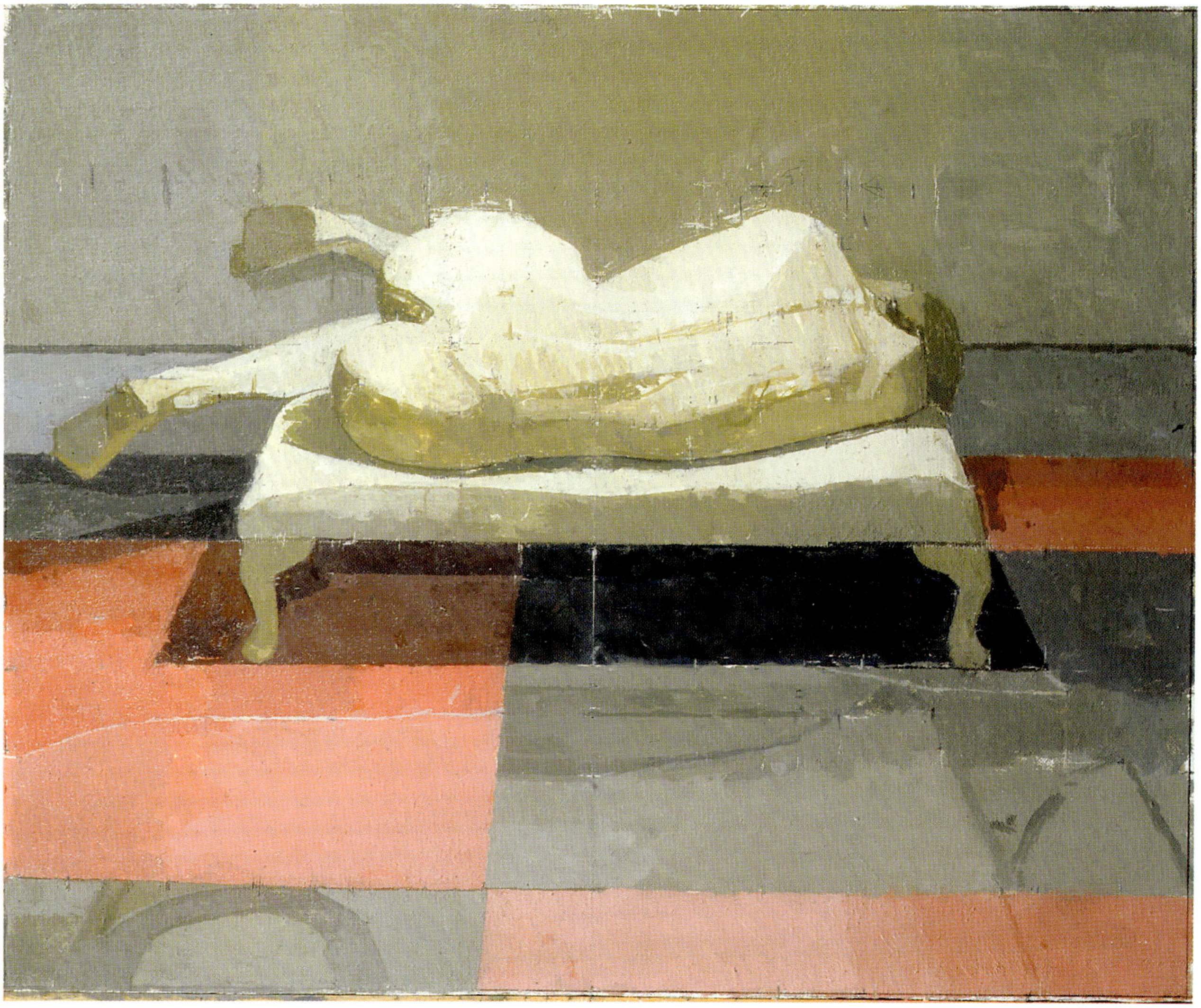

Jana, 1996-97
oil on canvas, laid on panel 14 x 16¾ inches

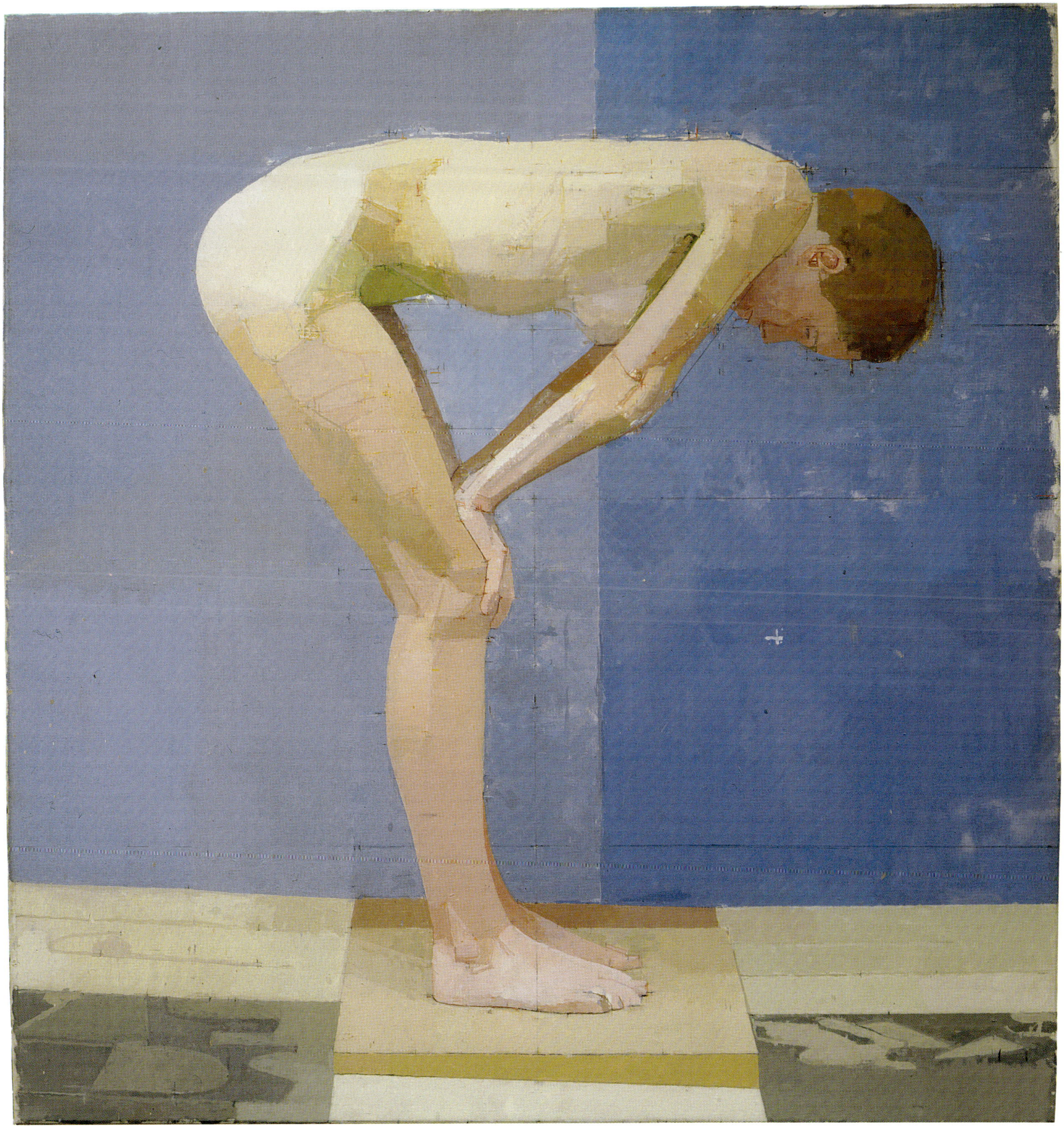

Ali, 1995-97
oil on canvas   32 7/8 x 30 3/4 inches

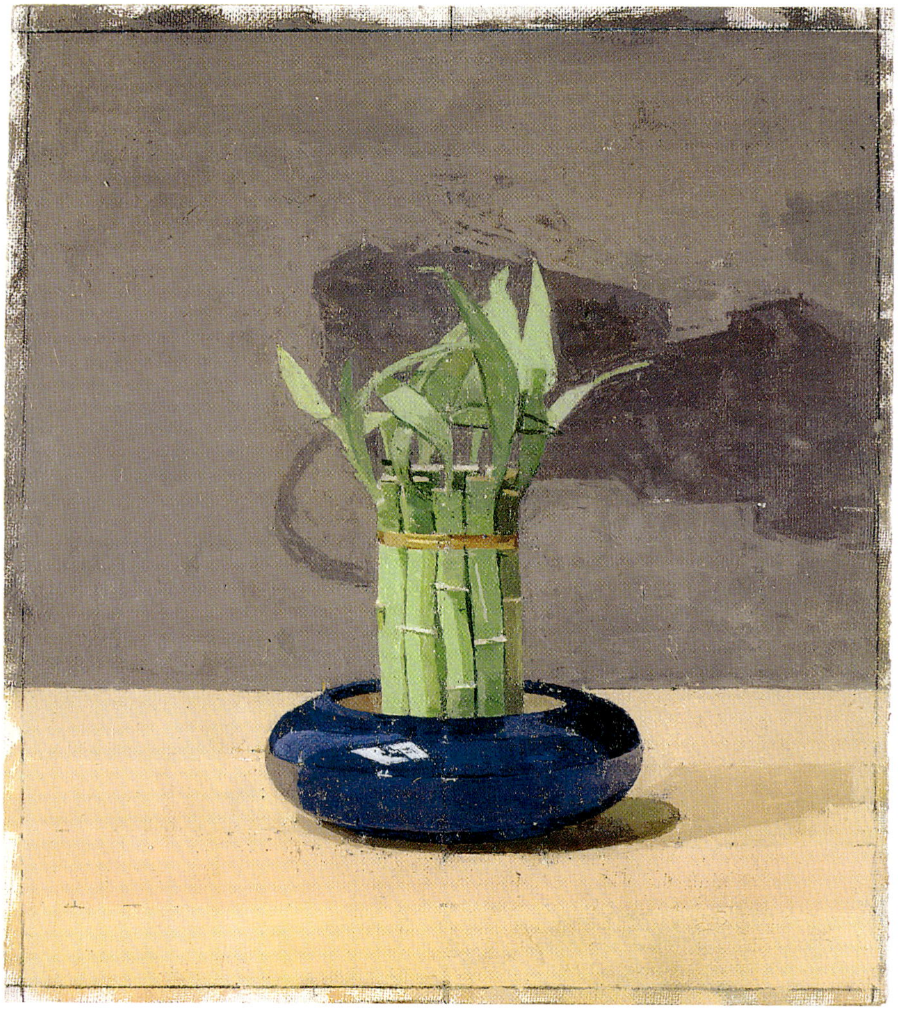

Letty's bamboo, 1997
oil on canvas, laid on panel $8^{3}/_{4}$ x $7^{3}/_{4}$ inches

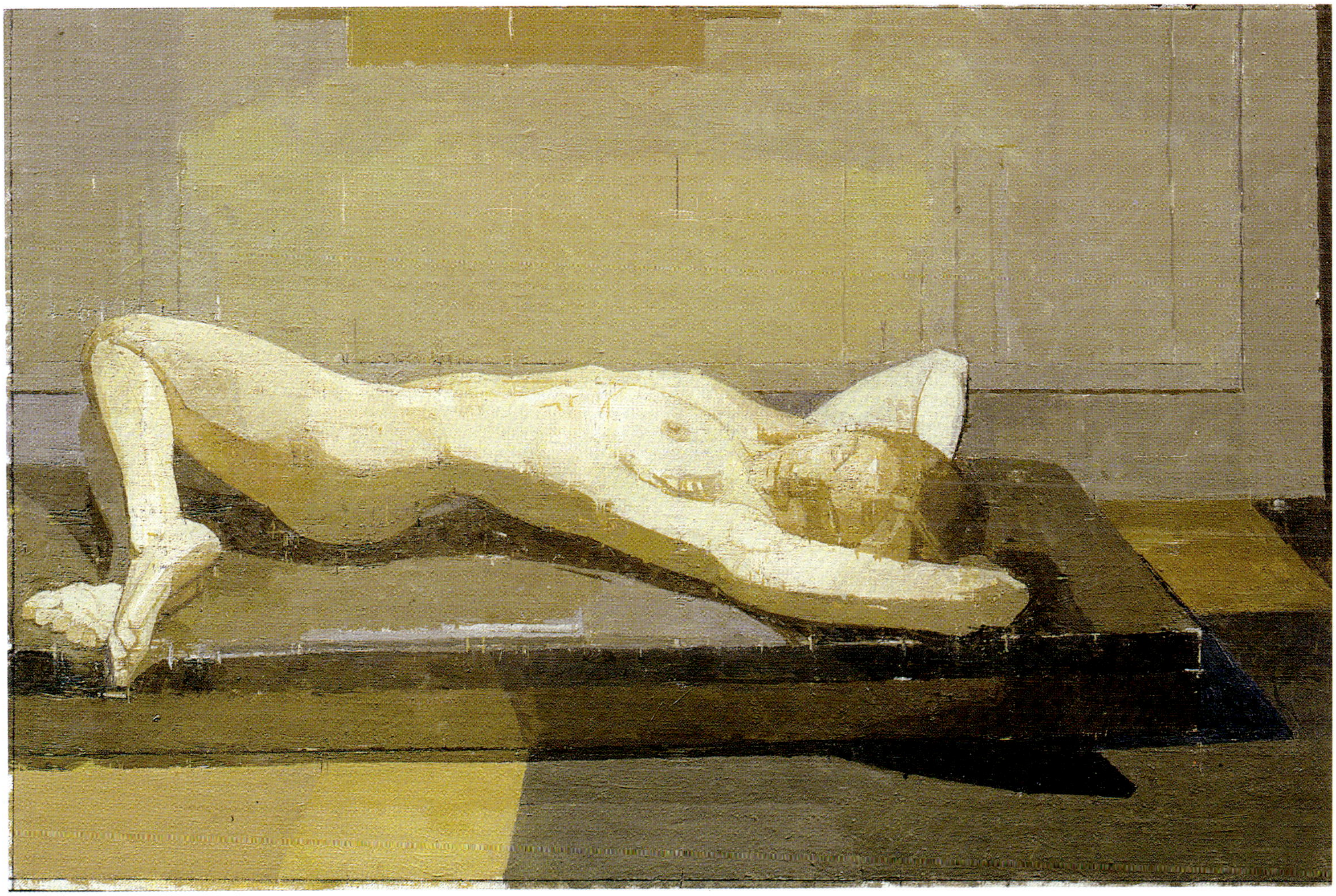

Propellor, 1994-96
oil on canvas, laid on panel 14 x 21 inches

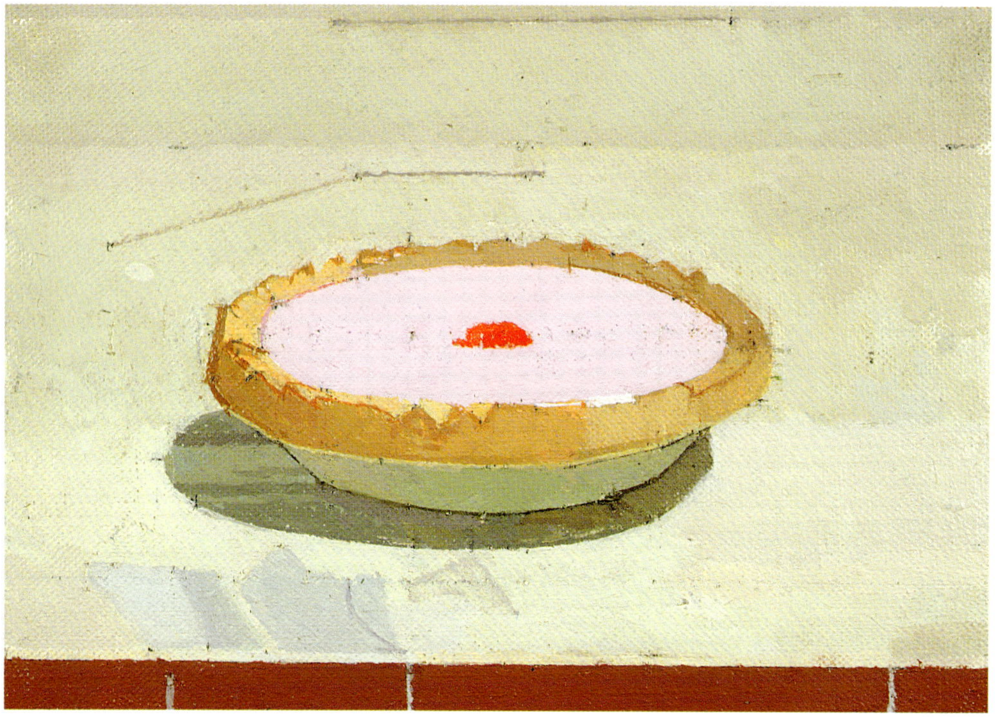

Is it a tart, or is it Ayers Rock? 1998
oil on canvas, laid on panel 5 x 7 inches

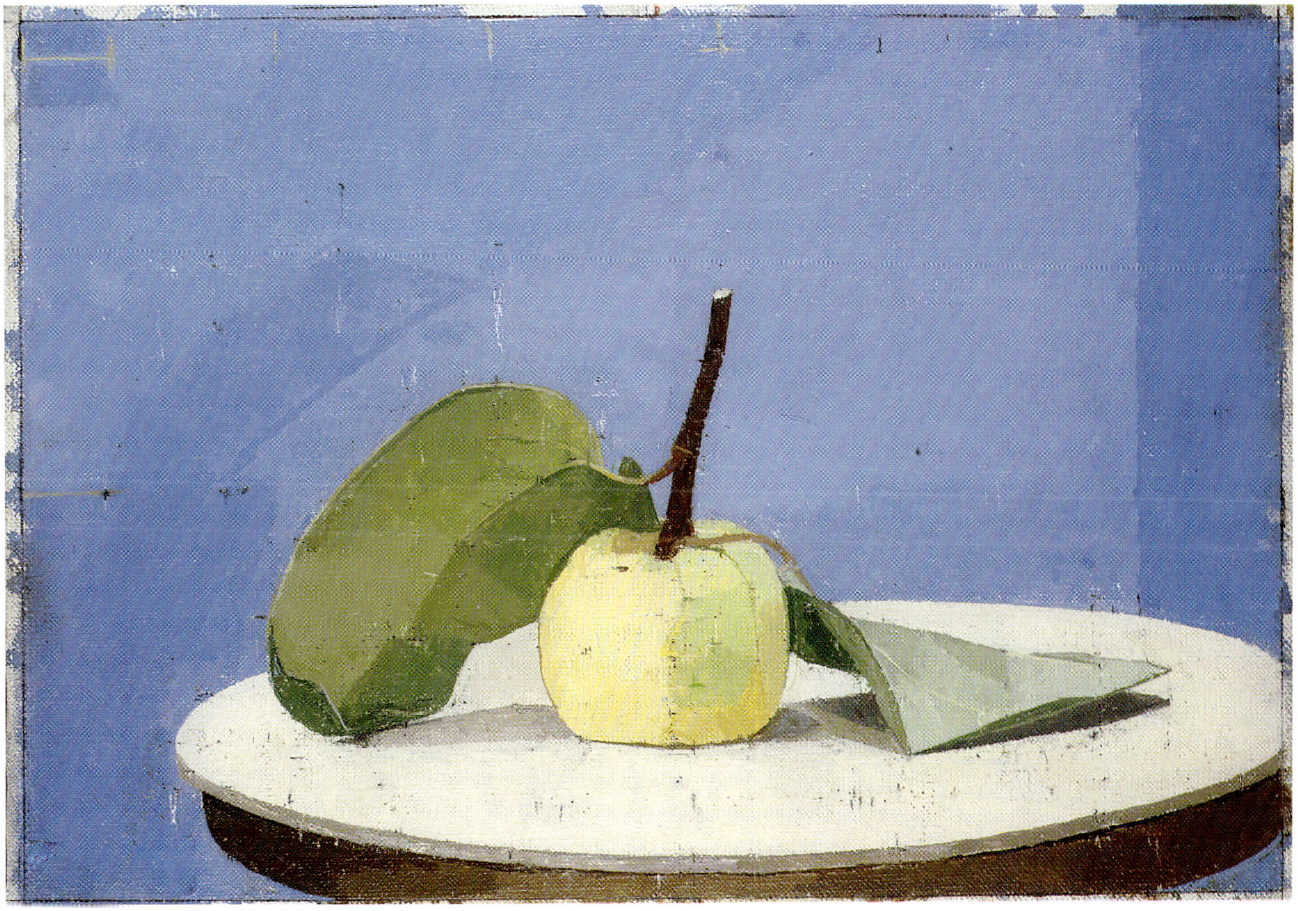

Quince, 1998
oil on canvas, laid on panel 10 x 14 inches

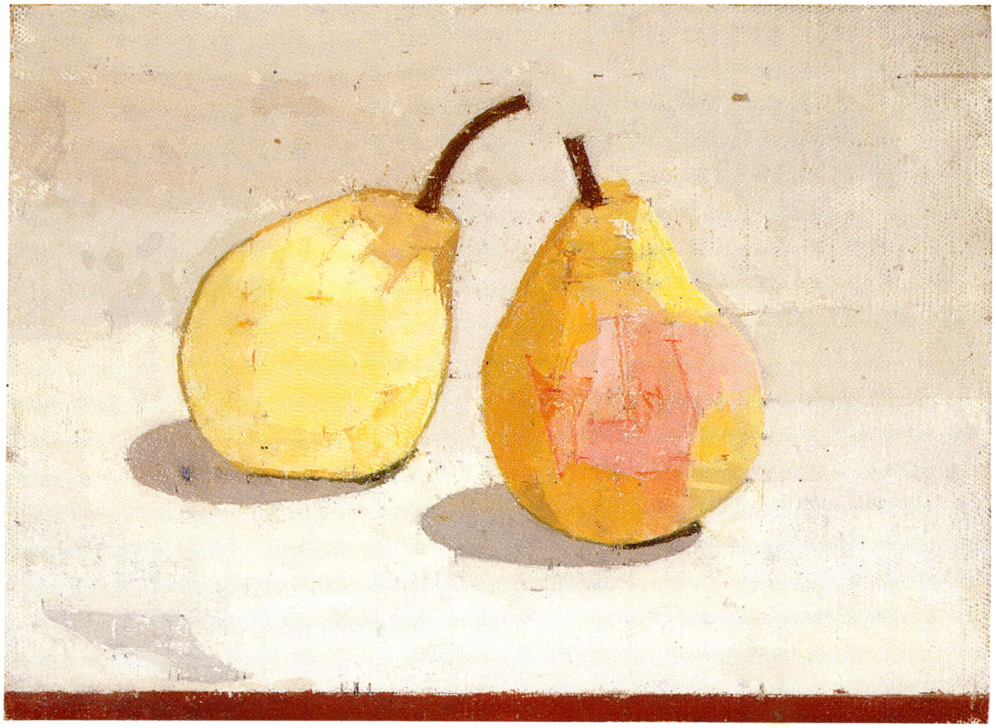

Two pears, 1998
oil on canvas, laid on panel 5 x 7 inches

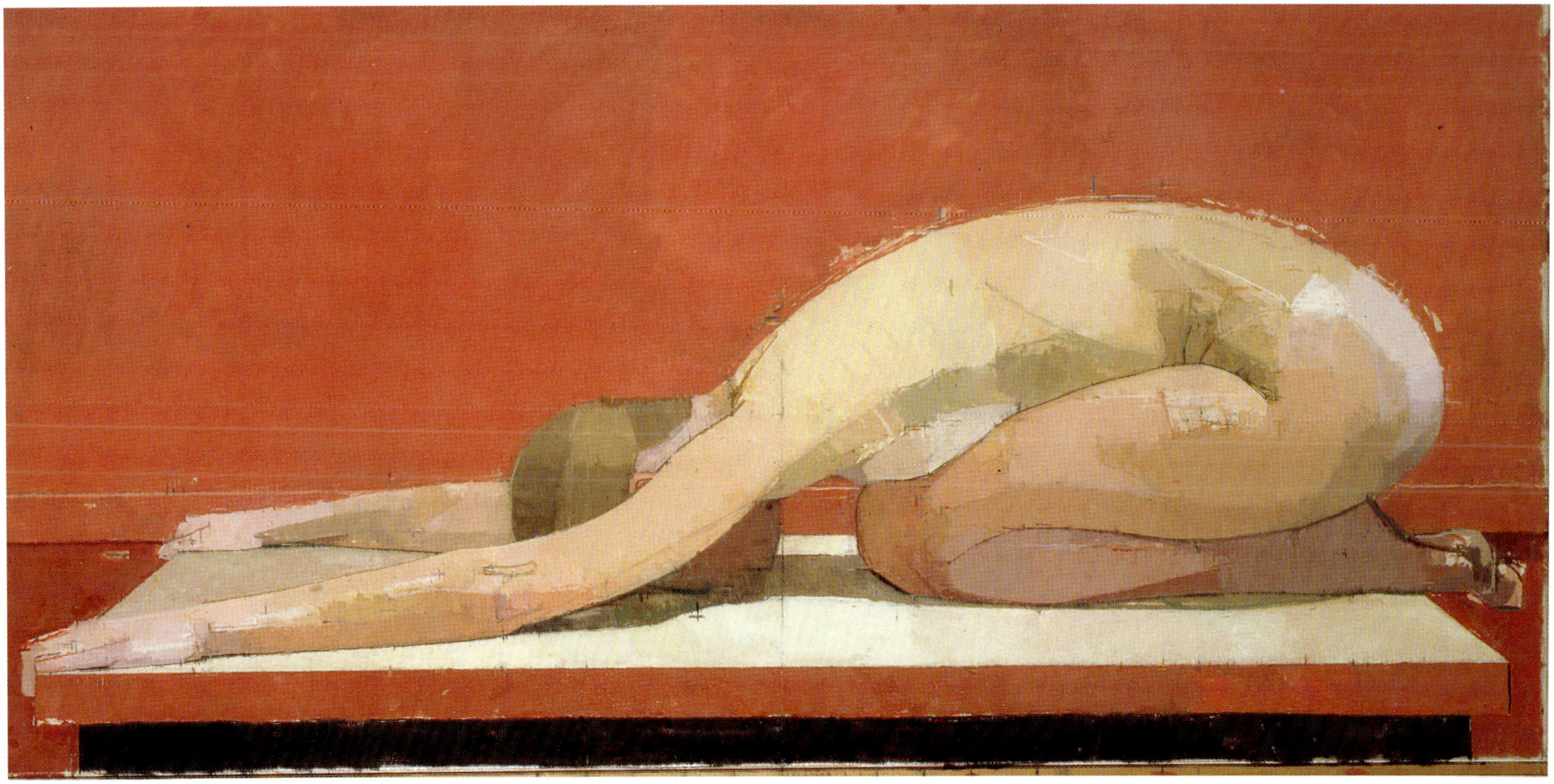

The wave, 1991-97
oil on canvas $19\frac{3}{4}$ x $39\frac{1}{2}$ inches

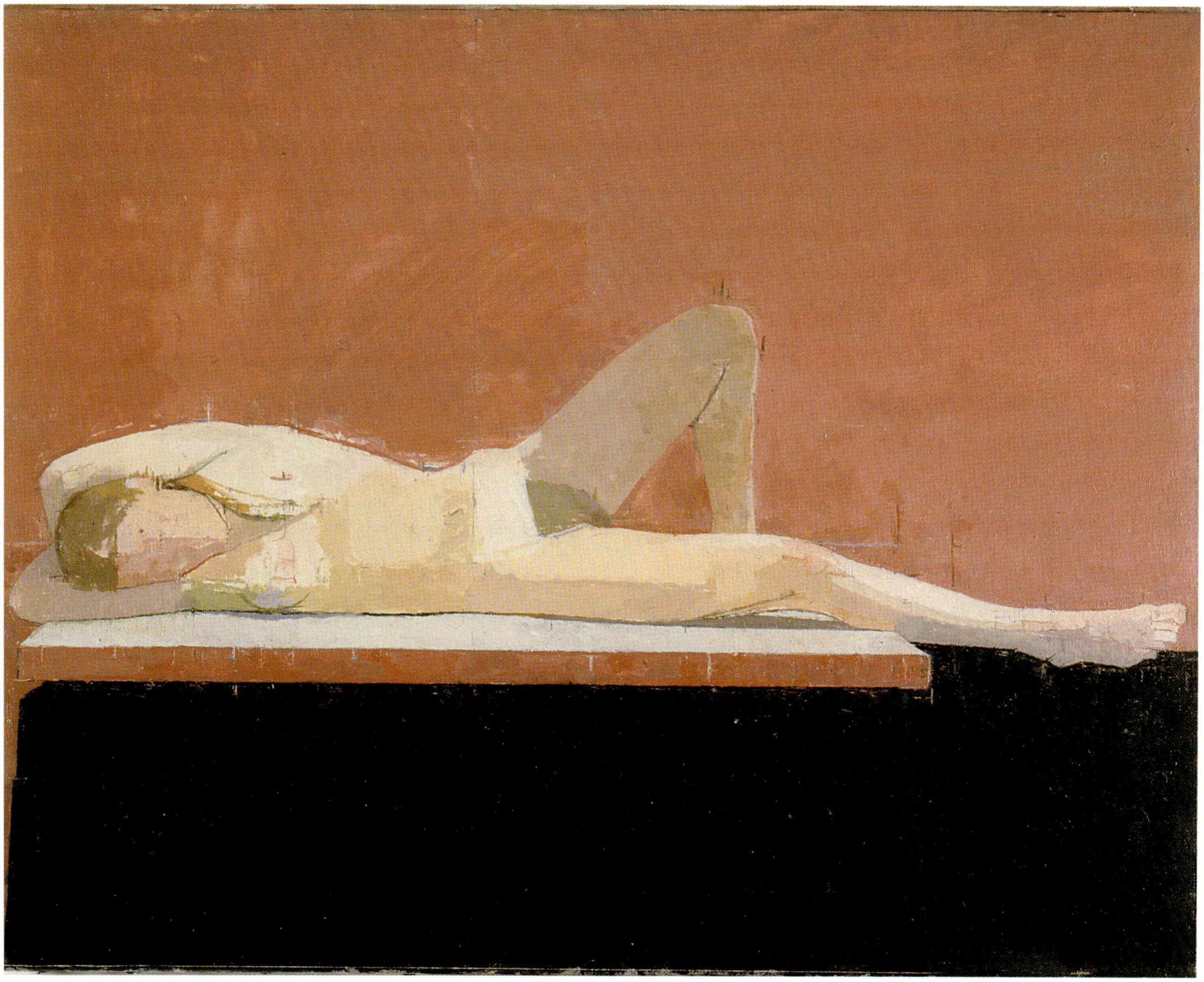

K and L, 1998
oil on canvas 15.7 x 19.628 inches

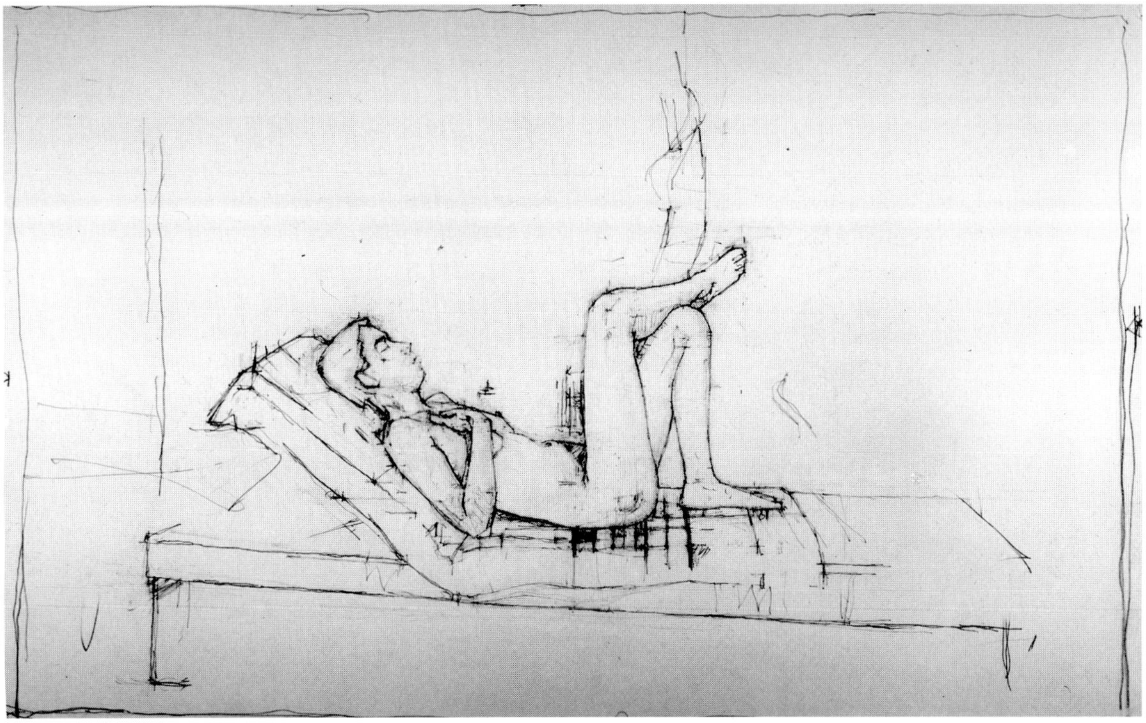

Reclining Nude, 1988
pencil 6 x 14 inches

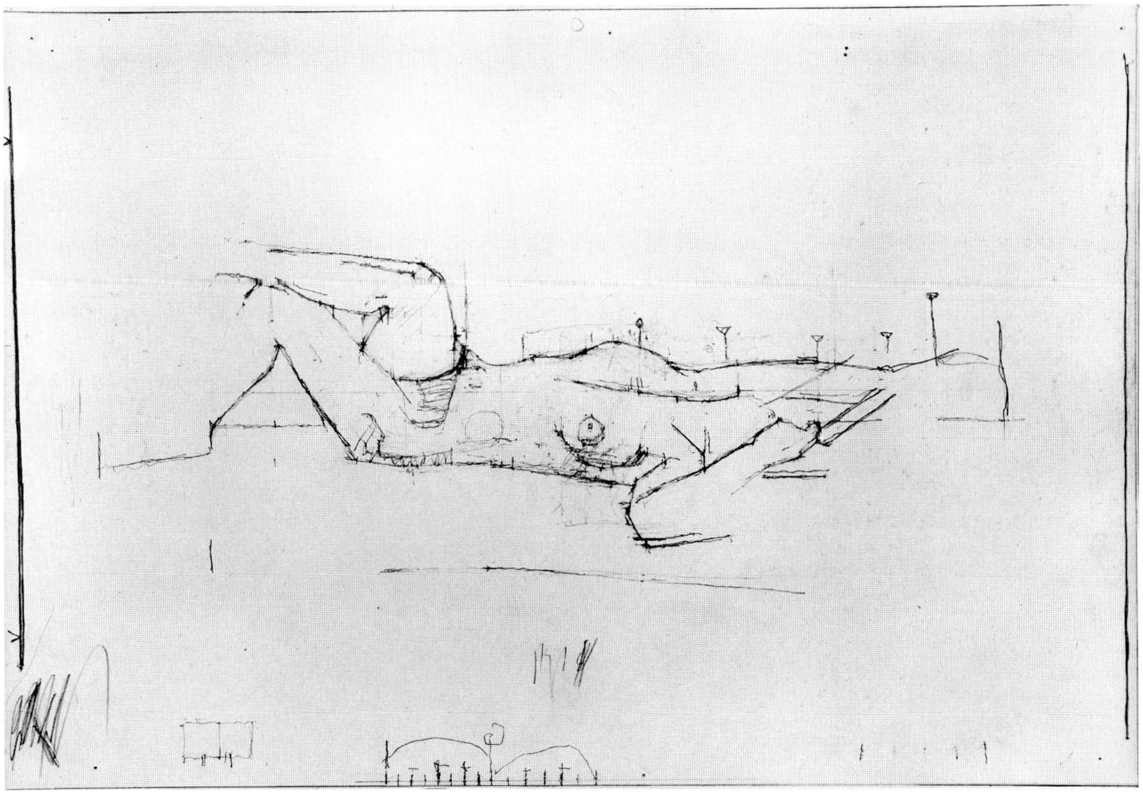

Rachel, 1997-98
pencil 12 x 17½ inches

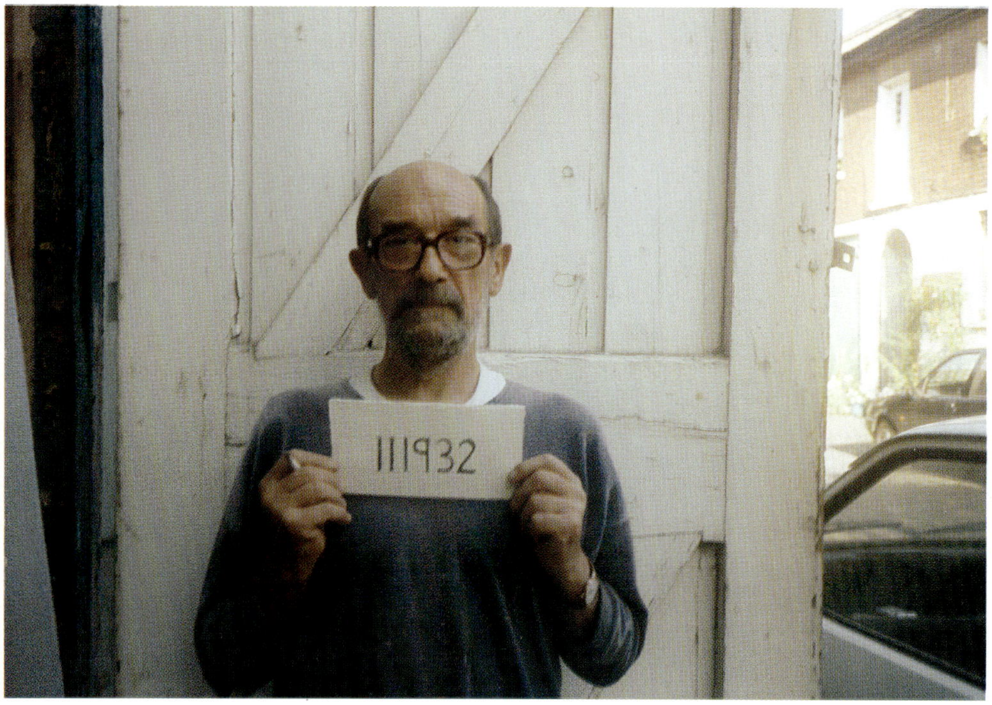

1998 *photograph by Georgia Georgallas*

EUAN UGLOW

1932	Born 10 March in London
1948-50	Attended Camberwell School of Arts and Crafts, awarded David Murray Scholarship
1951	Received State Scholarship for the Slade School of Fine Art, University College, London First exhibited with the London Group
1952	Received Spanish State Scholarship to work in Segovia, Spain
1953	Awarded Abbey Minor Scholarship (Prix de Rome). Travelled to France, Holland, Belgium; spent six months in Italy
1954	Did building work and farming as a conscientious objector
1957	Worked in Spain and France. Visited Giacometti with David Sylvester
1959	Moved to studio in Battersea
1960	Elected member of the London Group
1961	Part-time teaching at the Slade and Camberwell School of Arts and Crafts Second prize in junior section of John Moores exhibition, Walker Art Gallery, Liverpool
1962	Worked in France and Italy
1963	Worked in Morocco
1968	Worked in Turkey
1970	Won Edwin Austin Abbey Premier Scholarship
1972	Won first prize for the painting *Nude, from Twelve Regular Vertical Positions from the Eye 1967* at John Moores 8, Walker Art Gallery, Liverpool
1972-74	Worked in Italy during the summer months
1976	Worked in Italy
1980	Worked in Cyprus
1983	Worked in Cyprus
1984	Invited by the British Council to visit India for the exhibition The Proper Study, Lalit Kala Akademi, New Delhi
1985	Worked in Cyprus
1987	Invited to teach and work in China
1990-95	Artist Trustee, National Gallery, London
1997	Honorary member of The London Institute
2000	Died 31 August in London

One-man Exhibitions

1961	*Paintings and Drawings*, Beaux Arts Gallery, London
1969	*Drawings*, Gardner Centre, Sussex University, Brighton
1974	*Euan Uglow*, Whitechapel Art Gallery, London, and tour (Arts Council exhibition)
	Euan Uglow: Drawings, Colnaghi, London
1977	*Euan Uglow: Recent Paintings and Drawings*, Browse & Darby, London
1983	*Euan Uglow: Paintings and Drawings*, Browse & Darby, London
1989	*Euan Uglow: Euan Uglow's Nudes*, Whitechapel Art Gallery, London
	Euan Uglow: Drawings, Browse & Darby, London
1991	*Euan Uglow: Ideas, 1952-1991*, Browse & Darby, London
1993	*Euan Uglow*, Salander O'Reilly Gallery, New York, in association with Browse & Darby
1997	*Euan Uglow*, Browse & Darby, London
1999	*Euan Uglow: Drawings*, Browse & Darby, London
2001	*Euan Uglow: Night Paintings*, Browse & Darby, London
2002-3	*Euan Uglow*, Bury St. Edmunds Art Gallery, and tour (Arts Council exhibition)
2003	*Euan Uglow: A Retrospective*, Abbot Hall Art Gallery, Kendal, Cumbria
	Euan Uglow: Drawings, Browse & Darby, London

Selected Group Exhibitions

1960-61	*Modern British Portraits*, The Arts Council Gallery, Cambridge, and tour (Arts Council exhibition)
1961	*New Painting 1958-61*, Torquay Art Gallery, and tour (Arts Council exhibition)
	John Moores 3, Walker Art Gallery, Liverpool
1962	*Drawing Towards Painting, Six Young Painters*, Cheltenham Art Gallery and Museum
1964	*London Group 1914-64*, Jubilee Exhibition: Fifty Years of British Art, Tate Gallery, London, and tour (Arts Council exhibition)
	Six Young Painters, Blackburn Art Gallery, and tour (Arts Council exhibition)
1968	*Helen Lessore and the Beaux Arts Gallery*, Marlborough Fine Art, London
1971	*Painting and Perception*, The MacRobert Arts Centre Gallery, University of Stirling
	The Slade 1871-1971, Royal Academy of Arts, London
1972	*John Moores 8*, Walker Art Gallery, Liverpool
1975	*Body and Soul*, Peter Moores Liverpool Project 3, Walker Art Gallery, Liverpool
1976	*The Human Clay*, Hayward Gallery, London, and tour (Arts Council exhibition)
1977	*British Painting 1953-1977*, Royal Academy of Arts, London
1979	*Hayward Annual*, Hayward Gallery, London (Arts Council exhibition)
	The Knot of Life, L.A. Louver Gallery, Los Angeles
1980	*The British Art Show*, Mappin Art Gallery, Sheffield, and tour (Arts Council exhibition)
1981	*Eight Figurative Painters*, Yale Center for British Art, New Haven
	From Object to Object, Worcester City Museum and Art Gallery, and tour (Arts Council exhibition)

1984	*The Proper Study,* Lalit Kala Akademi, New Delhi (British Council exhibition)
	The Hard Won Image, Tate Gallery, London
1984-85	*The Singular Vision,* Royal Albert Memorial Museum, Exeter, and tour
1985	*British Artists in Italy,* Canterbury College of Art
1986	*Studies of the Nude,* Marlborough Fine Art, London
1987-88	Invited artist, *8th International Drawing Biennale,* Cleveland County Museum, Middlesborough, and tour
1990	*The Pursuit of the Real,* Manchester City Art Gallery, and tour
1991-92	*Bacon to Now: The Outsider in British Figuration,* Palazzo Vecchio, Florence
1992-93	*British Figurative Painting of the 20th Century,* Israel Museum, Jerusalem
1994	*Five Protagonists,* Browse & Darby, London
2000	*La Mirada Fuerte. Pintura degurative de Londres,* Mexico City (British Council exhibition)
	Encounters, National Gallery, London
	The School of London and their Friends, The Collection of Elaine and Melvin Merians, Yale Center for British Art, New Haven
2002	*A Measure of Reality,* Kettle's Yard, Cambridge

Selected Bibliography

Coldstream, William, Laughton, Bruce, *The Slade 1871-1971,* exhibition catalogue, Royal Academy of Arts, London, 1971

Cork, Richard, *The School of London and their Friends, The Collection of Elaine and Melvin Merians,* exhibition catalogue, Yale Center for British Art, New Haven, 2000

Feaver, William, *La Mirada Fuerte,* exhibition catalogue, British Council, Mexico, 2000

Forge, Andrew, *Painting and Perception,* exhibition catalogue, The MacRobert Arts Centre Gallery, University of Stirling, 1971

Forge, Andrew, *Euan Uglow, Paintings and Drawings,* exhibition catalogue, Salander O'Reilly Galleries, New York, 1993

Golding, Martin, *Euan Uglow's Nudes,* exhibition catalogue, Whitechapel Art Gallery, London, 1989

Gowing, Lawrence, *Eight Figurative Painters,* exhibition catalogue, Yale Center for British Art, New Haven, 1981

Kendall, Richard, *Manchester, London, Glasgow. The Pursuit of the Real,* Burlington Magazine, May 1990

Kendall, Richard, *Still Life Paintings (Ideas 1952-1991),* exhibition catalogue, Browse & Darby, London, 1991

Kendall, Richard, *Euan Uglow Drawings,* exhibition catalogue, Browse & Darby, London, 1999

Kendall, Richard, *The School of London and their Friends, The Elaine and Melvin Merians Collection,* Burlington Magazine, January 2001

Kendall, Richard, *Euan Uglow, Night Paintings,* exhibition catalogue, Browse & Darby, London, 2001

Kendall, Richard, *Euan Uglow, A Retrospective,* exhibition catalogue, Abbot Hall Art Gallery, Kendal, 2003

Kendall, Richard, *Euan Uglow Drawings,* exhibition catalogue, Browse & Darby, London, 2003

Kitaj, R.B., *The Human Clay,* exhibition catalogue, Arts Council of Great Britain, 1976

Lambirth, Andrew, *Snatches of Conversation,* exhibition catalogue, Whitechapel Art Gallery, London, 1989

Lambirth, Andrew, *A State of Emergency,* Modern Painters, Summer 1992

Lambirth, Andrew, *Five Protagonists,* exhibition catalogue, Browse & Darby, London, 1994

Lambirth, Andrew, *Encounters,* exhibition catalogue, National Gallery, London, 2000

Lambirth, Andrew, *Euan Uglow,* London Magazine, April/May 2001

Lampert, Catherine, *Painting from Life,* exhibition catalogue, Hayward Gallery, Arts Council of Great Britain, 1979

Lampert, Catherine, *Euan Uglow, The Proper Study,* exhibition catalogue, British Council, 1984

Lampert, Catherine, *Euan Uglow,* exhibition catalogue, Browse & Darby, 1997

McLean, John, *Euan Uglow, paintings and drawings,* exhibition catalogue, Salander O'Reilly Galleries, New York, 1993

Morphet, Richard, *The Hard Won Image,* exhibition catalogue, Tate Gallery, London, 1984

Murphy, Myles, *Euan Uglow: paintings and drawings,* exhibition catalogue, Browse & Darby, London, 1983

Piper, David, *Introduction, Euan Uglow, drawings,* exhibition catalogue, Colnaghi, London, 1974

Prendeville, Brendan, *A Measure of Reality,* exhibition catalogue, Kettle's Yard, Cambridge, 2002

Rothenstein, John, *Modern English Painters* (3 volumes), London, 1974

Seddon Jones, Julie, *Euan Uglow,* exhibition catalogue, Browse & Darby, London, 1989

Sylvester, David, *Getting it Right,* Modern Painters, Summer 1997

Troostwyck, *'New Work', Euan Uglow's, Diagonal,* The Studio, vol. 187, May 1974

Willing, Victor, *Opaque Perception,* Art Monthly, December/January 1978

Public Collections

Arts Council of Great Britain

British Council, London

British Museum, London

Ferens Art Gallery, Hull

Glasgow Art Gallery, Scotland

Government Art Collection, London

Kings College, London

Liverpool University

Metropolitan Museum of Art, New York

National Museum of Wales, Cardiff

Southampton City Art Gallery

Tate Gallery, London

Wakefield Art Gallery